Book Club
A Literature-Based Curriculum

Taffy E. Raphael, Ph.D.
Michigan State University

Laura S. Pardo, M.A.

Kathy Highfield, M.A.
Holly Elementary School

Susan I. McMahon, Ph.D.
University of Wisconsin, Madison

D1573224

Small Planet Communications, Inc.

Littleton, Massachusetts

Acknowledgments

Editorial: Liz Grube
            Melinda Hobausz
            Kim Leahy Beaudet

Graphic Design: Natalie MacKnight
                 Tim Metcalf

Production: Lloyd Herendeen
            Sarah Prince

Grateful acknowledgment is made to the following teachers who reviewed and tested our lesson plans in their classrooms:

Diane Lindbert, Cornell Elementary School, Okemos, MI
Kelly Campbell, Williamston Elementary School, Williamston, MI
Cindy Koch, Cushing Elementary School, Delafield, WI
Cindy Lafkas, Cornell Elementary School, Okemos, MI
Ellen Schwartz, P. S. 133Q, Bellerose, NY
Wendy A. Tamborrino, Binford Elementary School, Bloomington, IN
Melissa Thibault, Unity School, Delray Beach, FL

Thanks also to the staff and students at the Sheridan Road Elementary School and the Allen Street Elementary School in Lansing, Michigan, and the Holly Elementary School in Holly, Michigan, where much of the research, development, and filming of the Book Club program was conducted.

Picture credits are listed on page 296.

Small Planet Communications, Inc.
25 Porter Road
Littleton, MA 01460
www.smplanet.com

ISBN 0-9656211-0-3   1 2 3 4 5 6 7 8 9 10 05 04 03 02 01 00 99 98 97

Contents

About the Authors

Taffy E. Raphael

Taffy E. Raphael, a former classroom teacher, is currently a professor in the College of Education at Michigan State University. She received her master's degree in reading instruction at the University of North Carolina at Greensboro, and her Ph.D. from the University of Illinois, studying and conducting research at the Center for the Study of Reading. At MSU, she teaches courses about literacy instruction; conducts research on alternative methods for teaching reading, writing, and oral language in elementary school; and has coordinated the Master's Degree Program in Literacy Instruction for six years. Cofounder of the Book Club Project, Dr. Raphael has led the collaborative team of researchers and teachers who have developed the program over the past eight years. She has published her research in such journals as *Reading Research Quarterly* and *The Reading Teacher*, and she has coauthored and edited books including *Creating an Integrated Approach to Literacy Instruction* (Harcourt Brace, 1996), *Contexts of School-Based Literacy* (Random House, 1986), and *The Book Club Connection: Literacy Learning and Classroom Talk* (Teachers College Press, 1997). In 1997 she was selected as Outstanding Teacher Educator in Reading by the International Reading Association.

Laura S. Pardo

Laura S. Pardo spent fourteen years as a classroom teacher before taking her current position as an educational consultant. Her teaching has been highlighted in videotapes including the Center for the Study of Reading's *Reading Instruction in the Content Areas,* Silver Burdett Ginn's *Literature-Based Instruction,* and Small Planet's *Book Club: A Literature-Based Curriculum.* Ms. Pardo received her B.S. in education from Central Michigan University and her M.A. (with a concentration in reading instruction) from Michigan State University. She began her involvement with the Book Club Project in 1990 as a classroom teaching member. She has been a frequent presenter at the Michigan Reading Association, the National Reading Conference, and the International Reading Association. She has published the results of her Book Club research in numerous professional journals and books, and she continues to be interested in teacher research, literature-based instruction, and integrated language arts.

Kathy Highfield

Kathy Highfield received her B.A. in elementary education and French and her M.A. in literacy instruction (1994) from Michigan State University. Her more than ten years of teaching experience include instructing college freshmen in French language, tutoring students from first grade through adults in all subjects, and her current position as a fifth-grade teacher at Holly Elementary School. She has a keen interest in research, and she participates in a practitioner/research group with other teachers and Dr. Taffy Raphael. Ms. Highfield has been involved in the Book Club Project since 1991 and has made presentations about the program and her classroom research at meetings of the Michigan Reading Association, the Michigan Council of Teachers of English, and the International Reading Association. She is also interested in content-area instruction, the role of discussion in student learning, and teacher research. She coauthored the chapter "The Content-Area Connection" in *The Book Club Connection: Literacy Learning and Classroom Talk* (Teachers College Press, 1997).

Susan I. McMahon

Susan I. McMahon (Ph.D., Michigan State University), cofounder of the Book Club Project, is a faculty member within the Department of Curriculum and Instruction at the University of Wisconsin–Madison and Project Director of "Classroom Instructional Support for the Development of Literacy and the Learning of Literature and Social Studies," a study housed within the new Center for English Learning and Achievement. She has a total of twenty-six years of teaching experience at public and private schools and at the university level. Despite the different contexts, her teaching has consistently focused on literacy development and response to literature. Her research adopts ethnographic methods to explore literacy in urban, public-school settings where she collaborates with teachers to pursue areas of like interests. Currently, her research interests include literature-based instruction; the relationships between reading, writing, and oracy; the instruction of integrated content; and the use of student-led groups during instruction. She has published articles in *Teaching and Teacher Education, The Journal of Educational Research, The Reading Teacher*, and *Language Arts*. She also coedited *The Book Club Connection: Literacy Learning and Classroom Talk* (Teachers College Press, 1997). Recently, she won the Harold E. Mitzel Award for Meritorious Contribution to Educational Practice Through Research for an article based on Book Club.

A Letter from the Authors

Dear Colleague,

Wouldn't it be great if your students could maintain meaningful conversations about books? This is the goal we began exploring over eight years ago. We created a collaborative project (public school/university) to develop, research, and implement the Book Club program in elementary classrooms. What we worked to create was an alternative context for teaching reading: through writing and talking about excellent literature. The teacher's guide you're holding—and the related Book Club multimedia materials—are products of that research.

We developed *Book Club: A Literature-Based Curriculum* to help both beginning and experienced teachers create Book Club programs in their own upper-elementary classrooms. We support your efforts in several ways. First, this teacher's guide provides an overview of the program as well as specific tips on management and assessment. It also offers lesson plans for eight individual trade books, an author study unit, and a multi-book unit. Second, the videotape shows you exactly how Book Club works in real classrooms and includes interviews with Book Club teachers, program developers, and students. Third, the Book Club web site allows you to interact with the program developers and with other Book Club teachers, sharing your questions, ideas, and comments. You'll find our web site at:

http://www.smplanet.com/bookclub/bookclub.html

We hope you and your students enjoy using the Book Club program as much as we've enjoyed developing it. Let us know what you think—we look forward to hearing from you!

Taffy E. Raphael   Laura S. Pardo

Kathy Highfield   Susan I. McMahon

The Structure of the Book Club Program

New Ideas About Literacy

The Book Club program began as a collaboration between a group of teachers and researchers in 1989. Since then we've developed and refined a reading curriculum centered around small, student-led discussion groups. The children themselves assume responsibility for deciding the course of their conversations, but these conversations occur within a context of balanced literature-based instruction that fully integrates reading, writing, speaking, and listening.

The Book Club program is grounded in some exciting new ideas about literacy. As we all remember from our own school experiences, literacy was once defined as the ability to decode text and identify main ideas and details. Today, however, people have begun to view literacy as a process—a process of making meaning by interacting with text in a social context. In the Book Club program, we've incorporated two perspectives that have defined a new course for reading instruction: social constructivism and reader response theory.

A Social Constructivist Approach The social constructivist perspective defines reading as a complex mental process that takes place in a specific social, cultural, and historical setting. Knowledge, according to this theory, is constructed within the context of meaningful, collaborative activities. The meaning and purpose of these activities is determined by the cultural standards at a particular moment in history. At present, the standards for literacy in American schools emphasize constructing meaning, valuing a variety of textual interpretations, responding to text in personal and aesthetic ways, and responding to reading through writing and discussion. Social constructivist theory suggests that interacting with others not only enriches a reader's appreciation of literature, but in fact is the means by which children develop literacy. We reflect the social nature of literacy in Book Club's focus on student-led discussion groups and in whole-class discussions.

Reader Response Theory In the past, literacy instruction maintained a narrow focus on literal comprehension. Students were asked to read a text and identify the main ideas, which were defined by the people who created the curriculum. Reader response theory, one of the foundations of the Book Club program, suggests that reading involves more than extracting information from a text. Instead of assuming that meaning lies buried within text waiting for readers to unearth it, the reader response perspective recognizes that what readers *bring to* the text is just as important as what they *take from* it. Readers construct meaning by bringing their prior knowledge and their affective responses to the text. Discussing the text with others—asking and answering questions, debating, reflecting—forms another crucial aspect of constructing meaning. In Book Club, we try to incorporate all of these aspects of literacy.

Components of the Book Club Program

If you visited a typical Book Club classroom, you might see the teacher begin by reading aloud to the class. After the read aloud, the teacher might follow up with a brief lesson or whole-group discussion. Next, students would silently read that day's assigned pages in their trade book and write responses to these pages in their reading logs, or journals. As the children worked, you'd see the teacher move through the classroom, stopping to provide individual instruction and to respond to any questions that might arise.

Then the teacher would signal that it was time for the class to break into small groups. For the next fifteen minutes or so, you'd watch several groups of four to five students engage in animated discussions. As the students conversed, the teacher would be moving from group to group, listening and recording information that might inform instruction, assessment, and whole-class discussions. Finally, the teacher would reconvene the class and conduct a whole-group discussion to share ideas and clarify concepts.

While this is certainly what you *might* see if you visited a Book Club classroom, it is by no means the only way a Book Club lesson could proceed. Every Book Club lesson centers around students' small-group discussions and includes opportunities for students to read, write in their logs, and participate in whole-class activities. However, these components vary from day to day, from unit to unit, and from classroom to classroom. As we describe strategies and activities that comprise the Book Club program, we hope you'll recognize instructional elements that are familiar as well as some new and interesting ideas that you can incorporate into your own literacy instruction.

For purposes of discussion, we find it helpful to divide the Book Club program into four components: reading, writing, community share (whole-class discussion), and book clubs (small-group discussions). In actual practice, however, these components overlap constantly. For your convenience, we will describe each component separately and discuss how the instruction you provide for your students applies to each component.

Book Club Program Components

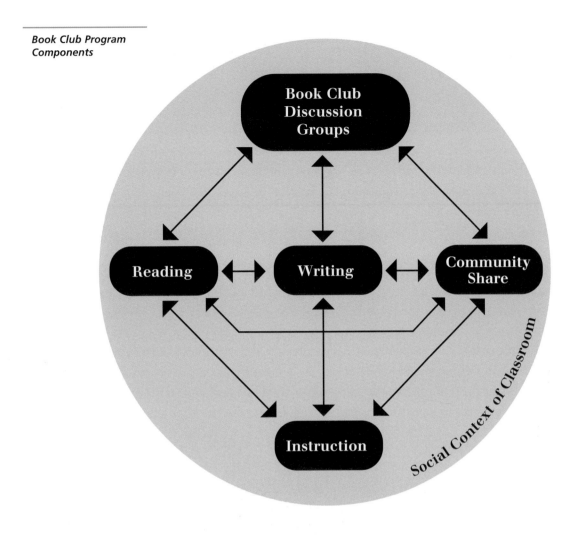

Reading

It's important to build a Book Club curriculum on a foundation of high-quality literature. Students should be able to connect the books they read in school with the experiences and ideas that shape their own lives. Book Club works best when you integrate many different types of literature and reading experiences.

A Variety of Excellent Literature We want our children to learn that literature can be a "mirror," reflecting issues, events, and ideas that children experience. As a mirror, this literature provides wonderful opportunities for students to reflect on decisions they have made or may someday have to make. Thus, we want our children to understand that books have personal relevance and can speak to real-life concerns. At the same time, we want our children to learn that literature can be a "window" as well, letting them see people, places, and events that they may never experience personally. Books can take them to faraway places, to times in the past or in the future. Books can give them a chance to meet presidents, kings, and famous people out of our history. Thus, we want our children to understand that books can help them learn about things they may never experience on their own.

When planning your Book Club curriculum, let your own expertise serve as your best guide for choosing books. As a teacher, you know which books you'd like your students to experience and which books students have enjoyed reading in past years. Some Book Club teachers also give their students a voice in selecting the books they'll read. For example, you might ask your students to select a favorite genre or author from which you will choose a book. Or you might offer several books that fit into a thematic unit and allow your students to choose among them.

We've found that the best books for the program deal with real issues—issues about which students can have authentic conversations and even arguments. Everyone agrees that the books should be well written and worth reading for their literary merit, but the element of controversy is just as important. Although a story may be beautifully written, if it doesn't confront serious issues, it probably won't fuel intense conversation in the classroom. However, this doesn't mean that texts must address strictly "realistic" issues. For example, the fantasy novel *Tuck Everlasting* (Babbitt, 1975) questions whether or not it would be desirable to live forever. While no one faces this dilemma in real life, we've seen the book inspire animated small-group discussions about what makes life precious and whether living forever is as wonderful as it initially sounds.

Opportunities for Many Types of Reading You'll want to encourage students to read independently, with peers, and in small groups, depending on their interests and needs. Each Book Club classroom period includes time set aside for sustained silent reading of the books students are discussing in their small groups. To prepare for their upcoming book club discussions, students read a specific section of their book—usually a chapter or two. If you were to wander through a Book Club classroom during this sustained silent reading, you would see some students sitting at their desks reading silently, while others might be seated in pairs or reading with their teacher. For some of the students, this reading may be "revisiting" sections that they've read earlier. Students sometimes read ahead because of their keen interest. Other students read ahead at home, prior to each day's activities, as a way to get a "jump start" on reading what might otherwise be too difficult for them.

Teacher Read Aloud The reading component of Book Club may also include the teacher's reading a theme-related book aloud. By sharing a read-aloud experience, you'll provide a common point of reference for the entire class, particularly when various small groups are reading different books. Reading aloud helps your students appreciate the beauty of spoken language and provides a model of fluent reading.

Reading Instruction The reading and writing components of Book Club are integrated in student's reading logs, which we discuss in the next section of this chapter. The logs provide ample opportunities to instruct students in reading skills and literary elements such as genre, story elements, vocabulary development, and comprehension strategies. By prompting students to apply certain skills and strategies as they write in their logs, you can reinforce important skills that traditional reading curriculums cover, as well as other strategies that might be missed. In the Book Club program, students will find this instruction immediately relevant to the ongoing discussions they are having about books.

A wide range of teaching opportunities emerge from the thematic or topical units around which Book Club is usually structured. For example, imagine that you are teaching a topical unit focused on the issues that led to the Civil War. Your students could read works of historical fiction whose characters grapple with some of the issues relevant to this topic. They could also read biographies that show how real people dealt with these issues. Your instruction might then include discussion about the genres of historical fiction and biography—what is different between the two and what readers can learn from each genre. Such a unit would complement and enrich your social studies curriculum as well. Your students might study topics related to the Civil War in preparation for beginning the literature unit, and they could continue to research topics or questions that arise from their Book Club reading and discussions. By integrating your curriculum around reading and discussing excellent, thought-provoking books, your instruction in all curricular areas becomes more meaningful and relevant.

Writing

Traditional reading workbooks usually focus on literal comprehension questions. This approach tends to turn reading into a hunt for the "right" answers, often to questions that are one-dimensional or even trivial. However, spending time scanning a text to find specific facts and record them on a worksheet is not likely to develop children's love of reading. The Book Club program moves beyond this traditional approach by encouraging students to respond to their reading in more open-ended ways. When students discuss books with their peers, the issues in those books become a part of their lives rather than just material for a worksheet.

The Book Club program emphasizes three categories of response to literature: personal, creative, and critical. Personal response includes a reader's emotional reaction to a text and the personal experiences that the text calls to mind. Creative response refers to the imaginative avenues a reader explores as a result of reading the text. Critical response involves analyzing the author's use of literary techniques. The chart on page 6 elaborates on these response categories, all of which are part of the writing component of the program.

Personal Response

Valuing Text Read	Feelings Evoked
	Degree of Enjoyment
Sharing Personal Stories	Related Texts
	Class's Experiences
	Family Experiences
	Personal Experiences

Creative Response

Engaging Creatively with Text	Self-in-Situation
	Altering Text Event
	Extending the Text
Engaging Creatively with Author	Letters
	Imagining Self as Author

Critical Response

Text Analysis	… of Literary Elements
	… of Author's Message
	… of Effect

Reading Logs As Book Club students read, they record their ideas, feelings, and questions in reading logs. Reading logs consist of both blank and lined pages, giving students the option of diagramming, drawing, or writing their responses. At the beginning of the year, you'll need to instruct and model for your students the range of possibilities for responses that are both appropriate and helpful to record in their logs. It's also important to encourage students' own creativity in inventing new ways of responding.

The main purpose of the logs is to focus students' attention on issues that can support lively discussion in their small groups. It's also a place where they can note vocabulary words and write down questions that they would like to have answered by their peers or by the teacher. Reading log maps (see "What can I do in my reading log?" in the Blackline Masters: Think Sheets section following page 261 of this guide) can provide students with a starting point for writing in their logs.

Think Sheets In addition to the reading logs, Book Club teachers can prompt students to respond to literature by using "think sheets." These open-ended worksheets introduce students to new ways of thinking about and responding to the texts they read and to new ways of organizing their thoughts. For example, in the think sheet reproduced below, a student synthesized ideas across three theme-related books. We've provided blackline masters for think sheets that have worked well with our students in the section following page 261.

Sample Think Sheet

A Book Club teacher created this think sheet to complement a unit that she was teaching on World War II. Especially in the beginning of the year, you may find that your students benefit from the guidance provided by such think sheets.

Name **Jennifer**   Date **November 5**

Bringing Ideas Together

Topics that <u>Sadako</u>, <u>Hiroshima No Pika</u>, and <u>Faithful Elephants</u> make me think about are:

War, Japan, People dying, people and animals; sadness, why people fight, bombs, Why did the US drop the bomb on japan, Why does did Japan and the US have a war, why are they friends now after they had a war.

The topic I want to share about is:

Why do people fight War

because   I want to now why people have war. I don't think that war is something to do. I dont think I need to grow up and see people fighting over something that can be solved by talking and communicating

---

You can use think sheets to guide your students in using many of the reading strategies and skills that school districts require. A think sheet might, for example, ask students to create a sequence chart, analyze literary elements, write a summary, predict outcomes, generate questions, or identify a theme. Once students have learned a method for responding to text from a think sheet, they can pick up or adapt this method to create original responses in their logs. We call log responses that students create themselves on blank or lined paper (instead of on preformatted think sheets) *share sheets.*

Expanding the Range of Reading-Log Options As your students gain experience with the role that reading logs play in the program, they'll be ready to create increasingly sophisticated log entries. You can support students directly by providing think sheets that encourage more complex skills, such as synthesizing ideas across texts and making broad connections to themes.

Many teachers have found, too, that the students themselves develop new possibilities for reading log entries. You might have your students brainstorm a share-sheet idea list that remains on display in the classroom throughout the year. Students can then add ideas to the list as they think of them. As students create these new possibilities and teach them to their peers, they'll develop a sense of ownership and voice in their own learning.

Community Share

Whole-class discussions, which we call community share, provide a context in which teachers and students can bring ideas from their reading, writing, and small-group discussions to the attention of the wider classroom community. Since we know that learning is a language-based social process, and that high-order thought processes have their origins in social interactions, community share forms an especially crucial aspect of the curriculum. Community share allows you, as both a leader of and a participant in the conversation, to introduce new ideas and skills, to initiate "repair activities" when students have blatantly misinterpreted information in their reading, and to share your own ideas and feelings with your students.

Community share enhances the feeling of community in the classroom, giving students the confidence to share their thoughts and allowing them to get to know each other. Since students will work in many different small groups throughout the year, it's important that they develop a level of familiarity and comfort with each of their classmates.

Community share can serve different purposes depending on its placement before or after students meet in their book clubs. (In fact, many teachers exploit all of these purposes by using community share both before and after book clubs.) A community share that precedes book clubs provides an opportunity for instruction. For example, you can use it to build background that will help your students get the most from their reading and small-group discussions. You might encourage students to review what happened the previous day or week, both to inform students who have been absent and to refresh the memories of everyone in the class. You might also focus students' attention on theme-related issues that will come up in the day's reading assignment. Students might raise questions about their previous reading that they hope will be answered in today's reading, and you might instruct them in new ways of writing about or discussing their reading.

In a community share that follows book clubs, students share the ideas and issues that came up in their small groups. They might discuss interesting insights that their group had, or they might present any questions that they were unable to answer. Some of these questions might be answered by their classmates in other groups, while others might inspire a lesson to develop a skill students need to understand an aspect of the reading.

During community share, you'll probably want to encourage students to make intertextual connections, linking the reading they've just done to other texts they've read and to their own lives. Community share gives you the chance to model for the class different ways of responding to texts and ways of participating in discussions about text. For example, you might share your feelings about a particular scene in a book and encourage students to share their own reactions. Other conversational skills you could model include asking follow-up questions, clarifying a point, and expanding on someone else's comment. Community share can also be a time to examine interesting or confusing words from the reading.

Book Clubs

All of the program components ultimately support students' small-group discussions, or book clubs. We want students to engage in real conversations in which they share their personal, creative, and critical responses to literature and take an interest in their peers' ideas and opinions. As students read, write in their logs, and build background in community share, they are preparing themselves to engage in just this kind of conversation.

During the development and classroom testing of Book Club, teachers experimented with different numbers of students in each small group. Six students turned out to be too many, since some students didn't get a chance to talk very often. On the other end of the spectrum, three students were too few. Although a group with three members often held good conversations with each student enjoying plenty of time to talk, an absence meant that the group was down to a pair, and teachers had to recombine groups nearly every day. Through trial and error, we learned that groups of four or five were best, providing both stability and a chance for everyone to participate. (For further discussion of grouping concerns, see the Classroom Management chapter, page 13.)

As in every other component of the program, instruction plays a crucial role in supporting students' small-group discussions. Putting children into book clubs and telling them to talk about a book is not enough to set real conversations in motion. Talking about literature requires a combination of skills and strategies in which students need instruction. The way you lead discussions during community share provides one concrete model for students to follow. You'll also want to conduct lessons in specific conversational skills (e.g., what kinds of questions work best to promote discussion) throughout the year to give students some guidelines. These lessons will focus on increasingly sophisticated conversational skills as students gain practice in discussing literature.

We often use audio taping as a tool for teaching students how to have successful small-group discussions. For example, we might record and transcribe one group's discussion and then have students analyze the transcript to identify ways in which the interaction could be improved. You can also use audio tapes for role-playing activities in which students perform the transcripts as plays. By assuming the roles of their peers, students can learn how it feels to spark a good conversation, to be left out of the conversation, to be bossy, or to ask silly questions. They can then discuss what they learned from playing these roles and apply this new knowledge not only in their book clubs, but also in other areas of social interaction.

In the same way that the components of the Book Club program overlap each other, the instruction you provide within a particular component often has a much broader relevance. For example, when you teach students discussion techniques—in the context of either small groups or community share—you are also teaching them about connections between spoken and written language. When you teach reading-log strategies, you are also teaching comprehension and response skills. Furthermore, the instruction you provide through the program reaches far beyond what takes place in the classroom. Because Book Club is structured around natural conversations about literature and the real-life issues it explores, the skills that students develop will enrich their whole lives.

The Flexibility of Book Club Components

We've already pointed out that you could use the community share component at different points in the program depending on the purposes you wish to accomplish. As you plan each daily lesson, Book Club offers the flexibility of spending as much or as little time on each component as you see fit. One day you might want to emphasize writing, for example, by having your students work on an extended synthesis activity or story writing connected to a book or theme. On another day, you might spend most of the Book Club period in community share, discussing the background and context of a book that the students are going to read.

Of course, external factors such as special programs (e.g., music, art, physical education classes), Title 1 integration, team teaching, resource room, and so forth inevitably affect the time you have for Book Club. The flexibility of Book Club allows you to shape your reading curriculum according to the practical requirements of your school day as well as the individual needs and interests of your students.

Classroom Management

Beginning Book Club

There are many decisions to make when using the Book Club program. This chapter is not intended to make those decisions for you but to provide you with information that will help you make your own decisions. Each teacher using the program will need to evaluate the issues and come up with answers that work in his or her own classroom. However, those of us who have been doing Book Club for a while have some suggestions for you to consider. The issues you will need to think about as you begin to implement Book Club include literature selection, grouping students, daily instruction, reading aloud, developing a special classroom library, and inclusion of special-needs students. Our suggestions will help you think about each issue more fully and will let you in on the things that have worked for us over time.

Literature Selection

Selecting appropriate books to use for Book Club is very important to the success of the program. You'll want to choose "quality literature"—books that are well written—but you should also consider several additional factors. These factors include potential for discussion, the background of your students, readability, curriculum, and availability.

First, and most importantly, a book should have potential for discussion. Look for books that raise some interesting questions or issues that students will want to talk about. When children read books that address serious, real-life issues, they can discuss and form opinions about these complex issues. At the same time, we would caution you to consider the developmental appropriateness of a book, since some issues are simply not appropriate for young readers. Many picture books today, while relatively easy to read, present very complex and mature issues. Books such as *Hiroshima No Pika* (Maruki, 1980) and *Pink and Say* (Pollaco, 1994) deal with serious issues that many lower elementary students could not handle. Even some fourth- and fifth-grade students struggle with the content. Use your own discretion when determining developmentally appropriate material for your students. You alone know your class and are best able to judge the kinds of materials they can handle.

Your own experience with a book will affect your success in using it for Book Club. When you use a book that you have read with students before, or a book that you have simply read and loved, your passion for the book will encourage students to look for the good in it. If you really love a book, your class will be able to tell, and they'll probably like it, too.

Another factor to consider when selecting literature is content. The book's content should be something about which students have some prior knowledge. If you want students to make connections to books, they need to know something about the topic from the start. In some cases, you may decide to provide this knowledge in a brief unit on the topic of the story, thereby providing your students with the appropriate knowledge base.

Readability is another factor to think about. You should select a book that most of the students in your class can read. Since most classrooms contain a wide range of reading abilities, we suggest you look for a book at your grade level. You can provide support to lower-ability readers in many ways, since you'll probably have students who cannot read the text independently. (We'll discuss this issue in detail later in this chapter, under "Inclusion.") Students reading above level can supplement their reading with other books by the same author or within the same theme.

Yet another concern deals with curriculum. Book Club integrates very easily with other content areas. It's fairly easy to find books focusing on many social studies and science topics, and to build a unit focusing first on content building, then on literature with Book Club. Therefore, when you select literature, think about the curriculum or unit topic with which you may want to integrate Book Club. The Lesson Plans section of this guide, beginning on page 55, contains some sample units we've used, along with many suggested book titles and theme links.

Finally, there's a logistical issue to think about: Are the books available? Part of the success of the Book Club program depends on all students having their own copies of the book. Ownership of the story increases when students can hold the book and touch the words—both with their eyes and with their fingers. This act of physically "owning" the book is very important. Students also use the book during small-group discussions to reinforce points they are making or to support their opinions. Therefore, you'll want to obtain multiple copies of the book(s) you plan to use for Book Club. In our quest to acquire books, we've found that some districts or county offices house classroom sets of books for loan. We've purchased books with money from our instructional funds. We've saved bonus points from commercial book clubs (such as Troll, Scholastic, or Trumpet) to purchase books. We've put together sets borrowed from various libraries. We've found colleagues who were willing to share book sets, and sometimes we've even bought books ourselves. (See page 42 for more tips on acquiring books.)

Selecting the best literature to use with your students is a decision you'll revisit several times a year, since you may read four to eight Book Club books yearly. Remember to consider the factors we've discussed here: quality of literature, potential for discussion, students' background knowledge, readability, curriculum, and availability. This will help get your program off the ground and running smoothly. Our lists of suggested books (in the Lesson Plans section) are not exclusive, and you should always pre-read any books that you plan to use with children.

Grouping the Students

Book Club is unique in its focus on student-led response groups. Typically, a book club group contains four to five students. Group membership remains constant throughout the book or unit, and groups change for each new book or unit. It's important to orchestrate placement thoughtfully and carefully. We'll discuss here several factors to consider when forming groups: heterogeneity in terms of gender, ethnicity, and language abilities; student personalities and attitudes; and student choice. These issues will confront you every time you choose new groups—usually each time you start a new book. In addition, there are two other grouping options that we'll discuss briefly: same-gender groups and repeat groups. And since we are often asked about disruptive students and those who find it hard to function in groups, we'll discuss this topic as well.

Heterogeneity We often have to form groups for Book Club before we've met our students (i.e., before school begins), or when we don't yet know them well (i.e., the first few weeks of school). For the first groups, we suggest that you begin by grouping the students heterogeneously by gender and ethnicity. If you have information about their literacy abilities from previous teachers, consider that as well. If you're including special-education students, intersperse them throughout the groups. We've found that groups of four students work best at the beginning of the year. As the school year progresses, you'll learn much more about your students, and forming subsequent groups will be easier.

Heterogeneity is something to strive for each time you form new groups, and you'll find a significant amount of research that promotes this kind of grouping. Heterogeneous groups are especially effective in Book Club because children's unique backgrounds and experiences affect how and what they can contribute to their group's discussion. The more diversity among the members of the group, the more diverse their discussion. An ideal group, then, would include diversity of gender, ethnicity, and ability. Each person will be able to contribute something unique to the group, which adds to the quality of discussion, and the group's diversity will help to promote and develop social skills.

Attitudes and Personalities You'll also have to consider the attitudes and personalities of your students. We've noticed that best friends often don't work well in the same group; nor will children who really dislike each other. We want our students to have a chance to work with as many of their peers as possible throughout the school year, but some combinations are better left unmade. Sometimes the attitudes of the students toward school and reading must be taken into consideration. Putting together two strong personalities might inhibit the other two members from joining the conversation. On the other hand, four strong personalities might lead to some very good discussions. This kind of information is something you'll learn about your students as the year progresses, and how you factor it into your grouping decisions is up to you.

Student Choice If we want students to take ownership of their learning, we need to provide them with choices. Grouping is one area where this can happen in Book Club. You can allow for student choice by conducting a survey at the end of a book, prior to assigning new groups. Ask your students to list the members in their current group, tell how the group did overall and what things they did to improve the group, and set some goals for next time. Also ask students to list the names of two or three other children they would like to have in their book club next time. (Several self-assessment forms that cover these questions are available as blackline masters in the section following page 281.) As you compile and tally these results, you'll still have the final say over group composition, but you can allow most students to be placed with at least one person of their choosing. This has worked well for us in the past, and students feel comfortable and happy that their voices are being heard.

Other Grouping Options Throughout our experiences in implementing the Book Club program, we've considered the issues of same-gender groups and repeat groups. From a fifth-grade teacher's perspective, same-gender groups seem to work well in the spring, when boys and girls often become focused on impressing members of the opposite sex. By creating groups of all girls or all boys, this need to impress is gone, and the book club conversations become more authentic. At the same time, however, we would advise you to use caution with same-gender groups because cliques can form and the diversity of ideas may be lessened.

Repeat groups are those whose members stay together for more than one book. Occasionally the dynamics of a group will create such authentic and meaningful conversations that it may be worthwhile to keep the group together for a second book. When doing this we always ask all the group members if they want to stay together, and all must agree before we assign the new groups. We also recommend doing this for only two books, not more, so that students get a chance to work with all their classmates. While repeat groups are certainly an option, teachers who use Book Club report using it only very sparingly—once or twice during a five-year span.

Placing Difficult Students "Some students just can't work in a group." We hear this statement repeatedly as we talk to teachers about Book Club. Our reply is: "All students can participate in book club discussion groups." We admit that some students don't like working in groups, that some students are disruptive in groups, and that some students are shunned by many of their classmates so that no one wants them in their group. However, we've found that all students can and do participate in book clubs. This is where your role in organizing the groups becomes crucial. Our experience using Book Club in our classrooms has given us some insight into ways to integrate difficult students.

Think carefully about heterogeneity, personalities and attitudes, student choice, and same-gender options when placing difficult students. Consider the interactions that might occur, and what kinds of students in a group will provide the best support and learning environment for each child. Here are some strategies that we've tried with disruptive students.

- Have the disruptive student's permanent desk physically separated from the group, but during book club discussions have the student move to join his or her group.

- Place the responsibility on the student. For example, we've had students who must decide on a daily basis whether they can participate in the group in an acceptable manner, and they choose whether or not to stay for book clubs. Alternative activities are determined ahead of time by the student and the teacher, so the student can make an informed decision.

- Have the student study how to participate in book clubs in a positive way. This might be accomplished by having the student serve as an observer to other groups, taking notes on what they do well and how the group makes things work. Later, the student can talk to the teacher about what he or she observed. This can often serve to open the student's eyes to ways in which he or she can participate in a more appropriate manner.

These are only a few suggestions. You certainly have your own ways of handling disruptive students in other areas, and Book Club is no different. With patience and thoughtful planning from you, all students can learn to participate in Book Club.

Arranging the Classroom A final issue in grouping students concerns the physical placement of the groups. Many teachers already have students' desks arranged in clusters of four or five, and these become the setting for book clubs. Some teachers use tables in the room and have students move during Book Club. If your room is carpeted, we've found that students love to lie on the floor and form a circle facing each other as they discuss the book. Sitting on window ledges, in a book nook, or in the hallway are also favorite places for children to hold book club discussions. We don't usually use alternative meeting places until the routines are established and practiced, but once students learn the "how" of doing Book Club, the "where" is anywhere you or they decide it can be.

It may sound as if grouping is an overwhelming issue, but really it isn't. It is, however, an important decision, and we believe the success of your program centers around the ability of the book club groups to maintain meaningful conversations. Your role in composing the groups is therefore crucial, and we would caution you to approach it as such. When the right combinations of students are found, book club conversations become full of rich, meaningful dialogue.

Daily Instruction

Daily lessons during community share form the instructional core of the Book Club program. These lessons may take place either before or after students do their reading, writing, and discussing in book clubs, but they are always related to the day's reading assignment and to the writing students do in their logs. Because Book Club is a complete reading program—not just supplemental or enrichment—you'll need to provide direct instruction to your students through these daily lessons.

The Lesson Plans section of this guide (pages 55–260) contains outlines of lessons that we've actually used in our classrooms. We've provided lesson plans for eight individual titles: *Last Summer with Maizon* (Woodson, 1990), *Tuck Everlasting* (Babbitt, 1975), *Bridge to Terabithia* (Paterson, 1977), *The Fighting Ground* (Avi, 1984), *A Wrinkle in Time* (L'Engle, 1962), *Hatchet* (Paulsen, 1987), *Walk Two Moons* (Creech, 1994), and *Maniac Magee* (Spinelli, 1990). There's also an author study on Mildred Taylor that focuses on her books *Song of the Trees* (1975), *Mississippi Bridge* (1990), and *The Friendship and The Gold Cadillac* (1987). During these units, all students in the class are reading the same book at the same time.

Near the end of the year, when students are very comfortable with the Book Club format, we've often done multi-book units in which different book clubs are reading and discussing different books. All of the books are linked either topically or thematically, so that the entire class can discuss larger issues during community share. On pages 244–260, we've provided an outline for a multi-book unit on the Civil War and resource lists for multi-book units on the environment, World War II, and coming of age.

We've compiled the lesson plans in this guide over the past eight years. They've worked well for us. They are not, however, meant to represent a definitive list of topics and issues to be discussed during the reading of these books. Our lessons are focused on the four main curricular areas of the Book Club program: language conventions, literary elements, comprehension, and response to literature. (See the chart on pages 26–27 for more about these curricular areas.) We developed our curriculum based on several factors: the guidelines for our particular school districts, current reading research, and our experience with a wide range of commercial programs.

You'll want to compare your own curriculum statements and objectives with our lessons and add skills and strategies accordingly. You should always use your own judgment to determine what instruction your students need, and at what time.

Because we know you'll be adapting our lessons and the Book Club program generally to your own needs, we've provided the Curriculum Overview chart on pages 47–54 to assist your planning. The chart lists the titles of all the lessons in this guide, organized according to Book Club's curricular target areas. So, for example, imagine that you're doing a Book Club unit and you feel that your students could use a lesson on share sheets on a particular day. If you wanted to see a model of a share sheet lesson that we've used, you could consult the chart to find such a lesson. We hope that this chart and our model lessons will give you the support and inspiration you need to develop lessons based on your own favorite books and the needs of your students.

Reading Aloud

Throughout the course of each book, it's often helpful to read another novel aloud to the class. The novel usually relates in some way to the book students are reading and discussing with their book clubs. Perhaps it involves a similar topic, theme, genre, or author, depending on your focus or goal for the book. You can read aloud from this novel at any time during the day, and we usually spend 15–30 minutes a day reading aloud. We have found several reasons to justify this.

First, we can encourage the children to make intertextual links. If we want students to realize that a book can make us think of another book, or help us to understand another book, it's appropriate for the teacher to model how to make such links. Using a book for read aloud that has some connections to the book club book allows this to happen. It gives the classroom community a shared experience within which to make these connections. As a result of your modeling and explaining why people link ideas from different books, students will soon begin to do this on their own—both in their written responses and in their book club discussions.

Second, we can make connections to our own lives. We often model through the read-aloud book what we're thinking as we read. We talk about what the book makes us feel, and why this is important. This helps us show the children not only how to understand the story better, but also how to use a book to make sense of events in our own lives.

We stress understanding the book, but not forming a stagnant understanding of the book's literal content. Instead, we model how to develop a fluid understanding that's based on the context of the moment. We talk to children about how their background experience and their prior knowledge influence how they comprehend a story. Likewise, we stress the importance of the social setting within which the learning takes place. Since we take a social constructivist view of learning, we try to provide our students with the opportunity to see how meaning is constructed in a social, language-based context. Sharing a read-aloud book helps us accomplish this.

Third, listening to a read-aloud book helps children develop fluency and increases their language use in writing and speaking. Hearing the teacher read aloud with good intonation, inflection, and emotion allows children to hear what good readers sound like. It also introduces them to beautiful language that they might not be aware of in their silent reading, but which they can hear while listening. We notice that students' vocabularies and language use expand to include the words from our read-aloud books. We see it in students' writing and conversations. This alone is reason enough to read aloud to children every day.

Finally, reading aloud from an ongoing chapter book creates a common experience that we as a class share. It helps make us a community. It's a way to tie us together, because we've all read and learned about the book's characters, events, and issues together. It allows us to build content knowledge together, form opinions, express beliefs and feelings, and grow as a community of readers and writers. No other community can be exactly the same, because the comments and ideas that come forth while reading a book aloud are unique. This community feeling is instrumental in having children participate in authentic conversations through book club discussions. The things we model and do as a whole class carry over into their small-group discussions.

As teachers, our days are full and we face demands from many areas of the curriculum. However, the 15–30 minutes it takes to read aloud to our children is something we won't give up. Everyone loves to hear a good story and to get caught up in it. The positive outcomes from this simple activity are seen two and three times over. It is a favorite time of the day in our classrooms, and its benefits to the Book Club program are many. We strongly recommend that you include this practice in your own classroom.

Special Classroom Library

As part of the Book Club program, we also assemble a set of books for a special classroom library. These books relate by genre, theme, topic, or author to the current book club and read-aloud books. If there is a unit of study connected to social studies or science, the books will often focus on the specific content. We do this because we want the children to have choices during our silent sustained reading time each day, and we encourage them to read from the special classroom library. Having books arranged by topic or genre helps students learn about different kinds of books and identify books they like. We all know children express a wide range of interests through their reading materials, and by providing them with many different kinds of books, we hope to reflect this range.

We also have a regular classroom library that contains books and magazines of all types, from which children can choose materials for silent reading. Our special classroom library is in addition to the regular library, and it usually exists on a table or special shelf. It changes over the course of the year as our topic or unit changes. We've found that the special classroom library really helps get children turned on to good books. Many students are able to make inter-textual connections between these books and their book club books. They often learn interesting facts that they can share with their book club groups, which increases the quality of the conversations. Sometimes, as questions are raised in the group, a student will bring in a book from the special classroom library to help answer a question or settle a debate. Children begin to see practical reasons for reading books when they can use them to prove a point or to share something new and meaningful with their groups. Thus, the classroom library helps students fulfill the basic goal of any reading program: it encourages students to become lifelong readers.

Inclusion

Book Club fits the needs of the wide range of literacy abilities found in most elementary classrooms today. The program has helped the literacy development of children labeled Chapter One, English as Second Language learners (ESL), and many special-education acronyms (LD, ED, ADD, ADHD, EI, EMI, POHI). In this section, we'll discuss some of the adaptations we've made in order to include all students in the Book Club program.

The Concept of Inclusion Over the past few years, *inclusion* has become a buzzword in education. People use inclusion to mean many different things, and its definition is often vague. For the purpose of this chapter, inclusion refers to a continuum of services for students with special needs. The chart below illustrates this continuum.

Inclusion Continuum

| Full time in institution with special programming | Full time in resource room with support | Part time in resource room; part time in regular classroom with support | Full time in regular classroom with support |

There is an underlying goal in schools today to place students into an environment that will be minimally restrictive—that is, an environment that meets their specific educational, social, emotional, learning, and developmental needs. The continuum of services ranges from students being placed full time into the general education classroom with support from teacher consultants and specialists who team teach with the regular classroom teacher, to students being placed entirely out of the public school system in private programs. Those making the placement decisions for inclusion students keep in mind that the best place for any student is where his or her needs are met and where he or she has as much contact with peers as is developmentally appropriate.

There have been many students in our classrooms over the years that traditionally have been excluded from "regular education" classrooms. Students with special needs—such as the learning disabled (reading, writing, language, math), ADHD, ADD, emotionally impaired, educable mentally impaired, Chapter One, ESL, and Downs Syndrome—have all been included in Book Club and have had success in the program. There have been only a few students who could not participate in Book Club. For example, one student who was profoundly hearing impaired could not hear most speech sounds despite the use of hearing aids. Rather than participating in book clubs, this student followed an individualized language curriculum tailored to develop his language expression and improve his communication skills.

Reading Support Many students who are typically pulled out of the regular classroom for reading instruction are pulled out because they can't read (i.e., call the words) correctly. In the pull-out program, they often receive texts that are below their grade level and have very simple plots. Students often don't succeed in these programs, nor do they often learn to like reading. One benefit we've discovered with inclusion in Book Club is an increased desire and motivation to become better readers. Students in Book Club feel better about themselves because they're reading harder books—books with plots and real ideas—and because they're being challenged to think and make meaning appropriate to their age and grade level. They are also set on an equal footing with their peers, which often does not happen with low-ability and special-education students.

However, many of the students we include in Book Club require support for reading the text. There are several ways to accomplish this. Some students take the book home every night and pre-read with an adult the text that is assigned for the next day. Then, in class, they simply read as much as they can of the assigned reading, knowing they have already read or heard it once. Another way we support children is through partner reading. A child can pair up with a more able reader and follow along as the text is being read aloud. He or she can also read to the more able reader, who becomes a tutor and guide as well.

A similar idea is to put the book on tape. Occasionally allowing your students a choice of listening to the book takes some of the burden off them. Of course, we would allow any of our students to listen to the tape, not just the inclusion students. At times we have the resource room or Title One teacher pre-read or reread sections of the book club book aloud for one or several students. This reinforces the concepts and helps students get the flavor of the language. Occasionally we read aloud from an especially exciting or intriguing part of the book club book for the whole class. This sparks interest, allows the students to hear and see the language of the book, and reinforces the ideas presented in the story. By providing reading support for our inclusion students, we've been able to create interest and continued motivation, not just for Book Club, but for reading in general. Such motivation is important when students with reading problems are asked to read simpler texts and practice reading skills at other times during the day. Book Club helps them see why the development of these skills is so important—to see that reading is more than simply worksheets and answering questions.

Developing Social Skills Another obstacle often involves the lack of social skills necessary for working in a group, both for inclusion students and for students in general. We found that many of our students did not know how to work well in small groups, especially when the teacher wasn't present. We've been able to address this issue in several ways. First, many of our early lessons focus on how to talk in book club groups. Even though many students are able to work in task-oriented groups (i.e., cooperative learning groups), the focus of a student-led literature response group is different. Therefore, instruction in how to interrelate is crucial for the entire class. In these lessons, you should pay particular attention to the inclusion students to monitor their understanding.

Second, special-education teachers have been able to offer small-group instruction that follows up on our lessons for the whole class. Inclusion students can practice the elements of good group discussion in a small group, which is slightly less risky. This has helped students become more confident and able to meld more easily into the whole-class community. By doing these kinds of lessons, we've experienced success with emotionally impaired or learning disabled students who traditionally have found it difficult to adjust socially in a regular classroom setting.

We've seen students reap real benefits through their participation in Book Club. They are exposed to daily language learning in a social and cooperative setting that requires them to learn how to cope in these situations and practice appropriate strategies of coping. They experience the way in which students are expected to behave in social situations. This takes some patience, time, training, and trial and error on the part of the teacher. As we mentioned earlier, in the grouping section, decisions regarding the grouping of inclusion students is very important in light of these social factors.

Instructional Aides In some schools that use Book Club, instructional aides accompany special-education students into the classroom. Sometimes the instructional aide helps a student read the assigned text, or the child can dictate his or her journal entry to the aide. Often the aide's role is to provide appropriate language learning for the student (i.e., sign language). We've found the presence of an instructional aide in the classroom to be comforting to the inclusion student, and not at all a disturbance or hindrance to the dynamics of the small group.

Preparing the Whole Class for Inclusion When putting inclusion into practice, we've found some regular education students to be hesitant and unsure about working with students who have typically been removed for reading instruction. Overcoming this hesitancy takes some direct instruction on the part of the teacher. We often begin each school year with a discussion about abilities. First, we encourage students to define *abilities* as a class. Usually the students name things like roller blading, bike riding, drawing, reading, writing, and playing soccer. Then the class talks about disability—that *dis-* means "not," and therefore that *disability* means not having an ability that someone else may have. We try to stress that this simply means that some of us face challenges where others might not.

We stress that everyone faces challenges, has something that they feel they cannot do as well as others, or has something that they have to do differently from others. From there, the conversation moves to how it feels when we cannot do something as well as, or we have to do it differently from, our friends. This helps the class understand that everyone has the same feelings about abilities and disabilities. This type of socialization is extremely important. Students need to understand that a person is a person, no matter in which area of life their specific difficulty lies. Such a discussion establishes the norms of sensitivity, cooperation, and acceptance for the class, and it decreases the incidence of teasing, mocking, and cruelty. One important norm to stress is never to make fun of someone who is different. Because learning is a process that requires us to take risks, creating a classroom environment in which everyone feels safe to take these risks is essential.

Finally, we try to meet each child at the point where he or she will be able to participate and learn. It would be impossible for us to offer you all the possible scenarios for working with special-needs children. Every child is unique, and it's up to the teacher to decide what's best for each child. For example, one of our students with a language disability found it difficult to transfer his complex thoughts to paper. He would verbally record his responses and then translate them into writing on a word processor. In this way he was able to participate in Book Club with success, despite the challenges he faced. We believe that many special-needs children can participate in Book Club through modifications and with an effort to meet each child's individual needs.

Final Thoughts

We've found Book Club to be a fun, motivational, and learning-filled program—for teachers and students alike. We know from experience that the issues and decisions described above are complex but manageable, and that by devoting specific attention to them early, you can help establish a successful Book Club program. As you revisit each decision throughout the year, you'll find your outcomes will vary depending on your teaching style, your students' needs, and your instructional and content goals.

Assessment

New Ideas About Assessment

New ideas about literacy—such as the social constructivist and reader response theories discussed on pages 1 and 2—have already led to changes in the way we teach. It's often tempting, however, to resort to the same old assessment techniques to measure students' achievement and progress. The problem with this is that traditional tests, in particular, not only fail to reflect the new goals of literacy instruction but often stand in the way of reaching these goals.

When reading was seen as a collection of isolated skills, it made sense to test reading achievement by checking students' mastery of these discrete skills. In the context of our new understanding of reading, however, a focus on low-level skills no longer shows all that our students are learning. Worse, it sends a message to students that we value these skills more highly than the more authentic literacy events that take place in the classroom, because the results of such assessments can determine their grades, their placement in particular groups, or even their participation in special programs.

Thus, a dangerous gap exists between current instructional goals and the outmoded assessment methods still used to gauge the success of our instruction. Further complicating the matter, many districts continue to emphasize the standardized tests that equate literacy with the mastery of discrete skills. However, many educators have developed models that align assessment with instruction in today's classrooms. Two of the most prominent new approaches to emerge from this research are portfolio assessment and performance-based assessment.

Portfolio Assessment A student portfolio serves the same purpose as that of a professional artist or photographer. It provides samples of the student's best work at a particular moment in time. A typical portfolio would contain writing samples, art work, a student's own evaluations of his or her work, and so on. Portfolios have a number of advantages over traditional tests. Perhaps the most important of these is that portfolios reflect the true nature of learning, which involves many trials and errors on the road to one's "best work."

Tests create very unnatural situations in which students have one shot at coming up with predetermined right answers. The process of developing a portfolio, on the other hand, encourages students to stretch themselves, to try new things, and not to be afraid of making mistakes as they learn new skills. Students have time to reflect upon their work and the progress they are making, revise earlier entries in their portfolios, and develop new ones.

A second advantage of portfolios over traditional assessments is their flexibility. A portfolio can contain samples of a student's work from many different types of activities, including the complex activities associated with literature discussions. A student in the Book Club program, for example, might include in his or her portfolio an audio tape of a book club discussion along with an evaluation form on which the student has commented about what he or she did well in the discussion and what could be improved. This gives you a much richer source of information about the student than a list of responses to comprehension questions. Portfolios also allow you to collect data at any time by drawing on your students' ongoing work. This form of assessment provides an excellent general picture of a student's evolving skills.

Portfolio assessment does have some weaknesses, however. First, it does not facilitate in-depth analysis of students' work in any particular area. While a broad sampling of work in many areas provides a good overview of a student's progress, the amount of data potentially contained in a portfolio could become so overwhelming that you would not have time to evaluate any of it very deeply. Second, portfolio assessment offers few clearly defined scoring guidelines. Thus there is little data available for comparing different students' work or for comparing one student's work at different times of the year.

Performance-Based Assessment   Performance-based assessment shares some features with portfolio assessment. Both involve collecting a range of materials that demonstrate students' abilities in reading, writing, and discussing. Both methods draw these materials from authentic literacy activities. Performance-based assessment, however, is based on more controlled literacy "events" from which you can create a detailed portrait of each of your students at a particular point in time.

A typical performance-based assessment takes place in the context of a one-week unit similar to the instructional units of your regular curriculum. The assessment unit engages your students in all of the activities that they normally do in the classroom, from which you gather specific information to assess their achievement.

Performance-based assessment offers the advantages of clearly defined scoring criteria and in-depth analysis of your students' work. It's relatively easy for you to compare different students' performances and to compare a single student's work across time. On the other hand, performance-based assessment is time- and labor-intensive for the teacher. You must prepare for the assessment in advance, and you must analyze your data afterward. Since the assessment is part of a structured unit, data collection is less flexible and occurs only during the specific days or weeks set aside for assessment events.

Assessment in the Book Club Program

As we developed the Book Club program, we experimented with both portfolio assessment and performance-based assessment. With each, we found advantages and disadvantages. Of course, the two methods are not mutually exclusive and in fact work very well together. You may decide to combine the two, taking advantage of what each method has to offer. You'll also be complementing the data you collect in formal assessments with information you gather informally throughout the year. In our research, we decided that clearly defined scoring criteria and in-depth analysis were the features we most wanted in our formal assessment strand. In this section we focus on performance-based assessment and describe one successful format that evolved from our research. (For more information about recent research in assessment, consult the sources listed in our Bibliography, which begins on page 291.)

Book Club Curricular Target Areas We wanted our assessment strand to match the overall goals of the Book Club curriculum. The chart on pages 26–27 details the learning outcomes or "target areas" you'll probably want to monitor within the program. The four major areas on which we focus instruction are (1) language conventions, (2) literary elements, (3) comprehension, and (4) response to literature.

Language conventions focus on the way our written and oral language works. These include grammar and mapping sound-symbol relationships through conventional spelling and fluent reading. In the Book Club program, language conventions also include the social skills used in discussing literature. Comprehension skills focus on how we make sense of text. These include developing background knowledge, processing text (summarizing, sequencing, etc.), and monitoring one's own comprehension during reading. Literary elements focus on both the overall structure used in literary texts and the tools authors use to create texts. The literary elements we want students to recognize and appreciate include genre, story structure, author's purpose, theme, and point of view. The Book Club program encourages students to respond to literature in personal, creative, and critical ways, and you'll want to evaluate each of these response types during a performance-based assessment.

Assessment Events Book Club's performance-based assessment consists of two 2-day "events." Each event centers around a particular text related to the theme your students are studying at the time. During the two days of each event, students participate in all of the activities that would normally be part of Book Club: they read a selection, create written log entries in response to the reading, meet for small-group discussions, and engage in community share with the entire class. The chart on page 27 shows a sample schedule for a Book Club performance-based assessment.

Language Conventions

Conventions include the rules, skills, and strategies necessary for students to be successful in the tasks and processes associated with responding to text.

Sound/Symbol
- spells conventionally
- reads with fluency

Grammatical Conventions
Uses appropriate language choices—
- verbs
- syntax
- punctuation
—in oral reading, discussion, and writing.

Interaction Conventions
- works with peers to set goals
- interacts with peers in literacy contexts:
  - writing conferences
  - literary circles
  - author's chair

Literary Elements

Literary elements refer to the structure and elements of text that students should know to help them understand text.

Theme
- author's purposes
- connections to life

Point of View
- characters' point of view
- author's point of view

Genre/Structures
- story structure
- expository structures
- types of genres

Author's Craft
- style
- text features

Comprehension

Comprehension includes the strategies students use for the purpose of text-based verification and sense-making.

Background Knowledge
- prediction
- draws on prior knowledge
- builds knowledge if needed
- context clues
- intertextual connections

Processing Text
- summarizing
- sequencing
- vocabulary
- organizing and drawing on text structure knowledge
- analyzing/developing characters, setting, plot sequence, etc.

Monitoring Own Reading
- asking questions
- clarifying confusions

Book Club Curricular Target Areas, *continued*

Response to Literature

Personal Response

Impressionistic response to literature, one's own writing, or the writing of peers:

- shares experiences
- shares personal feelings
- places self in situation
- compares self to characters

Creative Response

"Play" in response to literature:

- "What if?" (change event in story plot and explore impact)
- dramatizing events, characters' attitudes or actions
- illustrations of events, characters

Critical Response

Analytic response to the "effectiveness," "purpose," or "coherence" of a text; intertextual connections:

- explains changes in beliefs or feelings
- uses evidence from text to support ideas
- critiques texts using specific examples
- discusses author's purpose
- identifies author's craft
- uses text as mirror of one's own life and as window into the lives of others

Sample Performance-Based Assessment Schedule

Event 1		Event 2		
Day 1	**Day 2**	**Day 3**	**Day 4**	**"Day 5"**
• Read Chapter 7 of *Hatchet*	• Read Chapter 8 of *Hatchet*	• Read first half of science article	• Read second half of science article	• Listen to audio taped book club discussions and assess own performance
• Write log entry	• Write log entry	• Write log entry	• Write log entry	
• Discuss in book clubs (audio tape groups 1 and 2)	• Discuss in book clubs (audio tape groups 3 and 4)	• Discuss in book clubs (audio tape groups 1 and 2)	• Discuss in book clubs (audio tape groups 3 and 4)	• Select one log entry and write self-assessment
• Community share	• Community share	• Community share	• Community share	

Choosing the Texts When choosing the texts for your performance-based assessments, you should keep several factors in mind. First, the texts should represent the range of literature that you want your students to be able to read and respond to. We suggest one work of fiction and one work of nonfiction. Second, the texts should be embedded in the theme your students are studying at the time of the assessment. Some teachers use Book Club to integrate their curriculum, choosing themes and literature that relate to the science and social studies topics they are covering. Thus the nonfiction text for a performance-based assessment might be a chapter from a content-area textbook, or you might use an article from a magazine like *Cricket* or *World.*

Third, if you're planning to use a section from a longer trade book as an assessment text, you'll probably want to avoid using the very first chapters in the book. At this point, students may have recently formed new book clubs and may not be completely comfortable talking in these small groups. Their conversations will also be less rich because they are just learning about the setting and characters in the story. Once they get to the "heart" of the novel, they'll have prior knowledge from earlier chapters to bring to their discussions. The story's conflict will be developing and building to a climax, which will also liven up their discussions and give them more to talk about. For all of these reasons, we recommend you select a section from the middle of a chapter book for an assessment event.

You might decide not to use a chapter book at all during your assessment, but instead have students read a theme-related short story. During our research, we compared the data collected during a novel reading to the data collected during a short story reading. The differences between these two types of narrative fiction were not enough to yield different results in the performance-based assessment. Either type—the novel or the short story—provides a good sample of students' accomplishments in Book Club.

Assessment Tasks During a 2-day performance-based assessment event, students engage in six basic Book Club tasks: (1) reading a selection, (2) writing in their reading logs, (3) discussing in small groups, (4) sharing the results of their small-group discussions with the whole class, (5) assessing their own group participation, and (6) assessing their log entries. With the exception of students' independent reading, each of these tasks yields some concrete evidence of their performance that you can evaluate. We call these concrete pieces of evidence "artifacts." The chart on page 29 lists the number of artifacts collected from each task in a typical Book Club performance-based assessment.

Artifacts Collected in a Performance-Based Assessment

Artifacts	Expository Nonfiction	Narrative Fiction
Small-group book club discussions (audio taped)	1	1
Written journal entries	2	2
Whole-class community share (audio or videotaped)	2	2
Written small-group discussion self-assessments	1	1
Written journal entry self-assessment	Students select one journal entry that they think is the best of the four they have written, and they assess it.	

Student Self-Assessment In the past, assessment has often been a one-way street. Students submitted their work to a teacher, and the teacher's opinion of the work was the only opinion that went on record or counted for anything. We believe that students' opinions about their own work are a crucial element of assessment and growth. It encourages students to be clear about criteria for high-quality participation. It also encourages them to assume some responsibility for their own learning and their Book Club participation. A performance-based assessment in the Book Club program gives you several opportunities to elicit students' assessment of their own work.

For example, students can assess their performance in small-group discussions by listening to audio tapes of the conversations that took place during an assessment event. Since most classrooms have limited equipment for audio taping, you'll probably tape each group once during each 2-day event. Students can later assess their taped book club discussions by working in small groups with you or during a special community share.

Self-assessments that take place in the community share context can build on each other as each group's tape is played, and you'll also be able to guide and prompt the discussion. Alternatively, you might decide to have students gather in their small groups without you to assess their discussions. No matter what method you choose for listening to and discussing the tapes, each student should create a written self-assessment that describes both what was good and what needs improvement in his or her interaction.

Student self-assessment is also applied to the writing students do during an assessment event. In the model we are recommending, students select from their four log entries the one entry that they believe represents their best work. Then they write an explanation of why they thought it was the best.

Scoring Criteria One of the major advantages of performance-based assessment over portfolio assessment is the scoring criteria. For Book Club, we established a set of criteria that was in alignment with the learning goals of the program and was applicable to the kinds of artifacts collected in each 2-day assessment event. A suggested scoring rubric, based on a five-point scale, appears on pages 31–33. We applied the scoring rubric to students' journal entries and small-group discussions; information from students' self-assessments and from the audio taped community share sessions was used to support or raise questions about the conclusions we drew from the first two sources.

Assessments Throughout the Year A performance-based assessment requires planning beforehand and analysis afterward, so you won't want to be doing one every few weeks. However, Book Club lends itself to more frequent, informal assessments that can take place at any time. Students' reading logs provide information about their performance in Book Club, and you can collect these as often as you like to check on students' progress. During small-group discussions, you'll be moving around the classroom and can monitor individual students' participation. Community share is also a good time to notice which students have a lot to contribute and which ones might be falling behind for some reason.

Student self-assessment is just as valuable during regular Book Club units as it is during performance-based assessment events. We've developed several forms that ask our students to gauge their own performance and to set goals for improvement. (See the Blackline Masters: Assessment section following page 281 for some examples.) Some forms are used at the end of a unit, and others can be used any day of the week. Sometimes a dialogue between student and teacher takes place right on the form: The student completes the form, the teacher writes back with questions, and the student responds with more details. An example of such a dialogue is shown on page 34.

Modified Report Cards When we started using Book Club in our classrooms, we found that traditional report cards did not reflect many of the skills that our students were learning through the program. You may run into the same problem when you try to incorporate the rich information you have collected from a performance-based assessment into the report cards used by your school system.

In the Blackline Masters: Assessment section is a Reading Competencies Checklist that we developed and attached to district report cards in the Lansing, Michigan area. The

Score: 1

Journal Entries

- Focuses on major themes, issues, questions, or characters
- Effectively uses evidence from text, content area, and/or personal experience to support ideas
- Produces multiple, related, and well-developed responses
- Writes for a clear purpose
- Generates a well-focused, connected, and coherent response
- Dates entry

Book Club Discussions

- Focuses on major themes, issues, questions, or characters
- Effectively uses evidence from text, content area, and/or personal experience to support ideas
- Appropriately introduces new ideas
- Builds/expands on others' ideas
- Respects others' ideas
- Talks for a clear purpose
- Appropriately supports less active members of the group

Score: 2

Journal Entries

- Focuses on some major themes, issues, questions, or characters
- Effectively uses some evidence from text, content area, and/or personal experience to support ideas
- Produces several related responses
- Purpose for writing is fairly clear
- Generates a focused, connected, and generally coherent response
- Dates entry

Book Club Discussions

- Focuses on some major themes, issues, questions, or characters
- Effectively uses some evidence from text, content area, and/or personal experience to support ideas
- Occasionally introduces new ideas appropriately
- Occasionally builds/expands on others' ideas
- Respects others' ideas
- Purpose for speaking is usually clear
- Sometimes supports less active members of the group

Score: 3

Journal Entries

- Focuses on secondary themes, issues, questions, or characters OR lacks detailed discussion of major themes
- Uses little evidence from text and/or personal experience to support ideas OR use of evidence is less than effective
- Demonstrates some sense of purpose for writing
- Generates a somewhat focused, connected, and coherent response

Book Club Discussions

- Focuses on secondary themes, issues, questions, or characters OR lacks detailed discussion of major themes
- Uses little evidence from text and/or personal experience to support ideas OR use of evidence is less than effective
- Demonstrates some sense of purpose for speaking
- Builds some on others' ideas but may resort to round-robin turn taking
- Demonstrates some respect for others' ideas
- Less than effective at introducing new ideas

Score: 4

Journal Entries

- Makes few references to important themes, issues, questions, or characters OR lacks detailed discussion of any themes
- Uses little evidence from text and/or personal experience to support ideas OR use of evidence is ineffective
- Purpose for writing is unclear or lacking
- Response has inadequate focus, connection between ideas, and overall coherence

Book Club Discussions

- Makes few references to important themes, issues, questions, or characters OR lacks detailed discussion of any themes
- Uses little evidence from text and/or personal experience to support ideas OR use of evidence is ineffective
- Purpose for speaking is unclear or lacking
- Seldom builds on others' ideas and may resort to round-robin turn taking
- Demonstrates little respect for or attention to others' ideas
- Seldom introduces new ideas
- Speaks infrequently

Score: 5

Journal Entries

- Superficial response with minimal reference to the text or personal experiences
- Writing is a string of trivial textual details
- Demonstrates no clear purpose for writing
- Generates an unfocused, unconnected, and incoherent response
- Does not date entry

Book Club Discussions

- Superficial response with minimal reference to the text or personal experiences
- Talks about trivial textual details or irrelevant personal experiences
- Perseverates on ideas—does not build on them
- Does not introduce new ideas
- Demonstrates no clear purpose for speaking
- Speaks very infrequently
- Raises hand before speaking and/or resorts to round-robin turn taking

checklist focuses on some of the specific skills that students practice in Book Club, provides space for more open-ended comments on students' achievements, and allows for additional areas of focus to be added over the school year. We received positive feedback from parents whose understanding of what their children were doing in school was greatly enhanced by the information on the checklist. You may want to adapt this checklist or create a similar attachment that reflects what you and your students are accomplishing through Book Club.

Adapting Your Own Assessment Methods We don't want you to think that the ideas we're presenting in this chapter are meant to be prescriptive or set in stone. You'll inevitably want to adapt the format of the performance-based assessment to suit your own teaching style, your students' needs, and your curricular goals. The scoring rubric can serve as a starting point from which you can develop your own standards. If you already use portfolios in your classroom, you may want to integrate a performance-based assessment with portfolio assessment. And you'll certainly have your own list of questions you'll want to ask students on a self-assessment sheet. Your professional experience and creativity are the most powerful tools at your disposal, and the Book Club program offers many opportunities for you to use them to their full advantage.

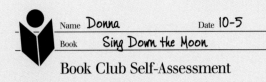

Name **Donna**   Date **10-5**

Book   **Sing Down the Moon**

Book Club Self-Assessment

1. How did your group do today?

   We did really good today.

   What parts were good?

2. What did you do to contribute to the group's success/failure?

   I tried to do good but I done better.

   I don't understand what you mean—?

3. What can you do to improve the group's level of success tomorrow?

   I can talk more about the book more than I did today

   OK.
   Donna, I think you are doing a very
   nice job. Keep working hard! A

Sample Book Club Self-Assessment Sheet Showing a Dialogue Between Student and Teacher

Name **Donna**   Date **10-5**

Book Club   **Sing Down the Moon**

Book Club Self-Assessment

1. How did your group do today?

   We did really good today.

   What parts were good?

   The questions I asked Maria and I said "That your logs where good."

2. What did you do to contribute to the group's success/failure?

   I tried to do good but I done better.

   I don't understand what you mean—?

   I mean that I couldn't read my log because I was at library!

3. What can you do to improve the group's level of success tomorrow?

   I can talk more about the book more than I did today

   OK.
   Donna, I think you are doing a very
   nice job. Keep working hard! A

Teaching Tips

It's always a challenge to start a new instructional program with your class. We hope that the preceding chapters have provided the background information to understand how the Book Club program works. This chapter is designed to address some of the specific questions that beginning Book Club teachers often ask us. You can use this chapter as a quick reference guide to find the practical information you need to get your own Book Club program under way. For your convenience, we've divided the questions into three categories: curriculum, management, and student diversity. At the end of the chapter is a curriculum chart that outlines all of the lessons in this guide according to the Book Club curricular target areas.

Curriculum

How can I make cross-curricular links in the Book Club program?

- Select books, both fiction and nonfiction, that deal with content-area material.

- Encourage students to make intertextual links between Book Club books and the materials they're reading in other subject areas.

- Build a special classroom library with books in the content areas that are also related to the Book Club books you're using.

- Use community share as an opportunity to point out cross-curricular connections and to model intertextual links.

- Create thematic or topical units that involve content-area studies and related Book Club readings. (See the outline for the Civil War unit that begins on page 244.)

- Include research components in Book Club units to increase the depth of students' understanding about content.

- Use a teacher read-aloud book as a way to link Book Club with a content-area discussion.

- Spelling: Draw on district guidelines, published programs, students' own writing, and students' interests to develop class and student spelling lists. Sources for interesting words can include students' writing and Book Club books.

How can I integrate my district's curriculum requirements within the Book Club program?

- Obtain a current copy of your district or school curriculum guide prior to beginning Book Club. Mark specific curriculum guide areas in terms of the four Book Club curriculum areas: language conventions, literary elements, comprehension, and response to literature. Use lessons, community share, and the reading log as opportunities to work district requirements into the Book Club program in a meaningful way.

- Pre-read the Book Club book prior to a unit and highlight sections of the book that lend themselves to lessons related to the district curriculum.

- As you look through the Book Club suggested thematic units and trade books, compare them to those recommended within your district. Where themes intersect, draw on district-provided materials to supplement or replace those recommended in the Book Club program. Look for book titles in the district materials that relate to thematic units you are teaching in Book Club.

- As you examine your district curriculum guide requirements, consider other areas of your day where you address areas listed in the guide. Book Club should not be the sole site for language and literacy instruction within your classroom.

Management

What are some of the guidelines for good book club discussions that I should share with my students?

- Help students generate their own list of guidelines for talking about texts. Ask them about conversations they've had on the playground and what makes the conversations work. Have them compare those conversations to conversations at home, in the lunch room, in the classroom, about television programs, or about movies. Discuss what helps make a conversation interesting, what kinds of interactions students enjoy, and some different ways of participating.

- Share some guidelines other students have generated (in previous years, or in other classrooms) for good book club discussions. For example, students in one of our classrooms generated the list on page 38.

– Overlapping speech is acceptable when you can still understand the whole conversation. It's not acceptable when the overlapping speech makes it hard to follow what is said.

– Listen carefully to what group members say, and then respond.

– Avoid asking questions that can be answered with a simple *yes* or *no*. Questions that are open-ended or that generate discussion make for better conversations.

– If you notice that any of your group members are not participating in the book club discussion, make an effort to include them. You could, for example, direct a question to a person who has not spoken for a while.

– Keep your conversations focused on the book you're reading—don't wander off the topic. If you do wander off, it is the responsibility of the group to get back on task.

– Keep your voices at a reasonable level. Don't shout.

– Have respect for your fellow group members and their ideas.

– Your discussions should all "connect" together. Avoid just reading your log and saying, "I'm done." Try conducting a discussion with your logs put away!

What are the guidelines for good reading log entries?

• Share examples of high-quality reading log entries with students. Using large chart paper or an overhead projector makes it easier to highlight the strengths of particular entries. If your students are willing to share their own entries (anonymously, if they prefer), you can display their entries and have the class add to, expand, and critique them. Talk about what is good about an entry and what might be done to make it better.

• Develop a chart of suggestions for good reading log entries. These suggestions can be both substantive—leading to thoughtful and complete entries—and formal—such as including the chapter, date, and page numbers to which the entry refers.

• Some guidelines that one Book Club class generated are:

– Your reading log should contain ideas that will inspire good conversations in your book club group.

– If you have any questions about the story, write them down and ask your group if they can answer the questions. Yes/no questions don't make for interesting discussions.

– Your feelings and reactions are more interesting than a retelling of the story.

– Write the date, book title, and reading assignment (page numbers) on each log entry.

– Spelling and grammar are always important, but they are not the main focus of your reading log. Just get your ideas down on paper, and don't worry if it's not perfect.

– As you gain experience with Book Club, try to write several different kinds of responses in your log each day.

– Writing time is "hot pencil" time—don't stop writing until time is up. When you finish an idea, start a new one.

What's the difference between a think sheet and a share sheet?

- A think sheet is a handout that prompts a particular type of written response to literature. For example, you might distribute a think sheet that asks your students to compare and contrast two books or two characters. The Blackline Masters: Think Sheets section following page 261 in this guide provides more examples.

- A share sheet is a blank sheet of paper that students use to respond to literature as they see fit. Normally a student will write his or her name, the date, and the day's reading assignment in the center of the sheet, and then divide the rest of the sheet into sections (also called "spokes"). In each section, the student will write one type of response to the reading—such as a list of questions for his or her book club group, an intertextual connection with another book, a critique of the chapter, and a response to a writing prompt that you've provided.

- Share sheets allow students to combine several response types on a single page. This is helpful during their book club discussions, because they won't need to flip through their logs looking for entries that they've written on different pages.

- Students will use share sheets only after they've learned a wide variety of response types and feel comfortable choosing their own ways to respond based on what they've read on a particular day.

- As the year progresses, you can expect students to create their own original formats for share sheets, as well as original response types. You should encourage this creativity, since it will help students take ownership of their learning and organize their logs in ways that make the most sense to them.

- The share sheet format was borrowed from an idea by Kathy Short (NRC presentation, 1992). Examples appear on pages 166 and 218.

What methods of formal and informal assessment work well with Book Club?

- Ongoing formal and informal assessments should inform daily instructional decisions that you make. Begin by establishing your specific purpose for any assessment used.

- Informal assessments include teachers' observations and anecdotal notes. These can be recorded in a spiral notebook kept for each unit. Notes recorded about individual students may be made on large self-adhesive notes and kept in individual student files. Notes can also be written on index cards for each student.

- Informal writing assessments include samples of students' written work, such as reading log pages, essays, and inquiry project notes. Evaluating students' progress on these materials guides your decision making about specific lessons to teach to the whole class or to small groups of students.

- Informal reading assessments include measures of fluency, comprehension, and response to literature. Asking students to read short segments of text during the reading component of Book Club provides information about fluency. Information about students' comprehension and response to literature can be obtained from book club and community share discussion (either during class or listening to audio tapes of these events) as well as from reading log entries.

- Following are some specific suggestions for informal assessments.

  - Walk around the room daily and read what students are writing. Ask probing questions of individual students who are not thinking very deeply.

  - Collect students' reading logs at the end of each week and assess their written responses to the literature.

  - Walk around the classroom during book clubs to assess students' conversations for reading comprehension and discussion skills. A simple checklist can help you do this.

  - Students can assess their own progress at any time during a Book Club unit. Sample forms are provided in the Blackline Masters: Assessment section following page 281.

  - Using a checklist during community share, you can assess how well students are understanding their reading and interacting with their peers.

  - Taking field notes or jotting down interesting comments or good intertextual connections in a journal can help you assess your students and can aid in planning further instruction.

  - Act as a facilitator when necessary. Even though Book Club is student-led, students will need guidance and direction from time to time.

- More formal assessments include the performance-based assessments described in the Assessment chapter that begins on page 23.

- Blackline masters for specific types of written responses may be used as a basis for both formal and informal assessments. (See the Blackline Masters: Think Sheets and Assessment sections following pages 261 and 281 in this guide.)

How do I get my students to talk in their book club groups, especially when they're just starting the program?

- Refer to the suggestions for creating guidelines for good book club discussions given on pages 37–38. Talking about your expectations regarding book club participation will help students overcome their hesitations.

- Model talking with a group, either with your peers or with former students.

- Use the overhead projector to present written transcripts of discussions. Highlight the kinds of words the students in the transcript are using to discuss text.

- Show a videotape of previous students doing Book Club. (This works especially well!)

- Share the following tips gathered from several Book Club teachers with your class:

  - Suggest that students begin by reading aloud from their logs and asking each other questions about the reading.

  - Enlist students who are self-confident speaking in groups to support their group members who are more reticent by directing questions to them and listening respectfully to their responses.

  - Explain to students that when adults read good books and discuss them, they apply the ideas in the books to their own lives.

  - Encourage students to move beyond reading aloud from their logs.

What are some good methods for selecting books for Book Club?

- Consult book lists in journals and magazines (e.g., *The Reading Teacher*, *Language Arts*) and publications such as *The Horn Book*.

- Choose a theme about which to find books or build a multi-book unit.

- Ask other teachers about books that they've enjoyed using with their classes.

- Consult the school or local librarian about which books children are borrowing.

- Review your curriculum for the year. Choose topics or themes that correspond to major themes for the year.

- Have students suggest books that they have heard about and would like to read. Of course, books that are chosen should have significant discussion value. Not all books that are a "good read" are appropriate for Book Club.

- Pick something *you* like! Your enthusiasm for a book will carry over to your class.

How can I get enough copies of a book for my classroom?

The expression "beg, borrow, or steal" comes to mind—actually there *are* some legal methods that might be more practical.

- Trade sets of books with fellow teachers.

- Buy a set with other same-grade teachers in your school or district.

- Ask the PTA to provide funds to purchase classroom sets of books.

- Call book distributors to ask about special prices on classroom sets. One distributor to contact:
    Keith Distributors
    1055 S. Ballinger Highway
    Flint, MI 48532
    Phone: 1-800-373-2366

- Use bonus points from commercial book clubs (e.g., Troll, Scholastic) to purchase extra copies.

- Borrow books from the local library and other libraries in the area or network.

- Ask your school administrators if there are funds available—often you can convince them to use monies previously spent on workbooks to purchase novels and picture books.

- Contact district or county resources. Many school systems already have lending options.

What amount of time should I allocate to Book Club?

- The amount of time that you allocate to different components of Book Club will vary according to the time of year, the complexity of the book, and classroom and individual needs. Initially, you will want to keep the time you spend on each component fairly short. A complete Book Club session will usually take more than an hour. Two options for a Book Club session are provided below.

	Option 1	Option 2
Curriculum Focus (Lesson)	8–10 minutes	15 minutes
Reading	20–25 minutes	15 minutes
Writing	5–7 minutes	15 minutes
Book Clubs	5–7 minutes	15 minutes
Community Share	5–7 minutes	15 minutes

How can I increase my students' repertoire of response types? Or, in other words, how do I get them to THINK about what they are writing and saying?

- Model response types for students. After you read a section from a read-aloud book, say what you are thinking about the book or write a model response on the chalkboard.

- Show actual student responses (after asking permission) that exhibit the kinds of responses you want to encourage.

- Review response types with students regularly. Hand out copies of the Response Choice Sheet(s) from the Blackline Masters: Think Sheets section starting on page 261 of this guide. You might try attaching the Response Choice Sheet to the front of students' reading logs.

- Use a transparency of the blank Response Choice Sheet to record types of responses that you and the class would like to focus on. Make a large copy and hang it in a prominent location in the classroom.

- Use community share as an opportunity to talk about the response types that you see students using in their reading logs. Discuss options for responding.

- Encourage students to create share sheets for original response types. Make copies of student-created share sheets and put them in folders where students can access them.

- Challenge students to use more than one response type for a reading selection.

How can I show what my students are learning if the mandated report card doesn't provide room to record observations of classroom talk and learning log entries?

- Examine the Reading Competencies Checklist in the Blackline Masters: Assessment section following page 281. This checklist was developed to augment a mandated report card. You may want to use or adapt this checklist to help parents and administrators understand the types of learning that are taking place in your classroom.

- Have each student gather a small sample of writing to show what they have been learning. Interpret the data for parents by writing notes or putting self-adhesive notes on the pieces of writing.

- Have students write what they are learning, in narrative form, as well as identify their best log response.

- Let students borrow audio tapes of book club discussions in which they have participated. Send home the tape and a small tape recorder (if necessary) so that parents can listen to it. You might also want to write a letter giving a summary of the book and telling parents how reading the book supports the class's curriculum goals.

Student Diversity

Are there any ways to group students who don't get along?

- Yes and no. There are some pairings of students that probably will never work. Identify these students and avoid placing them in the same group. Other pairs or groups may just need some coaching in how to work together.

- Talk to students (or groups) about expectations of behavior during Book Club. Create a bulletin board or posters with guidelines for participation in Book Club. (See also the response to the first question under Management, on page 37.)

- Role-play a Book Club discussion and a disagreement. Show students how they can and should give each other opportunities to explain their thinking. Explain what you are thinking as you ask the other students in the role-play group not to interrupt or to give another person a chance to talk. This kind of role-play can help students assume the role of mediators during their own discussions.

- Use a "fish bowl" to model a good discussion to the class. A "fish bowl" refers to setting up a Book Club group in the center of the classroom with other students placed around the central group. You participate in the central group, guiding and helping to demonstrate a good discussion.

- Ask students to name other students they would like to have in their book clubs. (NOTE: Friends don't always work well together. You will need to use your own judgment.) The End-of-Book Self-Assessment sheet in the Blackline Masters: Assessment section prompts students to name their preferences.

- Have students who haven't been getting along work on a very specific, finite project—creating a share sheet to respond to a particular book, for example. Working together in a fairly controlled situation may allow the pair to discover some area(s) of mutual interest, or at least give them practice in working toward a common goal.

- Although it sounds a bit trite, you may want to remind the class that working in a group is a skill that they will use throughout their lives. Being able to negotiate, compromise, and respect other people's opinions will help them be successful in their jobs and with their families.

What do I do if a student refuses to participate?

- Talk to the student individually. Try to pinpoint what is preventing them from participating. Do they feel shy about talking in front of the group? Is writing difficult for them? Is the book above or below their reading level? Do they find the subject of the book boring? Are they having trouble with a particular classmate? The answers to these types of questions can provide clues to motivating a student who's having a hard time participating.

How can I integrate inquiry-based learning with Book Club?

- To build background knowledge, have students complete an inquiry or research phase before they start the Book Club phase of a thematic or topical unit.

- Tell students the topic of the Book Club book they will be reading, and have them develop a list of related questions to research.

- Develop an inquiry unit to follow the Book Club phase and have students explore questions that arose during their Book Club readings.

- Divide students into their book club groups for the inquiry phase, so they can work together as research teams.

- Include books related to the inquiry questions in the special classroom library.

- Create a bulletin-board display of the information students have collected during the inquiry phase, and refer back to this information as students read the Book Club book.

- Draw on parents and community members as resources for interviews about topics related to a Book Club theme.

- Refer to page 247 in the Multi-Book Units chapter for more ideas about how to conduct the inquiry phase of a Book Club unit.

In addition to the language and literacy activities within Book Club, what other language arts events and activities should I include for a fully integrated language arts program?

- Silent Reading Time: Encourage students to read a variety of books, including those that they choose from the school and public libraries, from the classroom library, and from the special Book Club–related books. Make sure that the books they choose are ones that they can read independently.

- Process Writing: Encourage students to explore a wide variety of genres and topics, including personal-experience stories, personal narratives, inquiry papers, essays, letters, and so forth. Invite students to share their writing with peers during Author's Chair.

- Journal Writing: Encourage students to write daily in their personal journals. Invite them to select an entry that they would like to share with their peers.

- Whole-class Writing: Create class books, class stories, morning messages, and other class-generated written pieces.

- Grammar Instruction: Draw on district guidelines, published programs, and students' needs to include instruction on punctuation and grammar. Use students' writing as well as sentences from Book Club books for examples.

- Students with behavioral problems may respond to the following ideas.

  – Create a behavioral contract for a certain period of time that the student agrees to. Give specific goals, such as asking two questions per book club group, using at least one response type in a reading log, not interrupting when someone is speaking, etc. Review successes and discuss failures.

  – Give the student responsibility for an organizational aspect of Book Club. Ask them to collect reading logs or organize books—anything to get them involved.

  – Let the student decide if he or she can handle the group interaction each day. If the student chooses not to participate occasionally, have alternate activities set up.

  – If a student finds the book boring, ask the student to do some research about the same topic using media that he or she finds more interesting —CD-ROM encyclopedias, video, magazines, Internet, etc. Have the student present his or her findings to the group or class.

What kinds of additional support can be given to a student who finds a book too challenging?

- Refer to pages 19–22 of this guide for expanded information about inclusion.

- Make audio tapes or have students make audio tapes of selections from the book for the student to listen to and read along with.

- In the heterogeneous groups recommended for Book Club, students who need additional support can benefit from a wide variety of reading and discussion styles.

- Ask an adult (parent, Title 1, reading teacher) to pre-read the selection with the student.

- Invite the student to a private discussion about the book. Review and summarize the book so far and talk about what might be happening in upcoming sections. Clue the student in to the major plot elements to provide a context and additional background knowledge to assist him or her while reading.

- Peer partners work really well!

What about a student for whom English is a second or third language?

- Refer to pages 19–22 of this guide for expanded information about inclusion.

- All of the ideas listed under the previous question can also apply to a student new to English.

- Make sure that the classroom library contains books written in the child's primary language.

- Seek district assistance for a classroom bilingual aide.

- Look for translations of Book Club books written in the student's primary language.

- Use authentic multicultural literature as Book Club books for the whole class.

- Identify sources of help within the school or community. Communicate with the bilingual/ESL teacher about your Book Club plans. Ask the teacher to help you write a letter to a student's parents or guardians (in their home language, if necessary) about what kinds of learning experiences the student will be encountering in class.

- Find books in the student's primary language that have topical or thematic connections to the Book Club books. Invite the student to share (by drawing, writing, or speaking) how the book is similar to or different from the Book Club book.

- Post response choice terms in a student's primary language.

- Translate terms that are on the word wall. Make the student the "expert" who can teach the class how to pronounce the words in their first language. Other students in the class, in turn, can demonstrate how to pronounce the English terms.

- Give the student the option of drawing responses or writing responses.

- Encourage second-language students to write and speak in both their first language and English. Seek peer assistants to translate a student's writing from the other language to English and from English to the other language.

- Coach the class in how to help a student learning English. If the student makes a one-word response, encourage others in the group to demonstrate how to put that word into a sentence.

Curriculum Overview of Lessons

The following chart lists all of the lessons in this teacher's guide, organized according to the Book Club curricular target areas. Since our lesson plans are meant to provide you with ideas and suggestions, we hope that this chart will help you to develop your own curriculum. You can use it to locate lessons on topics you'd like to teach in your own classroom—perhaps with trade books other than the ones we've highlighted—and see how we've taught those lessons. Complete descriptions of the curricular target areas are provided on pages 26–27. (NOTE: The assessment lessons that come at the end of each lesson plan are not included in this chart. For model lessons, turn to the *Last Summer with Maizon* unit, page 80, or the *Fighting Ground* unit, pages 143–144.)

Curricular Area	Book Title	Lesson	Focus of Lesson	Page
Language Conventions • Sound/Symbol • Grammatical Conventions • Interaction Conventions	*Last Summer with Maizon*	1	Introduction to Book Club	57
	Tuck Everlasting	20	Process Writing—Essay	103
	Bridge to Terabithia	9	Fluency Review	114
	The Fighting Ground	9	Fluency Review	135
		15	Reader's Theater—Planning and Writing a Script	141
		16	Reader's Theater—Elements of a Good Presentation	142
	A Wrinkle in Time	3	Book Club Talk	150
		9	Fluency Review	155
	Hatchet	5	Qualities of a Good Book Club Group	169
		7	Use of a Self-Assessment Sheet	170
		8	Qualities of a Good Share Sheet	171
	Walk Two Moons	2	Elements of a Good Book Club Discussion	189
		5	Book Club Log Entries	194
		6	Assessing Book Club Log Entries	195
		14	Creating New Types of Reading Log Entries	204

Curriculum Overview of Lessons, continued

Curricular Area	Book Title	Lesson	Focus of Lesson	Page
Language Conventions	*Maniac Magee*	6	Review of Share Sheets	217
	The Civil War	14	Transition to Book Club Phase (Multi-Book Unit)	250

Curricular Area	Book Title	Lesson	Focus of Lesson	Page
Literary Elements • Theme • Point of View • Genre/ Structures • Author's Craft	*Last Summer with Maizon*	3	Character Map	63
		5	Author's Craft and Special Techniques	67
		7	Author's Craft—Point of View	68
	Tuck Everlasting	5	Author's Craft—Imagery and Foreshadowing	88
		8	Genre—Fantasy	91
		11	Recurring Images and Story Themes	95
		12	Point of View	96
		13	Recurring Images and Story Themes, Revisited	97
		14	Story Elements	98
		16	Story Graph	99
		18	Point of View, Revisited	101
		19	Time Change; Story Resolution	102
	Bridge to Terabithia	1	Discussing the Book's Title	106
		2	Characterization	107
		3	Use of Dialogue and Dialect	108
		5	Chapter Titles	111
		12	Point of View	118

Curriculum Overview of Lessons, continued

Curricular Area	Book Title	Lesson	Focus of Lesson	Page
Literary Elements	*The Fighting Ground*	2	Author's Purpose	127
		7	Point of View	132
		11	Building a Plot to a Suspenseful Climax	136
	A Wrinkle in Time	1	Elements of Fantasy	147
		2	Author's Craft—Character Development	148
		4	Author's Craft—Descriptive Language	151
		5	Elements of Fantasy, Revisited	152
		14	Genre—Fantasy	160
	Hatchet	11	Character Development	174
		13	Setting	176
		20	Author's Purpose	181
	Walk Two Moons	1	Author's Craft—Story Structure	189
		4	Author's Craft—Story Structure, Revisited	193
		13	Author's Craft—Characterization Through Actions and Dreams	202
		15	Point of View	204
	Maniac Magee	1	Point of View	211
		2	The Elements of a Story	212
		4	Theme and Plot	215
		5	Characterization; Point of View (Revisited)	216
		7	Setting	219
		9	Rising Action, Climax, Falling Action, Resolution	221

Curriculum Overview of Lessons, continued

Curricular Area	Book Title	Lesson	Focus of Lesson	Page
Literary Elements	Author Study: Mildred Taylor	1	Author's Craft—Imagery and Dialect	227
		2	Author's Craft—Characterization	228
		10	Theme	234
		13	Theme and Other Common Elements in Taylor's Books	239
	The Civil War	20	Point of View (Multi-Book Unit)	251

Curricular Area	Book Title	Lesson	Focus of Lesson	Page
Comprehension • Background Knowledge • Processing Text • Monitoring Own Reading	*Last Summer with Maizon*	9	Wonderful Words	73
		10	Sequence	75
		11	Interpretation with a Picture Book	78
	Tuck Everlasting	3	Characters and Character Maps	86
		9	Analyzing Character Development	92
		10	Comparison and Contrast	93
		15	Changes in Characters Over Time	98
	Bridge to Terabithia	4	Exploring the Concept of Kingdoms	109
		7	Vocabulary/Word Wall	112
		8	Making Connections to Characters	113
	The Fighting Ground	3	Vocabulary—Wonderful Words	129
		4	Vocabulary	130
		5	Word Web Around the Concept of Pain	130
		6	Summarizing and Reviewing Story Content	131
		8	Intertextual Connections	133
		10	Drawing Conclusions	136

Curriculum Overview of Lessons, continued

Curricular Area	Book Title	Lesson	Focus of Lesson	Page
Comprehension	*The Fighting Ground*	12	The Roles of the French and Tories in the Revolutionary War	137
		13	Predicting Outcomes	138
		18	Synthesis	143
	A Wrinkle in Time	6	Fifth Dimension and Time Travel	152
		7	Describing Our Town	154
		8	Reviewing Content and Making Predictions	154
		10	Sequencing	156
		11	Using Text Features and Prior Knowledge to Make Predictions	157
		12	Using Background Knowledge to Analyze Characters	158
	Hatchet	1	Elements of Survival	164
		4	Drawing Conclusions	168
		6	Summarizing	170
		9	Vocabulary—Word Wall	172
		10	Intertextuality	173
		12	Visualizing	175
		15	Vocabulary—Concept Web	177
		17	Sequencing	178
		18	Elements of Survival, Revisited	180
		19	Predicting	180
		23	Compare and Contrast	183

Curricular Area	Book Title	Lesson	Focus of Lesson	Page
Response to Literature	*Tuck Everlasting*	6	Revisit the Venn Diagram (Lesson 1)	89
		7	Feelings and Emotions	90
		17	Issues of Right and Wrong	101
	Bridge to Terabithia	6	Making Connections to Your Life	111
		10	Ways of Representing Thoughts on Reading	117
		11	Discussion of Death	118
		13	Talking About Difficult Emotional Issues	119
		14	Closure	121
		15	Flexible Discussion Groups	121
		17	Synthesis	123
	The Fighting Ground	1	Reading Logs and Checklists	126
		14	Analyze the Ending and the Story as a Whole	140
		17	Performing Reader's Theater	142
	A Wrinkle in Time	13	Author's Purpose	159
		15	Developing a Movie Script Based on a Book	161
	Hatchet	2	Use of Share Sheets	165
		3	Use of Response Choice Sheets	167
		14	Affective Responses (Me & the Book)	176
		16	Share Sheet Options	178
		21	Developing Ideas for Sequels	182
		22	Questioning; Letter Writing	183
		24	Process Writing—An Original Survival Story	185

Curricular Area	Book Title	Lesson	Focus of Lesson	Page
Response to Literature	*Walk Two Moons*	9	Personal Response—Family Sayings and Expressions	199
		11	Personal Response—Soul Drawings	200
		12	Creative Response—Drawing Pictures	202
		16	Personal Journals	205
		17	Free Writing	206
		18	Free Writing and Checking Comprehension	206
		20	Writing a Book Critique	207
	Maniac Magee	3	Empathizing with a Character	213
		10	Analyzing the Story's Resolution	223
	Author Study: Mildred Taylor	6	Feelings About the Story	231
		7	Analyzing the Author's Purpose	232
		9	Personal Response	233
		11	Critical Response; Process Writing	238

Last Summer with Maizon
by Jacqueline Woodson

Introducing the Book

The following lessons for *Last Summer with Maizon* can help guide the Book Club discussions about a novel that is a favorite of ours and that we hope will become a favorite of yours. Students will find that they can relate to the issues that best friends face, the existence of prejudice and unfairness, and the way that people change over time. *Last Summer with Maizon* can stand alone or be used to support themes and/or units that have to do with friendship, prejudice, and change.

Special Note: This set of lessons was created by a Book Club teacher who used *Last Summer with Maizon* as a first-in-the-year book. These lessons can be used as a **model** for you to follow with any book that you choose to use first in the year. You will notice that we have included many student examples to give you a sense of the kinds of responses that you might get during the first book of the year or from a class new to Book Club. Of course, these same lessons can be used later in the year with some modifications.

Summary Margaret and Maizon are best friends. They live on the same street in Brooklyn, wear the same clothes, and are often mistaken for sisters. The summer before they enter the sixth grade, however, presents many challenges to their friendship. Maizon has applied for a scholarship to a fancy boarding school in Connecticut, and Margaret dreads the thought of her friend moving away. Then Margaret's father dies, making everything seem empty and wrong. When Maizon does leave for school, however, Margaret finds herself growing in ways she never expected. Her teacher asks her to write down her feelings about the events of the summer. Margaret writes a poem she feels very proud of, and her teacher enters it in a city-wide contest. The other girls in school are more friendly to her now that she's no longer with "snotty" Maizon all the time. When her poem is

Paperback Edition, Dell Publishing, © 1990 by Jacqueline Woodson. ISBN 0-440-40555-6.

selected to be read in front of the mayor, popular athlete Bo Douglas is impressed and strikes up a friendship. Then Maizon calls and announces she's coming home. Margaret has to deal with her mixed feelings about Maizon's return and face the fact that both girls have changed in the time they've been apart.

Themes Author Jacqueline Woodson paints a wonderfully complex portrait of a friendship, exploring the tensions and jealousies that exist between even the best of friends, and showing how friends can both expand and limit each other's horizons. Other themes that are explored subtly in this book are those of prejudice and discrimination. There are references to why Maizon and her grandmother feel that she should go to school in Connecticut and a reference to the fact that the population of the neighborhood is changing in ways that make the residents uncomfortable. All of these themes provide reasons to discuss the issues that the novel presents as they relate to the students in your classroom.

Special Classroom Library There are two other books by the same author about the main characters in *Last Summer with Maizon. Maizon at Blue Hill* (Dell, 1994) and *Between Madison and Palmetto* (Dell, 1995) continue the story of the girls and how their lives and their friendship are changing. Several books about friendship and one about the effects of discrimination that you might also consider borrowing or adding to your classroom library are listed below.

Title	Author	Publisher, Date
The Incredible Journey	Sheila Burnford	Bantam Doubleday Dell, 1996
Number the Stars	Lois Lowry	Dell, 1996
Journey to Jo'burg	Beverley Naidoo	HarperCollins, 1988
Bridge to Terabithia	Katherine Paterson	HarperCollins, 1996
Sign of the Beaver	Elizabeth Speare	Bantam Doubleday Dell, 1995

Lesson 1

GOAL:

To introduce students to the parts of the Book Club program and to focus on one reading log option

ASSIGNED READING:

Chapters 1–3
(pages 1–23)

WRITING PROMPT:

Respond to two of the following prompts.

- Write whatever you're thinking or feeling about the book after having read or heard the first three chapters.
- Write about a part of the book that you especially enjoyed. Explain why you enjoyed this part.
- Write your thoughts about one or more of the following subjects: best friends, hospitals, sickness, knowing the future, family, and city life. You might relate one of the subjects to something you heard in the first three chapters of *Last Summer with Maizon*, or you might talk about a personal experience.

Language Conventions:
Introduction to Book Club

- NOTE: This lesson could be taught in two parts, if you have time limitations. On the first day, you could discuss the parts of Book Club and perhaps read the first three chapters aloud. On the second day, students could review the reading, write in their logs, meet in book club groups, and participate in community share.

- Assuming that this is your first Book Club unit of the year, one of the first and most important things you can do is introduce your students to the structure and special language used throughout the program. We find that it makes sense to begin by introducing the four program components. We explain that they will read chapter books. Each day during "reading" they'll read several chapters, or sometimes listen as the teacher reads aloud. They will respond to the reading by writing in their *reading logs*. Then they will meet in small groups called *book clubs* to discuss their reading and writing with other students. They will also have the opportunity to share their ideas with the entire class. This time during which the entire class shares ideas is called *community share*.

- We've found that students like a predictable structure, so we begin the year by describing the general pattern for each day (see below). We do let our students know that some days won't follow this pattern.

- Tell students that each day's Book Club activities will typically follow this order.

  - **Lesson.** The teacher will introduce a topic and discuss it with the students. Sometimes the teacher will present new information, and sometimes the teacher will ask students to contribute to a class discussion. The lesson can be related to the reading assignment that the students are about to begin or can focus on writing, talking, or management.

  - **Reading.** The students will read an assigned section of the novel.

  - **Writing.** Students will write in their reading logs about the section they've just read. In these logs they will focus on different parts of the story each day. One day they might write about their favorite or least favorite character, another day they might discuss any personal connections they have to the story, and so on. Often you'll display a

continued on next page

continued from previous page

writing prompt to give them a starting point for writing in their logs. After they've responded to the prompt, they should free write about anything else that they found interesting about the reading. Sometimes they'll use "think sheets" to record their responses to the reading. (Sample blackline masters follow page 261 in this guide.) You might show students a few of these think sheets to illustrate some different response options. Students will have a better understanding of these options after they've had a chance to try them during this unit.

– **Book Clubs.** Students discuss their thoughts about the reading and their log entries in book club groups. They will find that their reading logs are very useful during book clubs since their entries help remind them about ideas they might want to share. The students themselves will lead these small-group discussions, and some lessons will focus on strategies for making the discussions run smoothly.

– **Community Share.** After students have had their book club discussions, the whole class will come together for community share. In community share, students may introduce issues that were discussed in their book clubs, share their writings, and ask new questions about the reading. They will expand their thinking by making connections with other groups' discussions and exploring new ideas.

– Let students know that although this is the general format, it is likely to change occasionally. On certain days, they might read first and then have a lesson. On other days, they might skip a part, or stay longer in book clubs, or write longer, etc.

• To help students with ways to use their reading logs, you will probably want to introduce different options several times. One reading log option has to do with choosing a special story part. When a student finds a part in a book that he or she really likes, the student can write the page number(s) of the part in his or her log to help remember where to find it. Then the student can write a few sentences about why the part is so special. Remind students that writing helps them think before they talk.

• Read the first three chapters of *Last Summer with Maizon* aloud to students, or have them read with partners or silently. NOTE: Some Book Club teachers begin each book by reading the first few chapters aloud. This ensures that all students have access to the important stage-setting information and can hear the author's style and rhythm.

- Then have students respond to the writing prompt. You might choose to discuss some of the writing prompts with the class before asking them to begin writing.

- Beginning Book Club students are likely to write a quick response to the prompt and then put their pencils down, thinking that they're "done." If you find that this is happening, encourage students to use their logs as thinking tools by continuing to write until the writing time is over. One Book Club teacher calls it "hot pencil time" and tells her students that their pencils should not stop moving until time is up. Students may be surprised by the ideas that come out on paper if they just keep writing.

- Students should use their writing to help support their book club discussions. During the student-led discussions, walk from group to group, helping students get used to the format. In the beginning, you'll want to visit each group daily to do some facilitating. One Book Club teacher walks around the room with a clipboard, recording good discussion lines from each group. Later she shares these lines with the whole class as a modeling technique.

- In community share, you might want to think about two different discussion focuses. First, ask students to share their responses to the book: what they talked about in their book clubs. Second, ask students to share what they think about having book clubs as part of their reading program. What do they enjoy the most about meeting in small groups? What do they think will be challenging about working in these groups?

Teaching Tip

Early in the year, shorter times are better for each Book Club part. Expand the time given for each part as the year progresses. A sample schedule for a Book Club day early in the year is given below.

5–15 minutes	Lesson
25 minutes	Reading
5–7 minutes	Writing
5–7 minutes	Book Clubs
5–7 minutes	Community Share

Lesson 2

GOAL:
To help students learn and practice good critiquing skills that they can use as they read

ASSIGNED READING:
Chapter 4
(pages 25–30)

WRITING PROMPT:
Write a critique of the chapter. Support your critique with proof or evidence from the chapter or from your life.

Response to Literature:
Learning to Critique

- Talk to the class about why it is important to learn how to critique. Tell them that you want them to question what they read, learn how to evaluate books, and notice various author's crafts and how these crafts make a book work.

- Ask the class to name any famous critics in newspapers, magazines, or on television, and then invite them to discuss critiques that they have read or heard. You might ask them to name the parts of movies or books (e.g., characters, story, acting, design, special effects, language) that critics like to examine and discuss.

- Ask students if they have ever heard a critique that they thought was unfair or inaccurate. Our students have talked about critics who seemed too negative and critics who seemed to misunderstand the book or movie. What made the critique sound unfair to them? Ask if students have ever followed the advice of a critic who they thought sounded fair.

- Have the class discuss positive or negative aspects of the story so far. Remind them that a critic must provide reasons for his or her opinions. Encourage students to record page numbers for examples from the text that support their critique. You may want to use a chart like the one below to help students construct their critique.

What the Author Does Well	What the Author Could Improve Upon

- NOTE: Several examples of critiques with teacher annotations are shown on pages 61–62. These examples show the kinds of early responses that you might see in students' logs.

- After the discussion, have students proceed with the reading and writing portions of Book Club.

- When students get into their book clubs, they can discuss their individual written critiques of the chapter.

Curriculum Overview of Lessons, continued

Curricular Area	Book Title	Lesson	Focus of Lesson	Page
Comprehension	*Walk Two Moons*	3	Learning About Characters	190
		7	Background Knowledge—The Native American Peace Pipe	196
		8	Character Development; Wonderful Words; Background Knowledge—Snake Bites	197
		10	Vocabulary; Character Relationships	199
		19	Predicting the Story's Ending	207
	Maniac Magee	8	Sequencing and Summarizing	220
	Author Study: Mildred Taylor	3	Sequencing; Building Background Knowledge	229
		4	Building Background Knowledge; Point of View	230
		5	Comparing and Contrasting	230
		8	Making Intertextual Connections	233
	The Civil War	1	Start of Inquiry Phase (Multi-Book Unit)	249

Curricular Area	Book Title	Lesson	Focus of Lesson	Page
Response to Literature • Personal Response • Creative Response • Critical Response	*Last Summer with Maizon*	2	Learning to Critique	60
		4	Drawing Pictures from Imagery	65
		6	Overcoming Writer's Block	67
		8	Me & the Book	71
	Tuck Everlasting	1	Review Response Choices, Checklists, and Venn Diagrams	83
		2	Drawing the Book's Setting	85
		4	Me & the Book	87

• Today's discussions, both in book clubs and in community share, should present opportunities for you to assess students' understanding of the story so far. Observe comments made during community share, and also walk though the class as students are meeting in their book clubs. Make brief notes about the students' critiques of the chapter and the story so far. Some students may want to place their reviews in their portfolios.

Student Sample: Critique #1

Teacher Comment:

"Excellent early example of critique: Usually they just write that it was good or bad. I have to push them to say why. This student gives several reasons to support opinion, yet he lacks evidence and proof from the book. I'd push him to find proof in the book of emotion—where he had the best picture in his mind, evidence of where people could relate, and examples and excerpts of detail."

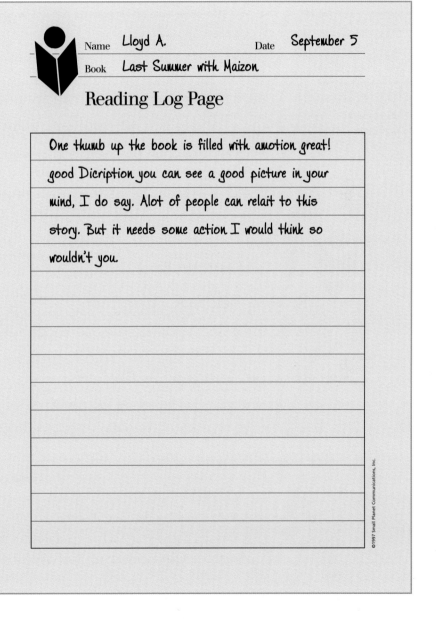

Name Lloyd A.   Date September 5

Book Last Summer with Maizon

Reading Log Page

One thumb up the book is filled with amotion great!
good Dicription you can see a good picture in your
mind, I do say. Alot of people can relait to this
story. But it needs some action I would think so
wouldn't you.

©1997 Small Planet Communications, Inc.

Name Lloyd A.   Date September 10

Book Last Summer with Maizon

Reading Log Page

I like the Book, why you might say, discription and that you get a purfect picture in your head when you read this book. Its sad in some ways and happy too. Another Reson I like it is because of detail this book has great detail. Its show how good freinds when there away there still best freinds. Maizon was very scared, Really for No Reson at all or mabey Not who knows.

Name Steve   Date September 5

Book Last Summer with Maizon

Reading Log Page

The part I liked in the book was the rain. I don't know why, but rain fascinates me. The thing I didn't like was Margaret's father died because he had another heart attack. I know just how she feels because when I lost my uncle. That's the saddest thing that ever happened to me. He was shot. It would be sad losing my Dad. Alot more sad to lose my dad. But I don't think that is going to happen though until he is really old.

Lesson 3

GOAL:
To teach students to think about characters and create character maps

ASSIGNED READING:
Chapter 5
(pages 31–37)

WRITING PROMPT:
Create a character map of a character in the story.

Literary Elements:
Character Map

- Explain to students that interesting characters who seem real or genuine to a reader are important to any story. Authors use characters as a way to help readers connect to a story. Authors also use characters to raise suspense about a story, or to remind readers of people they've known, which can help them make sense of story events. You might ask students to name interesting characters in other books that they've read. What makes these characters interesting and memorable to them?

- Brainstorm with students details about the different characters in *Last Summer with Maizon*. Tell them that they can learn about characters from direct descriptions of their personalities, their clothes, their hobbies, their homes, their families, and their thoughts and feelings. They can also learn about characters by noticing their words and actions and the ways in which other characters react to them.

- Tell students that one reading log option involves creating a character map. A character map is any kind of chart, list, or diagram in which students record interesting details about a particular character. (See student sample on page 64.)

- Explain that character maps will help students remember valuable details about characters as they read, and will help them to understand characters so that they can create good ones in their own stories. Authors tend to reveal more and more about a character over the course of the story, and a character map can also help students see how a character is changing throughout the story. All of this means that students will be better prepared to discuss these details in their book club groups. NOTE: You may want to model creating a character map on the chalkboard using a cartoon character or a character from a book you have read aloud.

- Have students complete the assigned reading and create the character maps that can serve as discussion starters in their book club groups.

Teaching Tip

At this point in the unit, students might feel more at ease with the Book Club format and with leading their own small-group discussions.

continued on next page

continued from previous page

However, you should be on the lookout for any "bad habits" that students may be forming. For example, one Book Club teacher found that her students were writing low-level recall questions—like workbook questions—in their logs and then bringing these questions to their book clubs for other students to answer. She decided to go over the different types of questions that avoid yes/no answers and that encourage thought, discussion, and more questions. This is an example of how a teacher adapted a lesson to fit the needs of a particular group of students. You can and should adapt each lesson to the needs of your own students on any given day.

Student Sample: Summary and Character Map

Teacher Comment:

"Early character profile— Many still have a tendency to summarize. I asked them why they write summaries if they don't know what to write and one boy said, 'We did it all the time last year and that was good enough thinking. We forget that we have to think deeper.'"

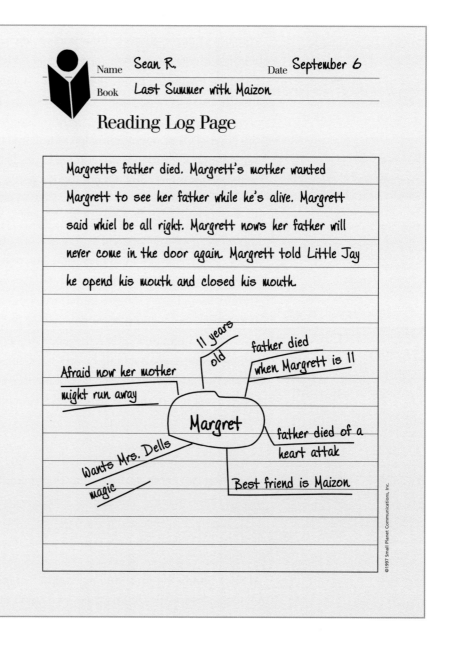

Name **Sean R.**   Date **September 6**

Book **Last Summer with Maizon**

Reading Log Page

Margretts father died. Margrett's mother wanted Margrett to see her father while he's alive. Margrett said whiel be all right. Margrett nows her father will never come in the door again. Margrett told Little Jay he opend his mouth and closed his mouth.

11 years old

father died when Margrett is 11

Afraid now her mother might run away

Margret

father died of a heart attak

Wants Mrs. Dells magic

Best friend is Maizon

Lesson 4

GOAL:
To help students use imagery to aid their comprehension and demonstrate their level of comprehension

ASSIGNED READING:
Chapters 6–7
(pages 39–54)

WRITING PROMPT:
Draw a picture as I read aloud. Then answer the following questions: What is your picture about? What in the reading inspired you to draw this picture?

Response to Literature:
Drawing Pictures from Imagery

- Discuss using imagery with students. Explain that when authors write they are often painting pictures with their words. As readers read, they use the author's words to create pictures in their minds. Tell students that one way to respond to a book is to draw the pictures that they see in their minds. This kind of response can be fun to talk about and compare with classmates.

- Explain to students that when people read the words that make up a story, they often form pictures in their minds. Introduce students to a reading log option that involves drawing pictures based on their reading. After they read a chapter of the book, they can draw pictures and then write one or two sentences below the picture to explain what their picture is about and why they drew it.

- Drawing pictures can help students to have a clearer understanding of what they have read. They can form pictures of characters and scenes in their minds, and then actually see how these characters and scenes look on paper.

Student Sample:
Picture #1

Teacher Comment:

"This share sheet and the one on the next page show the kinds of drawings students do to show the pictures that authors have created in their minds."

Joe
September 9

I due this because I could Clearly see it in my head that Margert and Maizon whear at the Tree where they bwas tikinahole.

continued on next page

continued from previous page

- Remind students that they need not be experienced artists to find this response option helpful and meaningful. Their pictures need only reflect their understanding of the story.

- Read today's assigned reading aloud to students. Ask them to draw pictures based on your reading. Another option is to have them do the reading independently and draw during the log writing period.

- Looking over students' drawings is an excellent way for you to assess their understanding of the events, characters, and details of the story. Noting a match or mismatch of text and pictures can be equally helpful. Samples of student responses to today's drawing/writing prompt appear on pages 65 and 66.

Student Sample: Picture #2

Teacher Comment:

"This is a typical early Book Club picture with sentences explaining what she drew and why."

Name Natalia K.   Date September 9

Book Last Summer with Maizon

Reading Log Page

I'm going to draw a picture of them doing there hand clap. How they clap ther palms together. I Drew this picture because it reminded me of How me and my Friends Do hand claps.

©1997 Small Planet Communications, Inc.

Lesson 5

GOAL:
To help students understand and identify the techniques an author uses in creating a story

ASSIGNED READING:
Chapter 8
(pages 55–58)

WRITING PROMPT:
Free choice

Literary Elements:
Author's Craft and Special Techniques

- Explain to students that an author uses different techniques to help readers enjoy a story. An author might use special words, create pictures in readers' minds with words, use funny language, and use interesting dialogue. All of these techniques of an author's craft draw a reader into a story and make the story more enjoyable.

- Tell students that you would like them to start keeping their eyes open for special author's techniques. As they read, they can record these techniques in their logs and explain why a particular technique helps them to enjoy a story. You might mention some specific author's techniques, such as: vivid imagery, humor, foreshadowing, flashback, dialogue, dialect, jokes, similes, metaphors, action words, and words or phrases that help a reader to see things.

- In this first Book Club unit, you can give brief descriptions of each author's technique. In subsequent units you might choose to focus an entire lesson on one of these techniques.

- After students read their assignment, they can write about any aspect of the book that interests them. They might want to focus on one or two author's techniques that they can identify in the book. Encourage students to discuss author's techniques in their book club groups.

Lesson 6

GOAL:
To help students develop strategies for overcoming writer's block

ASSIGNED READING:
Chapter 9
(pages 59–63)

Response to Literature:
Overcoming Writer's Block

- Make sure that students understand the phrase *writer's block*. Tell them that it is normal for people to experience writer's block from time to time when they are faced with a blank page. In a class discussion, ask if any students have ever felt "blocked" when they tried to begin a writing assignment. What does it feel like? What do they think causes it? You might compare a person with a frustrating case of writer's block to a car that keeps stalling, or to a computer that crashes and needs to be unplugged and then restarted. Invite students to think of other analogies.

continued on next page

continued from previous page

continued from previous page

WRITING PROMPT:
Practice free writing about anything related to the novel for sixty seconds. This is a technique that might help cure a case of writer's block in the future.

- Tell students that everyone who writes experiences writer's block, but since writing is a thinking tool, a writer needs to write *through* writer's block. Writer's block is no excuse not to write. Talk about specific strategies for dealing with writer's block. You might suggest that a "blocked" writer set a sixty-second time limit and write down whatever comes to his or her mind about a particular topic. Tell them that it is important that the writer keep his or her pencil moving during those sixty seconds and avoid the temptation to edit while writing. Remind students that they can always go back and edit later, but if they don't allow themselves to get their ideas on paper, they will have nothing to edit.

- You might also suggest that a student experiencing writer's block explore on paper why he or she might be having trouble getting started. The student might feel tired or sad on a particular day or feel intimidated or confused by a certain question. Getting these feelings out on paper might help the student to move past the writer's block and begin writing.

- Invite students to discuss as a class their own strategies for dealing with writer's block. You might make a list on chart paper so that students can refer to and use some of these strategies in the future.

Lesson 7

GOAL:
To focus on one technique that authors employ in order to help readers understand character's point of view in a story

ASSIGNED READING:
Chapter 10
(pages 65–73)

WRITING PROMPT:
Choose one of the following prompts:
- Write about Margaret's poem. How did it make you feel? Why did the author choose to include Margaret's poem and not just tell readers about it?

Literary Elements:
Author's Craft—Point of View

- Remind students of the discussion you had in Lesson 5 about author's craft and an author's special writing techniques. Tell them that one aspect of an author's craft is to express a character's point of view. To do this, an author might employ any of the techniques mentioned in Lesson 5, including humor, dialogue, foreshadowing, flashback, etc. One specific technique that an author can employ is having the character write something that expresses the character's point of view. In *Last Summer with Maizon*, Margaret writes a poem about her summer and tells the reader how she has really been feeling.

- Discuss with students what they think Margaret's poem might be about and why it might be interesting to hear her poem.

- Before asking students to read the assignment, you might spend some time discussing point of view. Ask students to identify who is telling the

- Write about the events of the chapter, taking another character's point of view.

story throughout this novel. Tell students that a character's point of view in a story shapes how a reader sees the events of the story. Explain that if *Last Summer with Maizon* were told from the point of view of a different character, it would be a different story. Invite students to discuss this idea as a class, or ask them to discuss it in their book clubs after they read the assignment and complete their writing activities. Two examples of point-of-view log entries by students in a Book Club classroom are shown on page 70.

- Encourage students to discuss in their book clubs both the writer's use of Margaret's poem and how it expresses the point of view of the story. They should touch on the subjects of both writing prompts even if all students in a particular group chose the same writing prompt.

Teaching Tip

This lesson presents an opportunity to assess students' comprehension of the story and of the concept of author's craft. Knowing what students are focusing on while reading the book can help you plan lessons in response to particular needs, or it can make the needs of individual students more apparent. Below are some suggestions for making this type of assessment manageable.

- Walk through the class during book club discussions and make notes about the level of understanding students show.

- You can also assess students' understanding during community share discussions.

- Examining students' reading logs can yield extensive information. One way to keep this manageable is to read one group's logs each day and write comments or questions on sticky notes in their logs. This starts a written conversation with students while not marking up their logs. Another way is to walk around the room and read students' logs as they write. You can ask individual students specific questions to prompt their thinking, and you can take notes on their progress.

Lesson 8

GOAL:

To encourage students to make connections between the book and their own lives

ASSIGNED READING:

Chapters 11–12 (pages 75–82)

WRITING PROMPT:

Make a connection between the book and your life. Can you relate to any of the characters? Why, or why not?

Response to Literature:
Me & the Book

- Ask students if any characters, events, or settings in the book so far have reminded them of people, places, and events in their own lives. Tell the class that making personal connections with characters and events in a book can help in their understanding and appreciation of the book.

- Tell students that another writing option for their logs is called Me & the Book. For this option, students may write about events or characters in the book that remind them of their own lives. Explain that writing about these events and characters can help them see the connections between the book and their own lives and that seeing these connections can help them think about the choices they can make about how to live their lives. For example, one student might understand what it's like to have a close friend move away and be able to better express his or her own feelings about a friend moving away. Another student might enjoy

Student Sample:
Me & the Book #1

Teacher Comment:

"Very typical early comparison of student's life to an aspect of a character in the book. Usually one or two points—a good beginning to build upon."

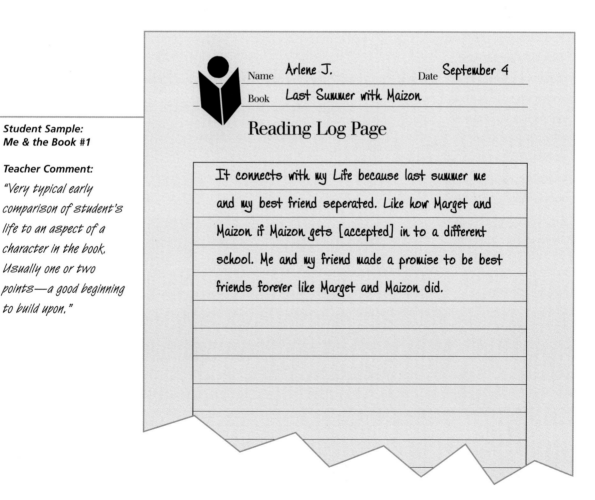

Name **Arlene J.**   Date **September 4**

Book **Last Summer with Maizon**

Reading Log Page

It connects with my Life because last summer me and my best friend seperated. Like how Marget and Maizon if Maizon gets [accepted] in to a different school. Me and my friend made a promise to be best friends forever like Marget and Maizon did.

continued on next page

continued from previous page

writing the way Margaret does and might think about what it means to be a writer. These types of connections help all readers understand a story and themselves somewhat better.

- Student examples of Me & the Book log entries are shown on page 71 and below.

- Remind students that they should choose any book-related topic that they are interested in writing about and that they don't have to share things that make them feel uncomfortable in their book club groups.

Student Sample:
Me & the Book #2

Teacher Comment:

"Another Me & the Book with more detail, more supporting points. It is better than the previous one (Arlene J.) because there is more depth of thinking. It's still immature, though, typical of early entries."

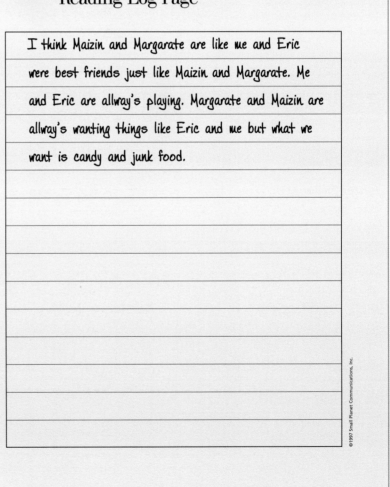

Name Zach   Date September 4

Book Last Summer with Maizon

Reading Log Page

I think Maizin and Margarate are like me and Eric were best friends just like Maizin and Margarate. Me and Eric are allway's playing. Margarate and Maizin are allway's wanting things like Eric and me but what we want is candy and junk food.

©1997 Small Planet Communications, Inc.

Lesson 9

GOAL:
To help students notice and record interesting, unusual, or confusing words and phrases as they read

ASSIGNED READING:
Chapter 13
(pages 83–87)

WRITING PROMPT:
Find some wonderful words in the chapter in the book. Why are these words wonderful to you?

Comprehension:
Wonderful Words

Teaching Tip

A word wall is literally a wall of words built throughout a unit of study, in this case a Book Club unit. The purpose of a word wall is to provide a place for the class to record words, phrases, and their definitions from the book and related readings. It provides a public arena where the connections between words and the meanings and connotations of words can be explored. A word wall can take many forms. There are only two rules—that the "word wall" be a safe place to store information for the duration of the unit and that the format be easy and convenient to use. Some formats that we are familiar with include large pieces of chart paper or butcher paper attached to a wall or chalkboard, a portion of a chalkboard reserved for this purpose, or a portable chart stand.

- Tell students that another way to respond to literature in their reading logs is to keep a list of "wonderful words"—words from their reading that they find interesting, fun, unusual, or confusing.

- Explain to students that this response choice might be helpful to them for a variety of reasons. Listing "wonderful words" can help students remember words whose meanings they want to learn. A "wonderful word" can also remind a student about an important idea or feeling that a character expressed. Thinking about these kinds of words can help everyone in a book club understand the characters and story more fully.

- Discuss ways to gather "wonderful words"—for example, recording words while reading, or looking back over the selection (after having read it once) to find interesting words. You might want to model some "wonderful words" that you have found in today's assigned reading. For example, the word *compromise* (page 86) is a challenging word. Even though it was used earlier in the book, you might want to look it up and discuss it again. The word *rumbled* (page 86) is interesting because it is a "sound" word—it describes what Margaret heard in the auditorium when she finished reading her poem. A student example of a "wonderful word" log entry can be found on page 74.

continued on next page

continued from previous page

- Ask students to look for your "wonderful words" as they read, and to find and record more of them to share during community share. Tell students that "wonderful words" collected throughout a unit will be added to a class "word wall." The word wall may be written on chart paper and posted on a wall or bulletin board in the room.

- NOTE: During the first Book Club unit of the year, it might be helpful to monitor "wonderful words" as a whole-class activity. After students have become familiar with the purpose of the word wall, they can use a think sheet to record words individually as they read.

Student Sample: Wonderful Words

Teacher Comment:

"Sometimes students do the 'assigned' entry, then get on with real thinking. I usually see this in good readers who think deeper than average students. Steve is ready for more challenging entries!"

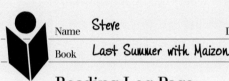

Name **Steve**   Date **September 13**

Book **Last Summer with Maizon**

Reading Log Page

Today Margaret read her poem it was really weird.

Anyway, We had to find a wierd word. I found

"snuck". I found snuck in a sentence saying She

snuck a look out the window. So that was my "wierd"

word. A thing that made me think is why Margaret

wrote that poem. Especially the begining "My pen

doesn't write anymore". That is one wierd begining. I

mean, who in the world would write something like that

begining? If I wrote that, I would [think] I was

crazy or something. But to put it this way, it's just

down right, absouloutly, positively, crazy weird.

"Phew." Know what? I bet the Auther did this to

confuse us.

©1997 Small Planet Communications, Inc.

Lesson 10

GOAL:

To make students see that understanding the sequence of events can help them to better understand the story

ASSIGNED READING:

Chapters 14–15
(pages 89–96)

WRITING PROMPT:

Make a sequence chart of important events in the book so far.

Comprehension:
Sequence

- Sequencing is an important ability that encompasses several strategies and skills. To sequence story events, students need to be able to identify key story events and distinguish them from minor happenings. Students should be able to put events in order—even if some are told out of order (e.g., flashbacks). Story sequences are critical to story comprehension.

- Explain to students that it is important to remember events in a story in the order they happened. Tell students that they can make a sequence chart, map, or list of these events in their reading logs to help them identify and remember the story events.

- Introduce the concept of sequencing by first referring to an experience that the entire class has shared. This experience might be a picture book, novel, poem, or movie, or it might be a class trip or some class routine.

- With the class, generate a list of four or five big events from this experience. You might need to help students distinguish between a big event and a small detail.

- Ask the class to place the four or five events in the order in which they happened. Tell students that this is called a sequence of events.

- Discuss with students why sequencing is useful. Mention that sequencing can help them to understand a story, and it can help them to retell or discuss a story. You might mention that sequencing can also be useful for planning and writing their own stories.

- You might want to model for students two or three types of sequence charts on an overhead projector. Types of sequence charts include charts made of squares, as in comic strips; squares with arrows, as in a flow chart; bubbles that connect; or lines as in a list. Basically, a sequence chart can be anything that graphically represents the order of events. Invite students to think of their own graphic organizers for sequence charts. NOTE: Examples of completed sequence charts are shown on pages 76–77.

continued on next page

continued from previous page

- While students are in book clubs, you may want to observe their discussions of the sequence of events in *Last Summer with Maizon.* You can learn from these discussions how well they are reading and understanding the book. It is also helpful to observe which events they list as important, and which they choose not to list, for insights into how they are making sense of the story.

Student Sample: Sequence Chart #1

Teacher Comment:

"This log entry reflects my lesson focus on BIG ideas. The double arrows Liz used are unusual."

**Student Sample:
Sequence Chart #2**

Teacher Comment:
*"Notice the snake
pattern this student
used to create her
sequence chart."*

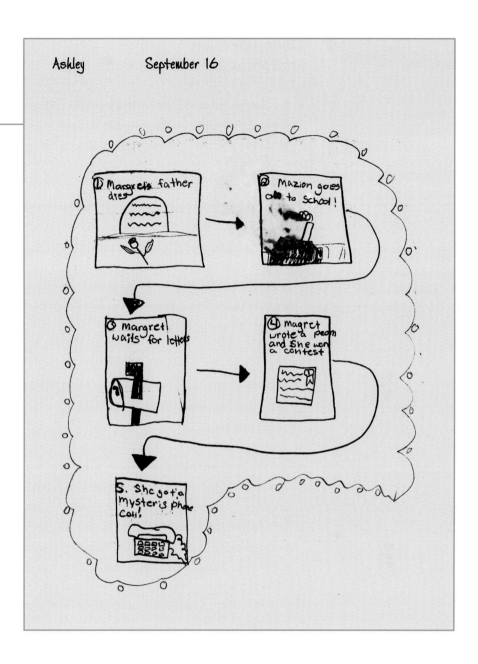

Ashley   September 16

① Margret's father dies

② Mazion goes off to School!

③ margret waits for letters

④ magret wrote a peom and she won a contest

5. She got a mysteris phone call!

*Student Sample:
Point of View #1*

Teacher Comment:

"I chose to teach a lesson on author's crafts in this chapter because of the poem. In beginning book clubs, students need guidance and examples or they have a difficult time finding author's crafts and techniques."

Name Margie Owen   Date September 13

Book Last Summer with Maizon

Reading Log Page

One of the tricks was when the athour had Marget write the poem. It could of been different the athur could of said and marget wrote a poem on how she felt but she didn't she had marget say what was in the poem. This author is a good author. And I think Maizon at Blue Hill is going to be as good a book as this one!!

Margets work isn't so good because her dad died and Maizon went away.

Name Mark   Date September 11

Book Last Summer with Maizon

Reading Log Page

Ms. Pizzle

Well today it was a good class but that Margeret, theres something wrong with her. I've talked to her 3 times today. She's got proplems.

*Student Sample:
Point of View #2*

Teacher Comment:

"Typical point-of-view entry in which a student tries to write a section from a different character's point of view."

Student Sample:
Interpretation

Teacher Comment:

"Ashley at first relied on summarizing to get going—her thinking improves as the writing continues. Typical early interpretation—simple."

Name Ashley   Date September 10

Book Last Summer with Maizon

Reading Log Page

Margret and Mazoin said good by to each other and hugged for a long time and Mazion said thanks to Margret for ceeping the trophe even thogh that they won 2nd place.

I learned that best freinds stay togeather no mater what! even like me and my freind. She moved to Rockford and I only get to see her 2 times every year! Me and my freind are like peas and carrets! But Margret and Mazion will allways be buddies!

Lesson 12

GOAL:
To help students think about their classroom experiences as they were reading *Last Summer with Maizon*

ASSIGNED READING:
None

WRITING PROMPT:
Fill out a self-assessment form.

Student Self-Assessment

- Explain to students that assessment, particularly self-assessment, is an important part of learning. Self-assessment is a chance to reflect on the work one has done, to think about what has gone well, and to decide what areas need extra work and improvement. A person who never stops to review his or her progress is bound to repeat mistakes and never grow as a reader and writer.

- You might want to distribute self-assessment forms. (A sample is provided in the Blackline Masters: Assessment section following page 281 in this guide.) Ask students to read the forms carefully and to think carefully about their responses. Answer any questions students might have about the forms.

Lesson 13

GOAL:
To discuss the grades and evaluations you've given each student, and to help students set personal goals for the next Book Club unit

ASSIGNED READING:
None

WRITING PROMPT:
Think about your self-assessment form and your grade and evaluation from me. What goals can you set for the next Book Club?

Teacher Evaluation

- Explain to students that your evaluation will give them another perspective on their work and progress.

- Evaluate each student's accomplishments and progress during the Book Club unit using information from the various assessments. Base your evaluations on information and evidence gathered throughout the unit. Allow observations made during community share and book clubs to inform your evaluations. (A sample Book Club Evaluation form is provided in the Blackline Masters: Assessment section.)

- If time allows, meet with each student individually and share your evaluation and grades for the student. (For other options, turn to Lesson 20 for *The Fighting Ground*, page 144.) Also discuss the student's self-assessment form. Ask the student to share his or her feelings about the unit and about how he or she has progressed. Then answer any questions that the student might have about the unit or about your evaluation. You might give the student a form on which to record his or her reactions to your conference and to set some concrete goals for the next Book Club unit. (A sample Reaction and Goal Setting form is provided in the Blackline Masters: Assessment section.) Tell the student that the goals they set will be revisited during the evaluation of the next Book Club unit.

Tuck Everlasting
by Natalie Babbitt

Introducing the Book

This chapter contains twenty-one lessons that you can use with *Tuck Everlasting*. The novel can be used with different levels and grades of students. You can increase or decrease the sophistication of discussion depending on your class. For example, the question of whether a person would want to live forever can be discussed at whatever level of sophistication and depth is appropriate for your class. With older students, you may decide to increase the number of pages they read each day. You might also want to consider including this book as a literature component to a science unit about life cycles.

Summary Ten-year-old Winnie Foster lives a privileged and protected life in 1880, but she longs to do something important. One morning she sneaks out into the woods her family owns. There she sees a handsome young man taking a sip of water from a spring at the base of a tree. When she asks if she can have a drink, too, Jesse Tuck nervously refuses. His mother and brother arrive, and before Winnie knows it, she is being kidnapped. Finally they stop to rest and tell her their story: the spring contains water that makes people live forever. Seventeen-year-old Jesse was born a hundred and four years ago. Unbeknownst to any of them, a strange man is listening to their tale and dreaming of profiting from the spring. The group proceeds to the Tucks' home, where Winnie meets the father. Tuck explains to her why living forever has been more of a curse than a blessing for his family, and why it's important that no one ever find out about the spring. Slowly Winnie begins to appreciate the natural cycle of birth, life, and death.

Meanwhile, the stranger is negotiating with Winnie's family, trading information of her whereabouts for ownership of the woods that contain the spring. When the man arrives back at the Tucks' house, states his plan to exploit the spring, and starts leading Winnie away, Mae Tuck hits him in the head with a shotgun. At that moment the constable arrives, sees every-

Paperback Edition, Farrar, Straus and Giroux, © 1975 by Natalie Babbitt. ISBN 0-374-48009-5.

thing, and takes Winnie back to her family and Mae to jail. After the man dies, the Tucks know that Mae will be sentenced to hang. It is impossible for her to die, and their secret will come out. They devise a plan to rescue Mae from jail, and Winnie insists on helping. Before the night of the escape, Jesse gives Winnie some of the spring water and suggests that she drink it when she turns seventeen so that they can get married and spend forever together. The next morning, the constable comes into Mae's cell to serve her breakfast and finds Winnie in her place. The Tucks are gone!

Seventy years later Mae and Tuck return to Treegap and find what they had both hoped and dreaded to find: a recent grave marker with Winnie's name on it.

Themes The cyclical nature of life and the purpose of death are two major themes in *Tuck Everlasting*. It is interesting to discuss both of these themes through the plot premise that the cycle of life which we take for granted is not necessarily the only way it could be. Other aspects of the novel that may come up in students' discussions are responsibility, maturity, loyalty, and friendship. In the course of the novel, Winnie Foster is forced to consider what she thinks is right and wrong, and to act on her beliefs. Not only does she decide to help her friend Mae Tuck escape from jail, but she later decides not to drink from the spring water. Both decisions have consequences and rewards. Many of the discussion points proceed from the question: Would you want to live forever?

Special Classroom Library With *Tuck Everlasting*, you will want to include books in your classroom library that are in the genre of fantasy or that deal with mortality and death. *A Wrinkle in Time* by Madeleine L'Engle (Dell, 1996) is one book that we have seen paired with *Tuck Everlasting*. Other books that you might want to consider are listed below.

Title	Author	Publisher, Date
The Lion, the Witch, and the Wardrobe/Chronicles of Narnia	C. S. Lewis	HarperCollins Children's Books, 1994
The Giver	Lois Lowry	Houghton Mifflin, 1993
A Summer to Die	Lois Lowry	Bantam Books, 1984
Lifelines: A Poetry Anthology Patterned on the Stages of Life	Leonard S. Marcus	Dutton, 1993
A Taste of Blackberries	Doris Buchanan Smith	HarperCollins Children's Books, 1988
Faithful Elephants	Yukio Tsuchiya	Houghton Mifflin, 1988
Charlotte's Web	E. B. White	Harper, 1952

Lesson 1

GOAL:
To review the range of
response choices and the
use of reading log check-
lists; to introduce a triple
Venn diagram format

ASSIGNED READING:
Prologue
(pages 3–4)

WRITING PROMPT:
- Use a triple Venn diagram
  to show how the events
  in the prologue are
  linked. (You won't fill in
  all of the sections now—
  just fill in what you learn
  in today's reading.)
- How does the author
  create a feeling of
  suspense in the prologue?
  Write down some ques-
  tions the prologue raised
  in your mind.

Response to Literature:
Review Response Choices, Checklists, and Venn Diagrams

- One of the goals of the Book Club program is to show students the wide range of responses they can have when they read literature. This lesson is an opportunity to review some of the different response types students have already learned and to discuss some of the new responses students have created. The lesson also provides an opportunity to introduce or review Venn diagrams and to use a Venn diagram as a thinking tool for reading *Tuck Everlasting*.

- Remind students of the types of response choices they have already learned how to use in their reading logs. If any students have invented new types of responses, ask them to share these with the class. (You may want to add the names and descriptions of these new response types to a chart or a bulletin board in the classroom.)

- Distribute copies of a reading log checklist that includes all the types of reading log responses covered in the previous discussion. Students may write in the response types that they and their classmates have created. (Sample Reading Log Checklist forms are available in the Blackline Masters: Think Sheets section following page 261.) Explain to students that the checklist can help them keep track of the types of responses they have used in their logs and can remind them of the range of possible responses.

- Review using Venn diagrams as a format for students' reading log entries. (A sample Venn Diagram form is available in the Blackline Masters: Think Sheets section.) Since one of the important areas of response to literature is making connections within and across texts, the Venn diagram can be a very useful way to make these connections visible. Discuss with students the various things that they could compare and contrast using two circles, such as two characters, two books, a book and a movie, and so on.

- Introduce the format of a triple Venn diagram, used to show links between three items. Explain that in the prologue they are about to read, the author describes three events that are somehow linked to each other. Suggest that they draw a diagram with three circles in their reading logs and fill it in as they read. Or, you might want to read the prologue aloud and model for the class how to use the triple Venn

continued on next page

continued from previous page

diagram. A sample diagram, along with a teaching tip from a Book Club teacher, is provided below.

- If you have asked students to read the prologue silently and fill in Venn diagrams in their reading logs, ask them to share their diagrams with a partner. Then, in community share, ask for volunteers to share their diagrams with the whole class.

- NOTE: Any Venn diagrams that have been started—whether by you or by the students—should be saved. You will return to them and fill in more information in Lesson 6.

Triple Venn Diagram:
Tuck Everlasting *Prologue*

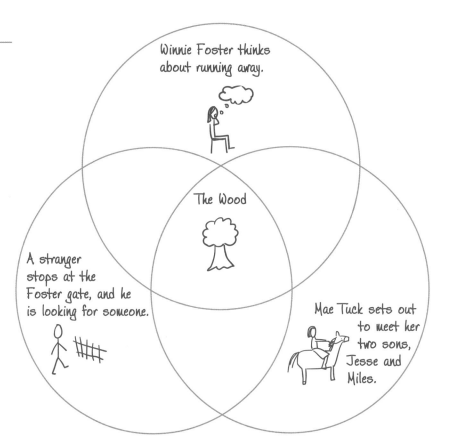

Winnie Foster thinks about running away.

The Wood

A stranger stops at the Foster gate, and he is looking for someone.

Mae Tuck sets out to meet her two sons, Jesse and Miles.

Teaching Tip

"I usually draw a Venn diagram on the overhead, and I read the prologue aloud. As I go through the three seemingly unrelated events, I add them to the diagram. Students can make their own along with the teacher, or the whole class can use the teacher's model. Students can then add events as the story unfolds."

Lesson 2

GOAL:
To understand how the vocabulary and phrases that an author uses help a reader picture the setting of a story

ASSIGNED READING:
Chapter 1
(pages 5–8)

WRITING PROMPT:
Listen to Chapter 1 again and draw what you picture as Treegap.

Response to Literature:
Drawing the Book's Setting

- An essential part of reading literature is forming mental pictures of what the author describes. Unlike television or movies, books require the audience to participate in the creative act. This lesson is an opportunity for you to discuss with your class how writers use carefully chosen words to create images in readers' minds, and how these images can (and inevitably do) vary from reader to reader.

- NOTE: You may choose to use an audio tape of Chapter 1 to teach this lesson. We've used different methods to obtain audio tapes of stories. We have purchased tapes, made tapes ourselves, and had students make tapes. However, a tape is not necessary—you can teach the lesson by simply reading Chapter 1 aloud.

- Have students complete the day's reading assignment **before** you conduct the lesson. The Book Club teacher who developed this lesson plan did today's drawing activity in place of book clubs. You may also decide to omit book clubs from today's session, or you can integrate the drawing activity with students' preparation for book club discussions.

- Reread Chapter 1 aloud. Ask students to help you identify words and phrases that describe the setting of *Tuck Everlasting.* List the words on the chalkboard or create a concept web with Treegap as the center and the words and phrases on the spokes. Possible words and phrases to explore include *easiness* (page 5), *touch-me-not appearance* (page 6), *otherworld* (page 6), and *dimness shot through with bars of sunlight* (page 7). Discuss how these and other phrases make the students feel and how the words help describe the setting of the story.

- After discussing the descriptive language, give students the writing prompt. Play the audio tape or read the chapter aloud several times while students draw their interpretation of Treegap and its environs.

- Hang the pictures along the chalkboard and discuss how different students have portrayed Treegap. Discuss how a person's experiences can affect the way they "see" something when it is described. Note both the similarities and the differences among the pictures.

Lesson 3

GOAL:
To model creating a character map and/or share new ways to create character maps

ASSIGNED READING:
Chapter 2
(pages 9–12)

WRITING PROMPT:
Make a character map of Mae Tuck.

Comprehension:
Characters and Character Maps

- Students' story understandings and interpretations are enhanced as they become more aware of the ways authors use literary elements to convey their stories. Characterization, one such element, can be highlighted through creating character maps. To introduce (or review) various map formats, we've used legends or folk tales, which tend to have simply drawn characters and little character development. If you are using this lesson early in the year, you'll want to model how to create a character map. We like to model by reading aloud a legend, folk tale, or short story.

- After reading aloud, create a character map with students' input on an overhead transparency or the chalkboard. A typical character map might consist of a bubble with lines extending out from it as shown on the student sample below. The character's name occupies the center with questions and supporting information placed around the page. Discuss personality traits, descriptions, and actions as possible sources of information about the character.

- Later in the year, this same lesson can be taught through a discussion about different ways of doing character maps—lists, flow charts, pictures and attributes, and so on. (See the format ideas given on the next page.) We like to begin by introducing students to specific formats, eventually moving to students creating their own maps.

- Have students read Chapter 2 and start their character maps of Mae Tuck. In community share, discuss what they've added to their maps so far and what they talked about in their book clubs.

Student Sample:
Character Map

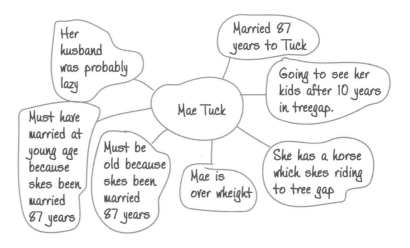

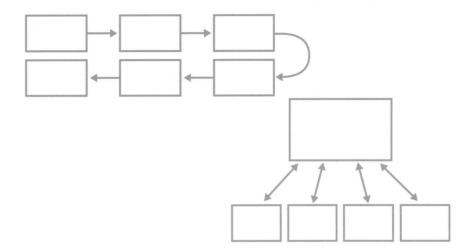

Lesson 4

GOAL:
To have students show how they have connected to the text

ASSIGNED READING:
Chapter 3
(pages 13–16)

WRITING PROMPT:
Have you ever felt like Winnie does—like running away? Describe how you felt and how your feelings were similar to Winnie's.

Response to Literature:
Me & the Book

- Making a personal connection to a book enhances both enjoyment and understanding of the literature. This lesson can be used to introduce or review the Me & the Book response type.

- Talk to students about books that they have enjoyed. Ask them to explain why they enjoyed them. Expand the discussion to include a book or books that you have enjoyed. Make the point that often the reason a reader enjoys a book is that there is an event or character in the book that the reader relates to, or understands.

- If necessary, introduce the Me & the Book response type to students. Have students give a few examples about how something that they've read made them think about their own lives. Tell them that when writing about these kinds of things, they should describe a character or event in the book and then tell what the character or event reminds them of in their own life. Writing about how they relate to a book can help them understand the book more fully. If this is later in the year, expand and challenge students' connections by encouraging complex comparisons and asking them to provide evidence from the story.

- During community share, ask volunteers to share their responses to the writing prompt.

Lesson 5

GOAL:
To provide students with the information to interpret imagery and flashback in a text

ASSIGNED READING:
Chapter 4
(pages 17–21)

WRITING PROMPT:
Whom or what do you think the man in the yellow suit is searching for?

Literary Elements:
Author's Craft—Imagery and Foreshadowing

- Students' appreciation of a text is greatly increased when they understand the literary devices that authors use to create certain effects. This lesson allows you to review imagery and foreshadowing with your students and helps them apply their knowledge to *Tuck Everlasting*.

- Have students complete the day's reading assignment **before** you conduct this lesson.

- Explain that imagery is language that an author uses to illustrate with words the characters and events in a book. Imagery can include both descriptive language and figurative language. Descriptive language uses precise nouns and verbs and vivid adjectives to describe something. Figurative language can consist of similes and metaphors. Remind students that a simile compares two dissimilar things and often uses the word *like* or *as* to make the comparison. A metaphor, on the other hand, suggests that one object or idea *is* another object or idea. Challenge students to find an example of a simile in the text, such as the one on page 18 that describes the man in the yellow suit as being *like a well-handled marionette*. Discuss how this imagery helps the reader understand how the man in the yellow suit looks and acts.

- Foreshadowing is another tool of the author's craft. An author uses foreshadowing to give readers a hint about something that will happen later in the story. This creates tension in the reader's mind and makes the story more exciting; it also helps tie the story together by relating early events to later ones. An example of foreshadowing occurs in Chapter 4 (page 18), when Winnie suddenly recalls her grandfather's funeral while talking to the stranger at the gate. You might want to discuss with your students how this imagery of the black funeral ribbons cautions the reader (and Winnie) about the character of the stranger, even though he seems perfectly harmless. Can students make any predictions about what might happen later in the story?

- During community share, return to the concept of imagery and ask students to share how the imagery in this chapter helped them make a prediction about whom or what the man in the yellow suit is searching for.

Lesson 6

GOAL:
To revisit the Venn diagram and add details from Chapters 2–5

ASSIGNED READING:
Chapter 5
(pages 22–30)

WRITING PROMPT:
Free choice

Response to Literature:
Revisit the Venn Diagram (Lesson 1)

- A graphic organizer can be used throughout the course of a book to record new information and relate it to what happened earlier in the story. Ask students to bring out the Venn diagrams they worked on in Lesson 1. Put your example on the overhead projector and, as a class, add a few details from Chapters 1 and 2.

- Have students add the details from your model onto their Venn diagrams and then work in pairs to add and discuss details from Chapters 3–4.

- After students complete the assigned reading and write in their logs, have them form pairs again to add details from Chapter 5 to the Venn diagram. A sample diagram with details from the Prologue through Chapter 5 is provided below.

- Both the Venn diagrams and free choice writing can form the basis of conversations in students' book clubs.

Triple Venn Diagram:
Tuck Everlasting *Prologue–*
Chapter 5

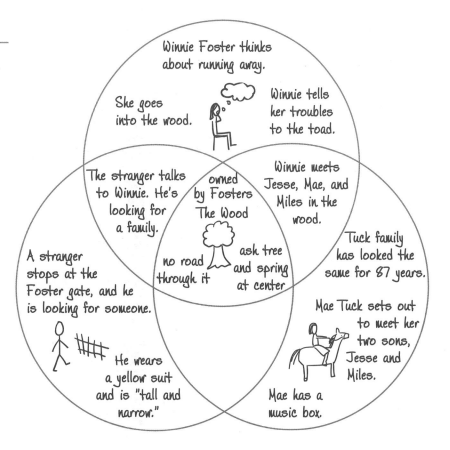

Winnie Foster thinks about running away.

She goes into the wood.

Winnie tells her troubles to the toad.

The stranger talks to Winnie. He's looking for a family.

owned by Fosters The Wood

Winnie meets Jesse, Mae, and Miles in the wood.

no road through it

ash tree and spring at center

Tuck family has looked the same for 87 years.

A stranger stops at the Foster gate, and he is looking for someone.

Mae Tuck sets out to meet her two sons, Jesse and Miles.

He wears a yellow suit and is "tall and narrow."

Mae has a music box.

Lesson 7

GOAL:
To discuss feelings and emotions as the author expresses them through the characters and as the reader responds to the story

ASSIGNED READING:
Chapter 6
(pages 31–36)

WRITING PROMPT:
Explore the characters' feelings. How do the Tucks and Winnie feel at this moment in the book?

Response to Literature:
Feelings and Emotions

- NOTE: The direction that this lesson takes depends to a great extent on the mood of the class, the time of year, and your goals and teaching style. You can choose to approach the lesson through a general discussion of emotions, a discussion of how authors show the emotions of their characters, a discussion of how readers respond to the emotions of the characters, or a combination of all three approaches.

- Approach 1: Discuss what role emotions play in books and in reading books. Start the discussion by raising some or all of the following questions: Why are emotions important in books? If authors chose not to describe any emotions, how would some books be different? What can the expression of emotions in books and our emotional responses as readers teach us?

- Approach 2: Introduce or review the several ways that authors can show emotion in their characters. Imagery, descriptions, and dialogue can all help convey a character's feelings. Look for examples of characters' emotions in Chapter 5. Point out phrases such as *instantly serious, dry as dust, plaintively,* and *very pale* on pages 28 and 29 as clues to what Winnie and Jesse are feeling.

- Approach 3: Lead a discussion about how the emotions of Winnie and the Tucks make the students feel. Do students feel sympathy or empathy with the Tucks' situation and Winnie's dilemma? What would students do in a similar situation?

- One or all of the above can be used to help students explore feelings and emotions in the context of *Tuck Everlasting*. After students have read Chapter 6, responded to the writing prompt, and met with their small groups, ask volunteers to share their writing in community share and discuss how their perceptions of the characters' emotions were similar or different.

Lesson 8

GOAL:
To explore the aspects of a novel that make it a fantasy

ASSIGNED READING:
Chapter 7
(pages 37–41)

WRITING PROMPT:
- What do you think about the Tucks' story? Back up your thinking with examples from the book.
- If you were Winnie, would you believe them? Why or why not?
- List some parts of Chapter 7 that are fantasy, and others that are realistic.

Literary Elements:
Genre—Fantasy

- *Tuck Everlasting* provides many opportunities to highlight the differences between fantasy and reality and to show how authors combine the two to create story lines that "work." This lesson can be used to highlight aspects of fantasy and the techniques that authors use to create the genre.

- It's best if students complete the day's reading assignment **before** you conduct this lesson.

- Read the section of Chapter 6 in which Winnie starts examining the music box (page 35, "When the tinkling little melody began . . .") aloud to students. Then read the section of Chapter 7 that concerns how the Tucks found out about the powers of the spring (page 40, "It hadn't changed, no more'n we had, . . ."). Begin a discussion about the differences that students notice in the two sections. Lead the discussion toward the conclusion that the earlier section of the book is something that really could have happened, while the portion describing the Tucks' story is fantasy, or something that could not possibly have happened.

- On the chalkboard or on an overhead transparency, create a compare-contrast chart with the column heads *Fantasy* and *Realistic Fiction.* Have students provide the characteristics of books that are realistic fiction versus works of fantasy. Look for intertextual connections that students use to illustrate their contributions to the chart.

- Have students continue their exploration of the fantasy genre while writing in their logs. Discussions about the aspects of fantasy can continue in students' book club groups and in community share.

Lesson 9

GOAL:
To follow the development of the characters in *Tuck Everlasting* over time

ASSIGNED READING:
Chapters 8–9
(pages 42–49)

WRITING PROMPT:
How does Winnie feel now? Give evidence from the book.

Comprehension:
Analyzing Character Development

- In Lesson 3, students created character maps to show what Mae Tuck is like. In this lesson, they will see that it is important not only to look at what a character is like at a particular moment in time, but also to watch how the character changes over time.

- Ask students to take out the character maps they created for Mae Tuck. If necessary, review some of the ways in which authors can show what a character is like: what the character does, what the character says, what the character looks like, and what other characters think and say about the character. Then ask students how an author could show that a character has changed during a story.

- Discuss the character of Winnie with students. What kinds of changes have students noticed in her since the beginning of the book? For what reasons has she changed?

- With the class, start a character-over-time chart on the chalkboard or overhead. (NOTE: Early in the year, you may want to coach students through creating a time line or a flow chart format for their character study. Later, have the class suggest and use a format.) Have students provide details of the changes in Winnie's character, including the reasons for the changes. Place or have students place changes/events on the chart. Discuss how the author has developed Winnie's character. (A sample time line is given below.)

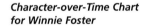

Character-over-Time Chart for Winnie Foster

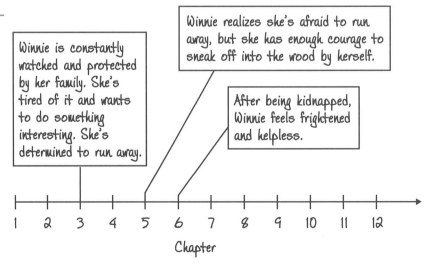

Winnie is constantly watched and protected by her family. She's tired of it and wants to do something interesting. She's determined to run away.

Winnie realizes she's afraid to run away, but she has enough courage to sneak off into the wood by herself.

After being kidnapped, Winnie feels frightened and helpless.

Chapter

- Have pairs of students repeat the process with one or more of the Tucks. One of the important details for students to notice is how little change there is in the Tucks and how this ties into their predicament.

- Discuss students' findings as a group before asking students to complete the assigned reading and the writing prompt.

- In community share, remind students to use their writing as a source of information while the class adds details to Winnie's character-over-time chart.

- NOTE: You will need a copy of the character-over-time chart for Lesson 10.

Lesson 10

GOAL:

To explore similarities and differences between Winnie's world and the Tucks' world and to apply this knowledge to under-standing Winnie's character over time

ASSIGNED READING:

Chapters 10–11 (pages 50–59)

WRITING PROMPT:
- Compare and contrast Winnie's home and the Tucks' home.
- How does Winnie feel now?

Comprehension:
Comparison and Contrast

- Comparing and contrasting is a comprehension skill that can be applied to understanding many aspects of a story, including setting, theme, and characters. By noticing similarities and differences between characters, students can understand what a character is doing and, more impor-tantly, why the character is doing it.

- NOTE: A copy of the character-over-time chart developed by the class in Lesson 9 is helpful when teaching this lesson.

- Start by discussing why it is helpful to compare and contrast two things. What can a person learn by thinking about how two things are alike and different? If you know a lot about one thing and not much about another thing, how can comparing and contrasting help you to understand the unknown thing? Ask students what sorts of character traits they could compare and contrast to understand a character better.

- Discuss ways to record these kinds of comparisons and contrasts. A Venn diagram is one method, but students may have better suggestions. Once again, it is very important to give students the free-dom to develop their own methods of response, particularly as the year progresses.

continued on next page

Lesson 11

Comprehension:
Interpretation with a Picture Book

GOAL:
To help students to understand the concept of interpretation and how they interpret lessons and ideas in their reading

ASSIGNED READING:
Chapters 16–17 (pages 97–105)

WRITING PROMPT:
Write about what you think the author wants you to learn from reading this book.

- As a story draws to a close, readers can reflect on all the events in the story, on the author's purpose for writing, and on their own lives to think about the kind of statement the author is trying to make.

- Interpretation is not an easy skill to learn. Although the goal is for students to interpret *Last Summer with Maizon*, the Book Club teacher who created and used this lesson plan in her classroom wanted to give the students some practice with a more controlled amount of text. She chose to have students interpret the messages in the picture book *Gluskabe and the Four Wishes* (Bruchac, 1995). *Smoky Night* (Bunting, 1994) is another possibility, although any picture book that subtly teaches its readers a lesson will work.

- Begin by reading the book aloud to the class. Then ask the students what the author wanted readers to learn from the book. Guide them with questions about the plot, the feelings of the characters, and the story's ending.

- Discuss how authors use their writing to teach lessons or to make statements about the world, even though they don't usually come out and say, "The moral of the story is…" Readers learn from a story by paying attention to language, the actions and words of the characters, and the pictures the writer creates with words. Explain that often a reader will learn something from a book that the author might not even have intended, because the story touched that particular reader's life in a special way. The message a reader takes from a story is that reader's interpretation.

- Tell students that they can write their interpretations of parts of *Last Summer with Maizon* in their reading logs. They can read their interpretations aloud in their book clubs and in community share, and they will also have the opportunity to hear other students' interpretations.

- An early example of a student's interpretation is included on page 79.

- You might want to walk though the class as book clubs meet and discuss students' interpretations of the novel.

Lesson 11

GOAL:
To examine the recurring images of the wheel, the hub, or the circle within the text and determine what kind of theme such images suggest

ASSIGNED READING:
Chapters 12–13
(pages 60–66)

WRITING PROMPT:
Do you notice any familiar or recurring images in Chapters 12–13? Where in the book have you seen them before? How are they related to the theme of the story?

Literary Elements:
Recurring Images and Story Themes

- There are strong themes throughout this novel, creating excellent opportunities to help students learn about the concept of themes in general as well as to identify particular story themes. One especially compelling theme is the idea that life is a natural cycle. Images of a wheel, hub, or circle recur throughout the text. You might begin to talk about theme by asking students what a story theme is. Reinforce ideas that relate to repeated images, a major idea, or the point of the story. You can point out to students that when they notice something that appears over and over again in a story, they should start to wonder what the author is trying to say through this device.

- After your discussion of story themes, students should complete the day's reading assignment.

- In a community-share setting, ask students to look through the first thirteen chapters of *Tuck Everlasting* and find examples of recurring images. Examples (from the prologue and Chapter 1) include the hub of the Ferris wheel, the wood as the hub of three seemingly unrelated events, and the giant ash tree at the center of the wood. Ask students what theme these images of a wheel might convey.

- Discuss the significance of an author using a recurring idea or image. What does its repeated use indicate about its importance to the story? Ask students to make intertextual connections to other books that they have read or movies that they have seen that employ recurring ideas or images.

- Next examine why the image of wheels, or cycles, is so important to Tuck and guide the discussion with the following questions: How important does this idea seem to Winnie? What does the constant movement of water symbolize for Tuck? Discuss why the author has used the wheel to help convey the theme of the book. You might ask students to identify any other idea or image that would convey the same theme to the reader.

- Finally, have students respond to the writing prompt and discuss their ideas in their book club groups.

Lesson 12

GOAL:
To understand how different characters' points of view make a story more complex and more realistic

ASSIGNED READING:
Chapters 14–15
(pages 67–75)

WRITING PROMPT:
Discuss the characters' differing points of view. How does the author use this to create confusion for Winnie?

Literary Elements:
Point of View

- Understanding different points of view is important both in real life and in literature. Because real people each have their own unique perspectives on the world, a realistic novel will explore the complexity of relationships between characters who have different beliefs, feelings, backgrounds, and personalities. Readers who are aware of these complexities will gain a deeper understanding of the characters and of the story itself.

- Ask students what they think point of view means. Guide them to understand that point of view is something that exists both in stories and in real life. Point of view is how a particular person or character sees the world. Point of view is influenced by the person's or character's background, experiences, beliefs, opinions, prejudices, and emotions. Someone's point of view can change over time. You might ask students to give examples of a change in point of view, either from their own experiences or from books such as *Tuck Everlasting*. Ask them what kinds of events and experiences can lead to a change in someone's point of view.

- You might also ask students to consider what happens when two people or characters have a different point of view about a matter that concerns both of their lives. How can this lead to conflict, or to growth? Can an individual have two different points of view about something at the same time? How would this make the person feel? What might be the outcome when a person wrestles with two points of view in his or her own mind?

- Suggest that students keep this discussion about point of view in mind as they complete today's assigned reading, respond to the writing prompt, and participate in book club groups and community share.

GOAL:
To note the author's use of recurring images and discuss what they add to the story

ASSIGNED READING:
Chapters 16–17
(pages 76–88)

WRITING PROMPT:
You may ask students to respond to one or both of these prompts:
• How does Winnie feel now?
• Do you see any more recurring images in today's reading? If so, what themes or ideas do the images suggest?

Literary Elements:
Recurring Images and Story Themes, Revisited

• Review the discussion of recurring images started in Lesson 11. Discuss how images of wheels have developed the themes of the book since Chapters 12 and 13.

• Students should now complete the assigned reading, write in their logs, and meet with their book clubs. During community share, you can continue your discussion of recurring images and story themes.

• Ask whether students have noticed any other recurring images in *Tuck Everlasting*. They may need to scan today's reading again to get some ideas. Two recurring elements are toads/frogs and water. Winnie spoke to a toad outside the fence of her own house, and she noticed the loud croaking of frogs at the Tucks' pond when she was in the boat with Tuck and then with Miles. Water is important to the story because it was water from the spring that gave the Tucks eternal life, and Tuck uses the ever-flowing water of the pond to explain to Winnie about the wheel of life. Remind students of their discussion concerning wheel imagery in Lesson 11.

• Guide students to see that the images of toads and frogs may represent nature. You might ask them to visualize the scene in which Miles and Winnie go fishing on the pond. Nature is all around them, and this is probably the first time in Winnie's life that she has been immersed in a natural setting. The croaking of the frogs is a vivid sensory image, and the discussion between Miles and Winnie about the frogs and the snapping turtles reminds readers of the cycle of nature—birth and death—that Tuck and Winnie discussed earlier. (Understanding the symbolism of the frogs will help students understand Winnie's encounters with toads in Chapters 22 and 25.)

• Remind students to look for frogs, toads, water, and any other recurring images as they continue to read *Tuck Everlasting*.

Lesson 14

GOAL:
To notice the structure of the story and analyze the story elements

ASSIGNED READING:
Chapters 18–19
(pages 89–100)

WRITING PROMPT:
Free choice

Literary Elements:
Story Elements

- Understanding literary elements can increase students' abilities to comprehend, interpret, and appreciate what they read. One of the key literary elements is the story structure or plot. There are several ways to describe this structure, and no doubt you have your own vocabulary for doing so. For example, you can say that a story has a beginning, in which the setting, main characters, and problem (or conflict) are established; a middle, in which the characters struggle to solve the problem; and an end, in which the problem is resolved. You can also say that a story consists of events leading up to a climax, a climax (the most exciting point in the story, when the problem or conflict demands action by the characters), and a resolution, when the problem is solved. It's useful to emphasize that in stories, there is usually some problem or conflict that characters must resolve.

- Ask students to define the central problem or conflict in *Tuck Everlasting.* You might point out that stories often have one big problem (e.g., the Tucks needing to protect their secret) and some related smaller problems (e.g., Winnie not knowing what to believe or whom to trust). You might ask them to briefly retell the story events that are leading up to a climax, and to predict what they think the climax will be.

- During community share, after students have completed the day's reading, written in their logs, and met with their book clubs, you might ask the class whether they think the story has reached its climax. Also ask them whether the central problem has been solved yet. Do they feel the dramatic tension created by the unresolved problem? Are they eager to continue reading?

Lesson 15

GOAL:
To understand how authors show changes in characters over time

Comprehension:
Changes in Characters Over Time

- In this lesson, students can add to their character-over-time charts and discuss how authors show changes in characters.

- Review the character-over-time chart developed by the class in Lessons 9 and 10. Ask students what kinds of details they would add to the chart

ASSIGNED READING:
Chapters 20–21
(pages 101–110)

WRITING PROMPT:
You may ask students to respond to one or both of these prompts:
- How has Winnie changed? Show proof for your answer. (You could create a before-and-after Venn diagram for this.)
- Why is Mae in danger? Support your answer.

at this point. Give them an opportunity to suggest other formats for presenting the information. For example, show the class how the same information could be presented in a Venn diagram format.

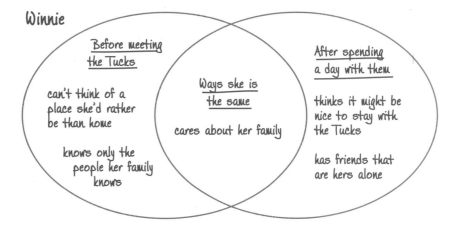

Winnie

Before meeting the Tucks
- can't think of a place she'd rather be than home
- knows only the people her family knows

Ways she is the same
- cares about her family

After spending a day with them
- thinks it might be nice to stay with the Tucks
- has friends that are hers alone

- To further explore the topic of characters changing over time, you could ask students whether they think stories are more or less interesting or realistic when the main characters undergo some change. How does this tie into the Tucks' dilemma—never being able to grow older or die?

- After this initial discussion, students can complete the assigned reading, write in their logs, and meet with their book clubs. Then, during community share, you can revisit the ideas about change that you discussed earlier, and relate them to the changes that are taking place in Winnie. If you wish to focus on the author's craft, ask them to give specific examples from the text of how Natalie Babbitt shows these changes in Winnie. Add these examples to the class character-over-time chart.

Lesson 16

GOAL:
To use a story graph as a tool for understanding a story

ASSIGNED READING:
Chapters 22–23
(pages 111–120)

Literary Elements:
Story Graph

- Readers' understanding of stories as complex as *Tuck Everlasting* can be aided by a story graph. The story graph helps students track changes in the story from beginning to end. It can be used to track characters' emotions, characters' relationships, readers' feelings about characters or about the story, or any other factor that changes over time.

continued on next page

continued from previous page

WRITING PROMPT:

Create a story graph for *Tuck Everlasting.*

- If you have not already done so earlier in the year, introduce students to the concept of a story graph. You might use an overhead projector or the chalkboard to model for students, using a story that is familiar to the whole class. Tell students that a story graph shows change over time. The vertical axis shows how much of something there is, and the horizontal axis shows at what point in time. The thing that changes might be, for example, a character's feelings, or the situation a character is in, or a reader's feelings about the story. A sample story graph for "Little Red Riding Hood" is shown below. However, in modeling with your class, you might choose one of the novels they have already read.

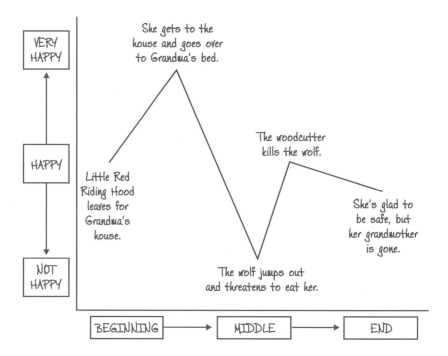

(Adapted from material in *After "The End": Teaching and Learning Creative Revision* by Barry Lane.)

- Suggest that students create a story graph for *Tuck Everlasting* as one of today's log entries. Remind them to be creative—their story graphs can show any kind of change that takes place in the story. For example, a story graph might track changes in more than one person or thing.

Lesson 17

GOAL:
To explore how the book brings up complex issues of right and wrong and personal responsibility

ASSIGNED READING:
Chapter 24
(pages 121–126)

WRITING PROMPT:
Write about responsibility and obeying the law. What are some variations and exceptions? In what ways is Winnie facing this issue?

Response to Literature:
Issues of Right and Wrong

- A theme that emerges throughout *Tuck Everlasting* is the complex relationship between being responsible and following the law. You can begin today's Book Club with a community share discussion about this theme. Questions you might use to promote discussion include: What are some different kinds of responsibilities that each person has? What are laws? How do the people who live in a community benefit when everyone knows and follows the laws? How important is your responsibility to do what you think is right? How important is your responsibility to obey the law? When your own sense of right and wrong goes against what the law says, what should you do? Why?

- Students should complete today's assigned reading, write in their logs, and meet with their book club groups. Then, during a second community share, you can continue your discussion of responsibility and the law. Ask students to share with the class their responses to the writing prompt and any related ideas that came out of their book club discussions.

- This lesson can also provide a curricular connection to social studies. If your students have studied citizenship or civic responsibilities, you can relate Winnie's situation to what they have learned about a citizen's responsibility to obey the law.

Lesson 18

GOAL:
To review the concept of point of view and to discuss how this literary element is used in *Tuck Everlasting*

ASSIGNED READING:
Chapter 25
(pages 127–133)

WRITING PROMPT:
If you were Winnie, what would you have done— drink the water or not drink it? Why?

Literary Elements:
Point of View, Revisited

- In Lesson 12 (page 96) students focused on the points of view of various characters in the story. Point of view can also refer to the author's perspective on a particular topic. In *Tuck Everlasting,* the theme of whether or not everlasting life would be a good thing expresses the author's point of view. In this lesson, you can focus on both the author's and characters' points of view.

- You might begin by asking students to share what they know about point of view. If you taught point of view in Lesson 12, ask them to recall what they discussed and wrote about during that lesson.

continued on next page

continued from previous page

- Start developing a compare-contrast chart for Winnie and the Tucks using ideas and events provided by your students. Then have students read the assigned reading, respond to the writing prompt, and meet with their book clubs. A student sample of a response to the writing prompt is provided below.

- In community share, ask volunteers to share the similarities and differences they noticed between Winnie's home and the Tucks' home. Add details to the compare-contrast chart started earlier in this lesson.

- Add any developments that students have noticed in Winnie's character to the character-over-time chart. Discuss how the details in the character-over-time chart and in the compare-contrast chart overlap.

Student Sample: Compare and Contrast

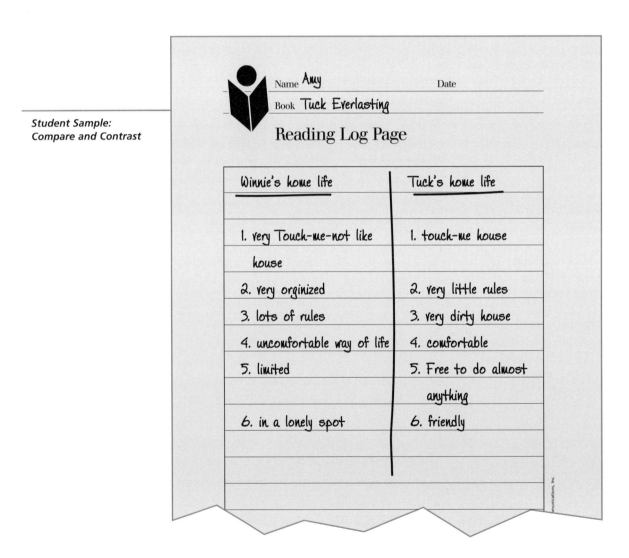

Name Amy   Date

Book Tuck Everlasting

Reading Log Page

Winnie's home life	Tuck's home life
1. very Touch-me-not like house	1. touch-me house
2. very orginized	2. very little rules
3. lots of rules	3. very dirty house
4. uncomfortable way of life	4. comfortable
5. limited	5. Free to do almost anything
6. in a lonely spot	6. friendly

continued from previous page

- Once the idea of point of view is clear, you can ask students to identify through which character's point of view this story is being told, and why Babbitt chose to do this. In discussing Winnie's point of view and how it influences the way the story is told, students might find it useful to talk about how the story would differ if, for example, readers learned of the events from Jesse's point of view.

- After students have completed the day's reading, written in their logs, and met with their book clubs, you can continue your discussion of point of view.

- Ask students to share their responses to the writing prompt. Be sure that students back up their positions for or against drinking the water with reasonable arguments. Also ask them to predict whether they think Winnie will go back to the spring when she is seventeen, and why they think so. Do they feel they know Winnie well enough to predict what her point of view will be seven years from now?

- You might also ask students whether they think the author has a particular point of view about whether it would be good to live forever. What evidence reveals Natalie Babbitt's point of view?

Lesson 19

GOAL:
To note how the author uses a time change in the Epilogue to resolve the questions still lingering in readers' minds

ASSIGNED READING:
Epilogue
(pages 134–139)

WRITING PROMPT:
Free choice

Literary Elements:
Time Change; Story Resolution

- Good readers have an instinctive sense of when a story is finished. It's important to help your students develop this sense by discussing in concrete terms the elements that come together to make a story complete. If you taught Lesson 14 (page 98), you have already laid the foundation for this lesson by discussing the basic story elements.

- You can begin today's Book Club by asking students whether they think the central problem or conflict in *Tuck Everlasting* has been resolved. They may conclude, for example, that the main conflict *is* resolved, because the man in the yellow suit is dead and Mae Tuck has been rescued from prison, so the secret of the spring is safe. Ask them what questions still remain unanswered. Do they expect these questions to be answered when they read the Epilogue? You might want to ask students how they would define an epilogue.

- After students have done the reading, written their responses, and discussed in their book clubs, you can return to the topic of story resolution during community share.

- Ask students whether the Epilogue answered the questions still lingering in their minds. Do they feel that the story is truly resolved now?

- Ask students to name the techniques Natalie Babbitt uses to show what Winnie decided about drinking the spring water. Be sure that your discussion includes mention of the time change between the story and the Epilogue. What clues does the author use to reveal when the events of the Epilogue take place? How does the author use the gravestone to give details about what happened to Winnie?

Lesson 20

GOAL:
To have students write a brief essay to be used for assessment purposes

ASSIGNED READING:
None

WRITING PROMPT:
You've decided to go ahead and drink the water. At what age would you drink the water, and why?

Language Conventions:
Process Writing—Essay

- The writing prompt for this lesson can provide a link between students' reading of *Tuck Everlasting* and process writing. A major theme of the book is whether it would be desirable to live forever, and students have had time to think about the issue and form personal opinions about it. Students now have a good context for writing an essay.

- Before students begin writing their essays, you might remind them of the steps in the writing process (e.g., prewriting, writing, editing, reviewing/proofreading, and publishing/sharing). Also remind them that an essay contains an introduction with a thesis statement, a body with arguments in support of the thesis, and a conclusion. (For a further discussion of essay form, see Lesson 18 for *The Fighting Ground,* on page 143.) Tell them that you will review their completed essays to assess how well they have understood *Tuck Everlasting* and how well they have mastered the process of writing an essay.

- Students should be given a reasonable amount of time to complete their essays, including all of the steps in the writing process. Be sure to tell them your expectations in terms of essay length and content.

Lesson 21

Self-Assessment and Goal Setting

GOAL:
To have students assess their performance during this Book Club and set some goals for the next one

ASSIGNED READING:
None

WRITING PROMPT:
Fill out the self-assessment form, and set some goals for your next Book Club.

- Have students fill out self-assessment forms and set goals for the next Book Club. Some options for completing this assessment are provided in Lesson 12 for *Last Summer with Maizon*, page 80.

- Below is a student example of a self-assessment form and goals.

- NOTE: Teacher evaluation and grading of a Book Club unit is also important. For a fully developed teacher evaluation lesson, please refer to *The Fighting Ground*, Lesson 20, page 144.

Student Sample: Self-Assessment

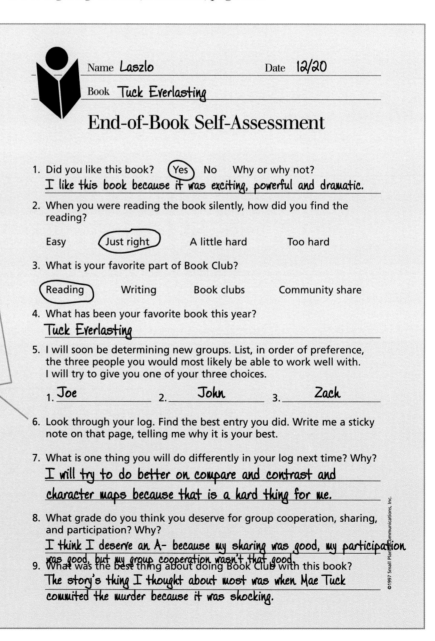

Name **Laszlo**   Date **12/20**

Book **Tuck Everlasting**

End-of-Book Self-Assessment

1. Did you like this book? (Yes) No   Why or why not?
   I like this book because it was exciting, powerful and dramatic.

2. When you were reading the book silently, how did you find the reading?

   Easy   (Just right)   A little hard   Too hard

3. What is your favorite part of Book Club?

   (Reading)   Writing   Book clubs   Community share

4. What has been your favorite book this year?
   Tuck Everlasting

5. I will soon be determining new groups. List, in order of preference, the three people you would most likely be able to work well with. I will try to give you one of your three choices.

   1. *Joe*   2. *John*   3. *Zach*

6. Look through your log. Find the best entry you did. Write me a sticky note on that page, telling me why it is your best.

7. What is one thing you will do differently in your log next time? Why?
   I will try to do better on compare and contrast and character maps because that is a hard thing for me.

8. What grade do you think you deserve for group cooperation, sharing, and participation? Why?
   I think I deserve an A- because my sharing was good, my participation was good, but my group cooperation wasn't that good.

9. What was the best thing about doing Book Club with this book?
   The story's thing I thought about most was when Mae Tuck commited the murder because it was shocking.

My best entry was the Me and the Book where you answered if you had ever ran away because it had the most detail.

©1997 Small Planet Communications, Inc.

Bridge to Terabithia
by Katherine Paterson

Introducing the Book

The following lessons provide support
and teaching techniques for using *Bridge to Terabithia* in Book Club.
This book is particularly well suited to Book Club because of the
number of discussion topics. Among other topics, students can discuss
the meaning of friendship, the need for understanding among people
and families, and how different people deal with the death of a friend.
Because one of the characters does die, this is a book that you will
want to use with fifth or sixth graders. You will need to gauge the
maturity and mood of your classroom to determine when *Bridge to
Terabithia* would best be introduced.

Summary Jess Aarons has been practicing for months over summer
vacation, intending to be the fastest runner in the fifth grade. Just as he's about to realize his dream,
however, the new girl at school beats him in the race. It's an unlikely start to a friendship, but Jess
and Leslie Burke do indeed become friends. Together they don't mind being different. The friendship
between Leslie and Jess really blossoms during the time they spend in Terabithia, an imaginary
kingdom where they are king and queen. Jess is astonished by Leslie's powers of imagination, and
Leslie encourages Jess to develop his artistic talents. The only other person who appreciates Jess's
drawing skills is Miss Edmunds, their beautiful music teacher.

One rainy day during spring vacation, Miss Edmunds offers to take Jess to
Washington, D.C., to visit some art galleries. Feeling slightly guilty over not inviting Leslie to go
along, Jess happily spends the day looking at paintings with his teacher. When he returns home, he
finds his family gathered in their kitchen and they give him the unfathomable news that Leslie has
drowned in the stream near Terabithia. At first Jess feels that he'll never recover from the tragedy,
but then he builds a bridge over the stream and invites his little sister to visit Terabithia. He's finally
ready to share the magic that he and Leslie created together.

Paperback Edition, HarperTrophy, ©1977 by Katherine Paterson. ISBN 0-06-440184-7.

Themes Friendship, death, and family are the main themes explored in *Bridge to Terabithia.* Jess's need for friends who understand why he expresses himself through art and the way that he does not feel a part of his family are both factors in his friendship with Leslie and the devastation and anger he feels when she dies. Although it is a sad story, it is also a story about hope—hope for understanding and hope for a meaningful life.

Special Classroom Library Other books by Katherine Paterson include *The Great Gilly Hopkins* (HarperCollins, 1987), *Park's Quest* (Puffin Books, 1989), and *Jacob Have I Loved* (HarperCollins, 1990). Each book explores the relationships that people have with each other and the kinds of misunderstandings, love, toleration, and anger that are present in every family or close group of people.

Three books that you might also consider using in conjunction with *Bridge to Terabithia* are *Missing May* by Cynthia Rylant (Dell, 1993), *Maniac Magee* by Jerry Spinelli (HarperTrophy, 1990), *Walk Two Moons* by Sharon Creech (HarperCollins, 1994), and *Part of Me Died, Too: Stories of Creative Survival Among Bereaved Children and Teenagers* by Virginia L. Fry (Dutton, 1995). All of these books explore the feelings that people have when they endure losses. They support *Bridge to Terabithia* thematically and could also be part of a multi-book unit. Lesson plans for *Walk Two Moons* and *Maniac Magee* begin on pages 187 and 209, respectively.

Lesson 1

GOAL:
To encourage students to think about and discuss the word *bridge* and its possible significance in the title *Bridge to Terabithia*, and to review response types

ASSIGNED READING:
Chapter 1
(pages 1–8)

WRITING PROMPT:
Free choice

Literary Elements:
Discussing the Book's Title

- Discussing the book title provides students with the opportunity to consider what the book might be about. This is also a good time to introduce themes that students will encounter in the book.

- Preview *Bridge to Terabithia* with students. Examine the cover and cover art. Discuss any other books that students have read by the same author.

- Discuss the word *bridge* with students. Ask them to describe the purpose of bridges and the different types of bridges. What images come to mind as they think about this word? Students should be encouraged to discuss bridges that are actual structures and bridges that are connections or links in a more abstract sense (e.g., "Reading is a bridge to knowledge and understanding").

- Ask students to predict what the word *bridge* might imply in this particular title. What do they think the book will be about? (Later, during community share, you might discuss whether the first chapter provided any clues as to why Katherine Paterson gave the title to this book.)

- If necessary, review the various options for log entries and go over the reading log checklist. (Sample Reading Log Checklists are provided in the Blackline Masters: Think Sheets section following page 261.) Lesson 1 for *The Fighting Ground,* page 126, provides a model lesson if you are introducing checklists for the first time.

- Remind all students to look for interesting words occurring in the story and to record them in their logs. Sample Vocabulary think sheets are available in the Blackline Masters: Think Sheets section.

Lesson 2

GOAL:
To help students notice and understand the techniques an author uses in writing about characters

ASSIGNED READING:
Chapter 2
(pages 9–18)

WRITING PROMPT:
Compare and contrast the two main characters, Jesse and Leslie.

Literary Elements:
Characterization

- Writers develop their characters by using a combination of techniques, such as describing characters directly, showing characters in action, and presenting characters' feelings and thoughts. Begin a discussion with students to highlight these three techniques.

- Within the discussion, bring out the idea that when an author describes characters directly, the reader learns about the character's appearance, dress, background, and personality through the voice of a narrator or another character. When an author shows a character in action, the reader learns about the character through his or her actions, speech, and interactions with others. When an author presents the character's feelings and thoughts, the reader learns about the character by reading about what he or she feels and thinks.

- Students can then look over the chapter of *Bridge to Terabithia* that they have already read as you point out examples of each technique. Highlight what they can learn about the characters, particularly Jesse, from these techniques. You may want to model the author's use of these techniques by creating a character map of Jesse on the chalkboard. A character map created by a Book Club student appears on page 108.

continued on next page

continued from previous page

• During book clubs, community share, or both, have students share their impressions of Jesse and Leslie after reading Chapter 2. How has the author added more detail to their characters?

Student Sample: Character Map

Name Ira   Date October 18

Book Bridge to Terabithia

Reading Log Page

Character Map

Has a crush on music teacher

Has a lot of chores

likes to run

Lonly because he's the only male child.

Jesse

Fights a lot with sisters

Has tough feet

loves to draw and wants to be an artist

Lesson 3

GOAL:
To help students understand how dialect adds a realistic flavor to a book and can provide clues about where the story takes place

ASSIGNED READING:
Chapter 3 (pages 19–28)

WRITING PROMPT:
What do you think the town of Lark Creek is like? Where might it be? Support your answers with details or dialogue from the novel.

Literary Elements:
Use of Dialogue and Dialect

• One way authors can increase the realism in their books is through the characters' use of language. *Bridge to Terabithia* provides numerous opportunities to illustrate how dialect adds to the telling of a story. Tell students that dialects are versions of a language spoken by different groups of people. A dialect can indicate a particular place, time in history, or group of people.

• Explain to students that everyone speaks with a type of dialect, and that variations of the same language can be interesting to notice. A dialect gives language a special, interesting flavor. Highlight these differences as being positive, since they help underscore the many varied and fascinating backgrounds of people in our country.

- Discuss examples of dialect used in Chapter 2. Some examples include *Ellie and Brenda come home,* page 15; *That ain't nothing to cheer about,* page 16; *Ain't 'cha gonna run?,* page 16. Compare these examples with how these same phrases are said in standard English and in your local dialects. Discuss how people tend to use standard English versus local dialects under different circumstances. Ask them to share their own experiences with the use of dialect.

- NOTE: Another good way to approach this topic is to play an audio tape of a folk tale told in dialect, such as one of the Rabbit Ears Folktales. This strategy ensures that the class doesn't disintegrate into poor attempts to mimic the dialect that you're discussing.

- Ask students to watch for other examples of dialect in the chapter that they are about to read. As they read, they should think about what the dialect tells them about the characters and where the story might take place. Does the dialect make the story seem more realistic to them?

Lesson 4

GOAL:
To provide a visual strategy—the word web—for students to use when exploring a new concept or vocabulary word

ASSIGNED READING:
Chapter 4
(pages 29–47)

WRITING PROMPT:
Draw or describe Terabithia. Use specific details provided by the author in the text.

Comprehension:
Exploring the Concept of Kingdoms

- Webs are a way to assist students in visualizing a concept, topic, theme, or the meaning of a word. A web can be very simple and quick, or it can be complex and completed over a period of time. Stress to students that webbing is a technique that they can use in their book club groups or in their reading logs.

- Begin a concept web on chart paper or on the chalkboard with the word *kingdom* in the middle. Have students brainstorm and share ideas that they have about kingdoms, such as people who live in a kingdom, where the different people live, and the activities that take place in a kingdom. Ideas that aren't agreed on by everyone can still be included and identified by either a different color marker, underlining, or a question mark. A sample is provided on page 110.

- Tell students that they can make webs using some of the interesting vocabulary they identify in the stories they read, and that they can include these webs in their response choices.

continued on next page

Lesson 5

GOAL:
To encourage students to notice and discuss the author's unique chapter titles

ASSIGNED READING:
Chapter 5
(pages 48–56)

WRITING PROMPT:
Write about some aspect of the author's craft exhibited in *Bridge to Terabithia*. (You may choose to focus on the author's choice of chapter titles, or you may focus on another example of the author's craft in the story.)

- Chapter titles are interesting tools that authors can use to tease their readers, create suspense, or sometimes just mark shifts and transitions. *Bridge to Terabithia* provides an opportunity to highlight the kinds of information titles can convey.

- Discuss with students the use of chapter titles and the purposes chapter titles can serve. How are chapter titles in a novel different from those in a nonfiction text?

- Guide students to notice that the chapter titles in *Bridge to Terabithia* are now changing to reflect the kingdom of Terabithia. Have students look at the Contents and discuss how they think the other titles relate to Terabithia. Some students may notice that there are some titles that are not related to Terabithia, and they can be asked to speculate what this means.

- Brainstorm why chapter titles that reflect the fantasy world of Terabithia are different from some of the other titles. Do students think it will be more difficult to predict what is going to happen in each of these chapters? Why, or why not?

- Ask students to explain why the author might have chosen to give some of the chapters titles that reflect fantasy events of the kingdom.

Lesson 6

Response to Literature:
Making Connections to Your Life

GOAL:
To encourage students to connect people and events from the story to their own lives to gain a clearer understanding of the story

ASSIGNED READING:
Chapter 6
(pages 57–64)

- Many of the events in realistic fiction are ones that readers can relate to. Realistic fiction can be like a mirror reflecting readers' own lives, or it can be a window through which to view lives that are different from their own.

- Talk about any characters, events, or settings in the book that have reminded students of people, events, and places in their own lives.

continued on next page

continued from previous page

continued from previous page

WRITING PROMPT:
Write about a special time you once spent with your family. It might be a holiday such as Christmas, or it might be some other event.

- Ask students to list in their logs any personal connections they have made to the book so far. Invite students to share their responses now (during community share) or later, in their book club discussions.

- Discuss how the personal connections that students have shared might help them to have a better understanding of the story.

Lesson 7

GOAL:
To encourage students to look for interesting vocabulary by creating a "word wall" for the story

ASSIGNED READING:
Chapter 7
(pages 65–77)

WRITING PROMPT:
- Add to the drawing or description of Terabithia that you started in Lesson 4.
- Write about the words you explored in Chapter 7.

Comprehension:
Vocabulary/Word Wall

- NOTE: A "word wall" is literally a wall of words built throughout a unit of study, in this case a Book Club unit. For further information about word walls, refer to Lesson 9 for *Last Summer with Maizon,* page 73.

- Prepare a large sheet of chart paper on a wall or bulletin board in your room, labeled with the title of the story and the author's name.

- Ask students to share some of the most interesting vocabulary words from the story that they've identified in their logs. Add these to the word wall. (If students are using a Vocabulary think sheet, you may want to model the format of date/word/page/meaning used on the sheet.) Talk about the words and determine their meanings, using either context clues, a person who knows, or a dictionary. Include concise definitions on the chart.

- Tell students that you will be adding interesting words to the word wall periodically throughout the story. Invite them to add words, too.

Teaching Tip

Alternative ways to organize vocabulary lessons include: define each word orally and write only the word, not the definition, on the word wall; give only the word and then have the class brainstorm a definition for the word wall; add words to the word wall in categories—have students make the connections between the words that they are finding interesting in the book, guiding them to form appropriate categories as needed.

Lesson 8

GOAL:
To use a small part of *Bridge to Terabithia* to help students understand the ways in which Jess's life is similar to and different from their own lives

ASSIGNED READING:
Chapter 8
(pages 78–85)

WRITING PROMPT:
Free choice. You might like to tie your writing in with the class discussion.

Comprehension:
Making Connections to Characters

Teaching Tip

This lesson was designed to help students understand that even though a person's life may be very different from one's own, the person can have similar feelings about people and situations. To accomplish this goal, the Book Club teacher chose to have students investigate an aspect of Jess's life that was unfamiliar to them—living on a farm and the chore of milking a cow. The lesson that follows focuses on farm life. However, you may want to choose another example from the book. For example, you may want to talk about what school is like in this community or how families seem similar or different.

- Tell students that comparing and contrasting Jess's life on the farm with their own lives can help them understand that even though Jess's life may be very different from their own, he has similar feelings.

- Start a discussion about life on a farm. Ask students to discuss one of Jess's chores—for example, milking a cow. What do students think is involved? How might it feel? How might it sound?

- Ask the class to work together to construct a flow chart of the process of milking a cow. Their job is to describe the process to someone who has no idea where to begin.

- Have the class begin by brainstorming information that they already have about milking a cow. Ask them to share information from *Bridge to Terabithia,* their personal experiences, and other sources. In particular, ask them to make intertextual connections to other books that they have read that contain information about the process. Write all the gathered information on the chalkboard or on chart paper.

- Next, have students help you organize the information in a flow chart. Make sure that students notice any gaps in the process. (If necessary, ask volunteers to research information to fill the gaps. Information can be added quickly at the start of the next class meeting.) A sample flow chart is provided on page 115.

continued on next page

continued from previous page

- Examine the flow chart and discuss how Jess's chore is similar to or different from chores that students complete at home. Talk about how Jess feels about doing this chore. Does he always want to do it or does he need to be reminded? How do students feel about doing their chores?

- In community share, revisit the idea that even though Jess's life may be very different, he has some ideas and feelings in common with the students in your class. Later in the story this idea will have a powerful impact, as students see that although Jess's life is different from theirs in many ways, he has similar feelings about death.

Lesson 9

GOAL:
To help students become fluent readers and recognize fluency in other readers

ASSIGNED READING:
Chapter 9
(pages 86–93)

WRITING PROMPT:
Think about the way Jesse and Leslie talk when they are in Terabithia. Why do they talk this way? How did the language sound as you read it with a partner?

Language Conventions:
Fluency Review

- Refer to Lesson 9 for *The Fighting Ground*, on page 135 of this guide, for a complete model of a fluency assessment lesson.

- Have students form pairs. Each student in each pair should read a section from *Bridge to Terabithia* (a section that takes place in Terabithia) to their partner. They should select a section that they have already read at least once, and they should be given time to practice their read-aloud independently, before they read to their partners.

- You can record assessment information from this activity on a checklist. A model Fluency Checklist is provided on page 116. A blackline master for this checklist is provided in the Blackline Masters: Assessment section following page 281.

Sample Flow Chart Showing the Process of Milking a Cow

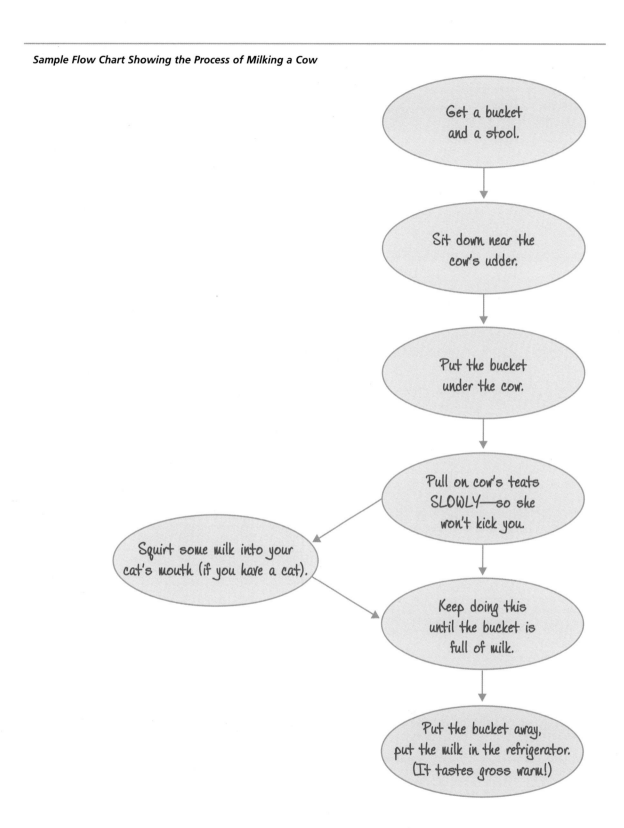

Sample Fluency Checklist

Date **October 4**

Book **Bridge to Terabithia**

Fluency Checklist

Student's Name	Uses Expression	Observes Punctuation	Smooth	Appropriate Speed/Volume	Uses Decoding Skills	Miscues	Self-corrects
Carmen Chin	✔	✔		✔	✔		✔✔
Donna Depietro		✔	✔		✔	✔	✔
William Haynes		✔	✔	✔	✔		
Mary Houlihan	✔				✔	✔✔✔	✔
Maria Perez	✔	✔	✔	✔	✔		
Fernando Ruiz		✔	✔	✔	✔	✔	✔✔
Anna Sorenson		✔		✔	✔	✔	✔
Rufus Thomas	✔	✔			✔	✔✔✔	✔
Kevin Washington	✔	✔	✔	✔	✔		✔
Ping Yu		✔	✔	✔	✔		

©1997 Small Planet Communications, Inc.

Teacher Comment:

"When I use this checklist, I write the students' names in once and then copy the sheet several times. Then I just date it at the top, write the name of the book, and put a check in each category that the child demonstrates. Under 'Miscues' I put a check for each one, and the same thing for 'Self-corrects.' I try to listen to each child read for approximately the same amount of time, so that numbers of miscues are for the same amount of time. This provides me with the information I need to offer additional instruction to some children and to report to parents. Another way you could do it is to have children all read the same page into a tape recorder, and then listen to it at a later time. Then they can share that with parents at conference time. I listen to students read aloud only once per book—and that seems to be enough for me."

Lesson 10

GOAL:
To help students learn various ways of representing their thoughts as they read

ASSIGNED READING:
Chapter 10
(pages 94–102)

WRITING PROMPT:
- What is a perfect day for you? Describe it in detail. What makes it so perfect?
- What do you think about the book so far?

Response to Literature:
Ways of Representing Thoughts on Reading

- Suggest to students that they keep track of their thoughts as they read this novel or any novel. This will help them to remember important or interesting details in the story, and it will help them keep track of their own thoughts and opinions about issues and events in the novel. They can use their notes for themselves or during book club and community share discussions.

- For students who are fairly new to Book Club, you will want to discuss the various ways of representing their thoughts. For example, they can:

  – Write a paragraph about something in the novel.

  – Create illustrations based on scenes or characters in the novel.

  – Generate charts, tables, or diagrams for keeping track of places and events in the novel.

  – Generate lists of important or interesting details as they read.

  – Draw a picture that expresses an emotion that the character(s) are feeling. Write a caption to explain the picture.

- Students who are more familiar with the ways of representing their thoughts might benefit from a brainstorming session in which they share ideas and create new ways of organizing their ideas about books. You may also want to talk about more formal methods of note taking that students might find useful when reading nonfiction texts.

- Ask students to try some of these activities as they read the assigned reading. Expect students experienced with Book Club to focus on using a variety of response types.

- NOTE: Although Leslie's death is revealed at the end of Chapter 10, you may want to wait to discuss the topic until the next Book Club session. The class discussion about this topic deserves to be given adequate time to develop.

continued from previous page

- Tell students that you selected the word *kingdom* for a special reason today. They can use the knowledge that they gathered during the lesson as they read the next chapter.

- Return to the web during community share and add information that students learned while reading Chapter 4.

Sample Concept Web for "Kingdom"

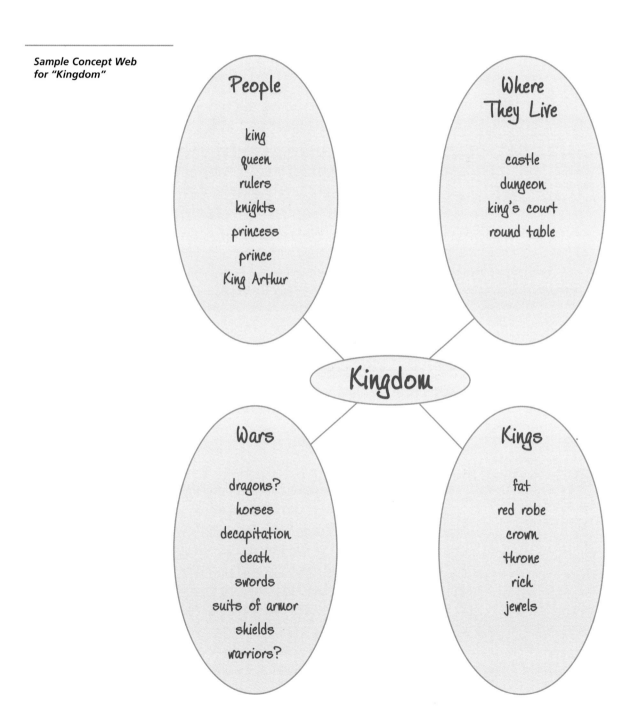

People

king
queen
rulers
knights
princess
prince
King Arthur

Where They Live

castle
dungeon
king's court
round table

Kingdom

Wars

dragons?
horses
decapitation
death
swords
suits of armor
shields
warriors?

Kings

fat
red robe
crown
throne
rich
jewels

topic through the story. In *Bridge to Terabithia*, the author expresses her point of view about the importance of allowing people to be who they are by showing how hard Jesse tries and succeeds in expressing himself artistically.

- Tell students that in some stories the narrator's point of view is limited, meaning that the narrator can reveal only the private thoughts and feelings of herself or himself or of a single character. In other stories the narrator's point of view is omniscient, meaning that he or she can reveal the private thoughts and feelings of any character. Use examples from books the class has read to illustrate the concept of limited and omniscient point of view. For example, *Tuck Everlasting* is a book in which the narrator sometimes has an omniscient point of view, while *A Wrinkle in Time* is told from Meg's point of view.

- Ask students to discuss the point of view used up to this point in *Bridge to Terabithia*. In what way does this point of view affect the way students think about the story?

- Discuss with students the ways in which *Bridge to Terabithia* would be different if it were being told from the point of view of a different character, such as one of the parents, one of Jess's sisters, or a teacher. What information would the reader no longer have? What additional information would the reader gain?

- After students have written in their logs and participated in book clubs, they may want to share additional insights into the role of point of view in *Bridge to Terabithia* and in other books they have read.

Lesson 13

GOAL:
To help students understand the different ways in which people handle difficult or emotional issues

ASSIGNED READING:
Chapter 13
(pages 118–128)

Response to Literature:
Talking About Difficult Emotional Issues

- One of the important reasons that people read is to learn how other people might feel about things. Knowing how a character feels can help a reader think about how he or she might feel in a similar situation. Books can make a person feel happy, sad, thoughtful, angry, and other ways. Give examples from your own reading experiences and invite students to talk about books they have read. Transition the conversation to emotions students have felt while reading *Bridge to Terabithia*.

continued on next page

continued from previous page

WRITING PROMPT:
Free choice. You might want to focus on the feelings of certain characters in the novel or on your own feelings about the events of the novel so far.

- Explain to students that everyone handles sensitive, difficult, or emotional issues in his or her own way. Some people like to share their feelings, while others do not like to share their feelings at all. Remind students that they should share difficult or emotional subjects in their groups only if they feel comfortable doing so. A share sheet done by one Book Club student who wanted to share a personal experience with death is shown below.

- Tell students that difficult and emotional times will be a part of all our lives. Some people deal with these times by sharing their feelings with friends who will listen to and support them. Today students might need to help classmates by being good listeners.

- Remind students that some people cry when they talk about emotional topics. Tears help these people to deal with and express their feelings. If someone in a group cries, students should offer the person a tissue and support, but try to focus on what the person is saying, not just on the fact that he or she is crying.

- NOTE: It is important to prepare yourself and your students for the possibility that some students might cry when they are discussing emotional issues. However, after teaching Book Club for several years, we have observed only one student actually crying in the classroom setting.

Student Sample: Feelings Response

Teacher Comment:

"This student was willing to share a personal experience with death that she linked to her Book Club reading. Other students will not choose to do so, and you should make it clear to the class that either response is OK."

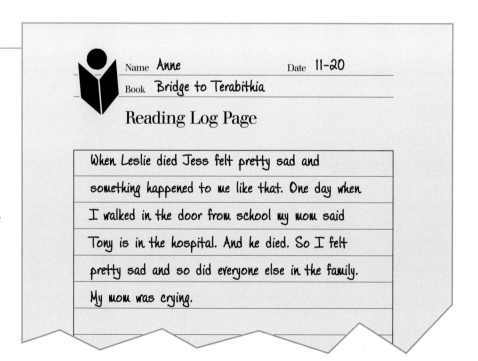

Name Anne   Date 11-20

Book Bridge to Terabithia

Reading Log Page

| When Leslie died Jess felt pretty sad and |
| something happened to me like that. One day when |
| I walked in the door from school my mom said |
| Tony is in the hospital. And he died. So I felt |
| pretty sad and so did everyone else in the family. |
| My mom was crying. |

Lesson 14

GOAL:
To encourage students to think about the story as a whole as they respond to a writing prompt, and to discuss any remaining issues or questions about the story

ASSIGNED READING:
None

WRITING PROMPT:
See lesson at right for writing prompts.

Response to Literature:
Closure

- Display the following writing prompts—or others that you think will allow students to synthesize their thoughts and feelings about the book as a whole—and ask each student to choose one and respond to it.

  1. What did Leslie's friendship mean to Jess, and what does Leslie's death then mean to him? What has he lost?

  2. How has this experience changed Jess's life? Why?

  3. Family seems to be a strong theme in this book. Explore Katherine Paterson's uses of family in the book. Is there a lesson there?

- Give students a large portion of the period to write their responses. Responses should then be discussed in students' book clubs.

- In community share, discuss the ending of the story. How does the ending make students feel about Jess and the people around him? Are they glad that Jess is sharing Terabithia with May Belle? Why, or why not?

- Ask students to discuss the story as a whole. Allow students to bring up any questions or issues they might have. What did they enjoy most about the book? What did they enjoy least? How did they feel at the story's end?

Lesson 15

GOAL:
To give students the opportunity to discuss their responses to yesterday's writing prompt with a different group of classmates

ASSIGNED READING:
Students should read the writing they did in their logs yesterday.

Response to Literature:
Flexible Discussion Groups

- Allow each student to spend at least fifteen or twenty minutes with his or her written response to yesterday's writing prompts. Students should use this time to reread, revise, change, and add to their work based on the discussions that occurred in students' book clubs.

- Tell students that they will be sharing their revised writing with a different group of classmates today. Form groups of four or five based on the writing prompts people chose the day before (e.g., all #1s together, all #2s together, etc.). If only two or three people responded to a particular prompt, it is fine to have them form one group.

continued on next page

continued from previous page

WRITING PROMPT:
You may revise your own writing from yesterday as you reread it. Then share this writing with the new groups you will form today.

- Give these new groups extra time for in-depth discussion. We recommend this for the following reasons:

  – The prompts and their responses often have special meaning to the students. As a result, the students' writing tends to be longer than usual.

  – Because they all answered the same question, students in each group will be interested in hearing how others thought and will probably want to spend time participating with each other around these ideas.

  – The students need to have closure on the story and to have the opportunity to discuss any topics that are still of interest to them.

Lesson 16*

GOAL:
To give students one last forum in which they may discuss the story and related issues

ASSIGNED READING:
None

WRITING PROMPT:
None

Whole-Group Discussion

* NOTE: The following is not actually a "lesson," but an opportunity to complete discussions that were begun in previous lessons. While giving this time to the class proved useful to the Book Club teacher who developed this set of lessons, you should use your own best judgment.

- Base today's lesson on previous whole-class discussion/community share times.

- In the discussion, allow students to discuss any lingering issues about the book.

- Some students might want to share reading logs from previous days. Death might still be on the minds of some students. You can have a discussion in which you address the idea that death is a sad part of life, but a part of life that people must deal with. Talk about how a person moves on when a part of his or her life is gone.

- Above all, allow students to say whatever they need to say about death and the book in general in this last group discussion.

Lesson 17

Response to Literature:
Synthesis

GOAL:
To have kids use the essay form to express ideas about the book that are important to them

ASSIGNED READING:
A favorite chapter or section of the book

WRITING PROMPT:
In a short essay, describe your favorite section or chapter of the book. You may make connections to your own life when it seems appropriate.

- At the end of this book, students have had many opportunities to consider various themes and issues that arose over the course of their reading and discussions. Themes that may have emerged are the importance and meaning of friendship; the unexpectedness and finality of death; the relationships that we can count on within our families, and so forth. Ask students to think individually about a big idea or theme that they found interesting. Ask them to think about their favorite story parts and how these parts can connect to the themes.

- Allow students time to browse through the book and collect their thoughts. Then have students use an essay format to write about the part of the book or the theme that they found most interesting and why.

- Tell or remind students that an essay is a writing format that allows a writer to tell why he or she thinks something. Students' essays should be about one-half to three-quarters of a page long. At the beginning, the essay should state the student's position, or main idea, about a theme or subject in *Bridge to Terabithia.* Then arguments or examples from the book should be given to prove, or discuss, the idea. Encourage students to stay focused on the main idea that they have chosen and to select their examples or arguments from the book carefully.

- You might need to give students a day for selecting their topic and writing their paper, and another day to do book clubs. You might also choose not to do book club groups with this particular lesson, but rather use the writing as another assessment tool.

Teaching Tip

Students often focus on subjects such as friendship, death, and family. Encourage them to think about the ways in which this story might affect their views of these topics. Did the story change them in any way? Do they think it will help them to prepare for life in any way? Will it cause them to think about their friends and family differently?

Lesson 18

GOAL:
For students to assess their own performance during the *Bridge to Terabithia* unit

ASSIGNED READING:
None

WRITING PROMPT:
Fill out the self-assessment forms.

Student Self-Assessment

- See Lesson 12 of *Last Summer with Maizon,* page 80, for a fully developed self-assessment lesson.

- Distribute copies of the End-of-Book Self-Assessment sheet, or a similar sheet of your own design. (A blackline master is available in the Blackline Masters: Assessment section following page 281.) Tell students what your expectations are regarding their completion of the sheet, and give them time to write thoughtful answers.

Lesson 19

GOAL:
To inform students about the grades they've received for *Bridge to Terabithia,* and to give them a chance to respond

ASSIGNED READING:
None

WRITING PROMPT:
Read over your grades and the comments I've written. Then fill out a Reaction and Goal-Setting sheet.

Teacher Evaluation

- See Lesson 13 of *Last Summer with Maizon,* page 80, for a fully developed teacher evaluation lesson.

- Distribute copies of your grades and any other comments. You can use the Book Club Evaluation forms in the Blackline Masters: Assessment section. Then allow students time to read your evaluation and to fill out a Reaction and Goal-Setting sheet, also available in the Blackline Masters: Assessment section. You can respond to students' comments as you're reading the Reaction forms later on. An example of a student-teacher dialogue on a self-assessment sheet is provided on page 34.

Lesson Plan

The Fighting Ground
by Avi

Introducing the Book

The Fighting Ground is a book that can speak to a large audience. Students can read the book from the perspective of someone living at the time of the Revolutionary War, from the perspective of a child who doesn't want to be controlled by a parent's decisions, or from the perspective of someone caught in events beyond his or her control. The possibilities for discussion are significant, and the book provides an opportunity for the class to explore history and the consequences of actions. Students of many different ability levels will find access points to this book.

Summary Thirteen-year-old Jonathan wants to fight against the British in the Revolutionary War, but his father, who fought in battle himself, will not allow his young son to join the army. Jonathan wants so much to carry a gun and be a soldier that one day when the tavern bell calls soldiers to arms, Jonathan rushes—without telling his father—to join. He proudly marches with his fellow soldiers into battle, where they encounter British allies, the German Hessians. Jonathan sees a family friend killed in the fight. He is then taken prisoner by the Hessians. While a prisoner, he helps a little boy whose parents were killed by American soldiers because they were Tory spies. Jonathan, who wanted to help defeat the enemies, was not truly prepared for the violence of war or the realization that his enemies are human too. In the end, Jonathan destroys the borrowed gun that he had been so proud to carry into battle. *The Fighting Ground* takes place over a twenty-four-hour period, and in this time Jonathan learns a valuable lesson about people and the harsh realities of war. He also learns about being a man and growing up.

Themes Themes that are introduced in *The Fighting Ground* include courage, cowardice, fear, and growing up. Jonathan learns through experience, rather than listening to his father, how terrible war is for everyone involved. He must learn the real meaning of war and come to terms with how his reactions range from courage to fear to cowardice in various battle

Paperback Edition, HarperTrophy, © 1984 by Avi. ISBN 0-06-440185-5.

Lesson 11

GOAL:
To encourage students to have a discussion about death and about how it has touched their lives

ASSIGNED READING:
Chapter 11
(pages 103–110)

WRITING PROMPT:
Why do authors choose to write about death? What details add to the drama of this story?

Response to Literature:
Discussion of Death

- Invite students to discuss the end of Chapter 10, when they learned of Leslie's death. What are some initial feelings that they had about this sad turn of events?

- Hold a community share in which you invite students to discuss their own experiences with death. Students might want to discuss the death of a family member, friend, neighbor, or pet. Have they ever been to a funeral? What was the funeral like? Remind students that they do not have to share—they should share only if they feel comfortable doing so. Students might be encouraged to share if they are able to hear you, the teacher, discuss a personal experience. With a topic this difficult, we have found that it is a good idea to be prepared to discuss the same issues that you are asking your students to discuss.

- If students have not had first-hand experiences with death, you might ask them to think of television shows, books, or movies in which they've encountered the subject of death.

- By the time students get into their book club groups, they should feel more comfortable discussing the topic of death than they did before the lesson began.

Lesson 12

GOAL:
To focus students on the story's point of view, and to help them understand the effect point of view has on the way a story is told

ASSIGNED READING:
Chapter 12
(pages 111–117)

WRITING PROMPT:
Explore the point of view of another character in the story (other than Jesse).

Literary Elements:
Point of View

- The literary element *point of view* is one that affects how a story is perceived by the reader. Point of view is literally the set of eyes through which the author tells the story. Stories can be written in the first person or third person. In a story written in the first person, the narrator uses words such as *I* and *we* and may participate in or directly observe the action of the story. In a story written in the third person, the narrator uses words such as *he, she, it,* and *they* and is usually outside the action of the story.

- An author not only chooses to tell the story from the first person or third person but may also express a personal point of view about a certain situations. Most of all he learns that war is not a glorious fight where one side is always right, but more a collection of people who are both good and bad and have both good and bad motivations for their involvement.

Special Classroom Library Other excellent books that are connected both topically and thematically to *The Fighting Ground* and that you may want to include in your classroom library are listed below.

Fiction Titles	Author	Publisher, Date
My Brother Sam Is Dead	James Collier and Christopher Collier	Scholastic, 1985
The Secret of the Seven Willows	Thomas McKean	Simon and Schuster, 1991
Sarah Bishop	Scott O'Dell	Scholastic, 1991
George Washington's Socks	Elvira Woodruff	Scholastic, 1993
Amos Fortune, Free Man	Elizabeth Yates	Puffin Books, 1989
Nonfiction Title		
The War for Independence: The Story of the American Revolution	Albert Marrin	Atheneum, 1988

Lesson 1

Response to Literature: Reading Logs and Checklists

GOAL:
To review the format of reading log entries and the use of reading log checklists

ASSIGNED READING:
9:58 A.M.–11:00 A.M.
(pages 3–15)

- NOTE: The fifth-grade teacher who developed this lesson plan had her students complete an inquiry unit on the Revolutionary War before beginning *The Fighting Ground* in Book Club. The first writing prompt for this lesson, as well as some of the writing prompts for subsequent lessons, presuppose this background knowledge. You might choose to integrate this lesson plan with your social studies curriculum or have students conduct an inquiry unit before they start *The Fighting Ground*. (For more information on inquiry units, see pages 247–250.) Background information about the roles of Hessian soldiers, Tories, and the French in the Revolutionary War is provided in Lesson 12 (page 137). You may decide to share this information with your students earlier in the unit.

WRITING PROMPT:

Do both of the following.

- Connect the ideas we've learned about the Revolutionary War to this story. Make several predictions about the story based on your knowledge of the war.

- Free choice—you might want to try a new response type.

- Remind students that there are many different ways that readers respond to the texts that they read, and that one of the class's goals for the year is to learn about as many different ways to respond as possible.

- Another goal is to learn to think about new ways of responding. Ask students to think about the different ways of responding that they have learned or that they have developed. If any students have invented new types of log entries, ask them to share these with the class. (You may want to add the names and descriptions of these new response types to a chart or bulletin board in the classroom.)

- Distribute copies of a reading log checklist that includes all the types of reading log responses covered in the previous discussion. Students may write in the response types that they and their classmates have created. (A blank Reading Log Checklist form is provided in the Blackline Masters: Think Sheets section following page 261.)

- Remind students that the checklist can help them remember the kinds of responses they've used before. They can monitor themselves to see if they are using the same type of response repeatedly. Let students know that there are many ways to respond to the same section of reading, and that the checklist can be a useful place to keep track of what response types they have attempted.

- After students have completed the assigned reading and responded to the writing prompts, ask them to share their predictions with their groups. Then have volunteers share their predictions during community share.

Lesson 2

GOAL:
To think about the book's style and the author's purpose for organizing the book in time units

ASSIGNED READING:
11:30 A.M.–1:05 P.M. (pages 16–28)

Literary Elements:
Author's Purpose

- Discuss how authors often have a purpose or a reason for writing. Remind students that the way an author writes often gives the reader a clue, or clues, as to why the author wanted to write.

- As a class, observe how *The Fighting Ground* is organized. Discuss why Avi might have decided to have the story take place over a twenty-four-hour period, with time markings rather than chapter titles.

continued on next page

continued from previous page

WRITING PROMPT:
- Have you ever done something against your parents' wishes? In what way was your experience similar to or different from Jonathan's experience in this section?
- Write about the author's purpose(s) in writing this book.

- Ask students what the author's purpose might be in leading the reader through the story minute-by-minute. If they need some help getting started, guide them with the following questions.

  – Why is it interesting to go through a day with one character who is experiencing war for the first time?

  – How is a story like this different from a history book?

- Ask students to note how the time markings help their understanding of the assigned reading. Have them share their impressions in their book clubs and during community share.

- Students should also share their responses to the writing prompts in book clubs and community share. An example of a student's log entry about the author's purpose is shown below.

Student Sample: Author's Purpose

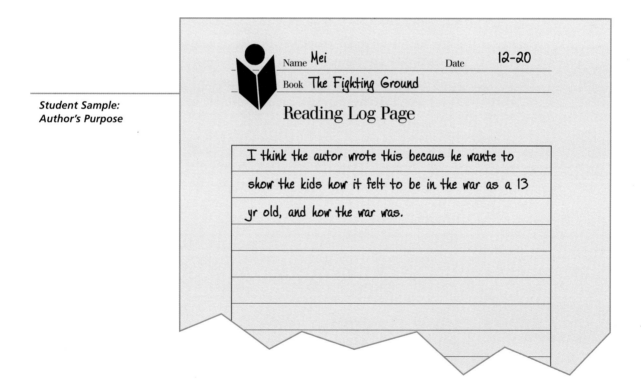

Name **Mei**   Date **12-20**

Book **The Fighting Ground**

Reading Log Page

I think the autor wrote this becaus he wante to show the kids how it felt to be in the war as a 13 yr old, and how the war was.

GOAL:
To help students notice and record interesting, unusual, or confusing words and phrases as they read

ASSIGNED READING:
1:30 P.M.–2:41 P.M.
(pages 28–41)

WRITING PROMPT:
• What do you think "the fighting ground" is in this story? Explain your response.
• Predict what the battle will be like. Remember to consider the factual information we've learned about this war.

Comprehension:
Vocabulary—Wonderful Words

• Remind students that one way to respond to literature in their reading logs is to keep a list of a selection's "wonderful words"—words that they find interesting, fun, unusual, or confusing.

• Discuss with students the reasons why this response choice might be helpful to them. For example, "wonderful words" might be terms for which students need to find definitions or words that students want to try in their own writing. "Wonderful words" can also remind a student about an important idea or a feeling expressed by a character. Thinking about these kinds of words can help everyone in a book club understand the characters and a story more fully.

• Discuss ways to gather "wonderful words"—recording words while reading, or looking back over the selection to find unusual or confusing words. Model some "wonderful words" that you have identified in today's reading. For example, the word *merci* (in the 1:30 P.M. time slot) is likely to be a new one for most of the class, and it's also a French word. This word could be discussed in book clubs, using context to figure out what it means, or students could check the dictionary. (Be sure that students know about the glossary of German terms at the back of the novel.) Another "wonderful word" is the phrase *nervous quiet* in the 2:10 P.M. time slot. This phrase tells how the soldiers are feeling and conveys how very difficult it must have been to stand there waiting for the battle to start and thinking about what might happen.

• Have students look for your "wonderful words" as they read, as well as noting others to share and put on the word wall during community share. (See page 73 for more about word walls.)

> **Teaching Tip**
>
> We've found it helpful to monitor new vocabulary as a whole-class activity during the first Book Club unit of the year. After students have become familiar with the purpose of the word wall, they can use a Vocabulary think sheet to record words individually as they read. The next lesson assumes that students are ready to be introduced to the Vocabulary think sheet.

Lesson 4

GOAL:
To introduce students to the use of a Vocabulary think sheet for keeping track of new words they encounter in their reading

ASSIGNED READING:
2:43 P.M.–3:05 P.M.
(pages 42–53)

WRITING PROMPT:
- Write about Jonathan's feelings during the battle. How would you feel in this situation?
- Write about interesting words in *The Fighting Ground*.

Comprehension:
Vocabulary

- Distribute copies of a Vocabulary think sheet like the one provided in the Blackline Masters: Think Sheets section following page 261. Tell students that they can use the Vocabulary think sheet to record "wonderful words" or words that they find interesting or confusing. When they finish reading, they can talk about their words in book clubs and community share, or they can check their dictionaries for the definitions of words they did not understand. Another option is for them to save their words for book club and then develop definitions based on their groups' discussion of the words.

- Prompt students to think about the kinds of words that they might be interested in discussing. Ask them to think about how their prior knowledge about the war affects how they read the book and what parts of the book they find engaging. Students might also find it interesting to notice which words from their inquiry into the Revolutionary War they are seeing in *The Fighting Ground*.

- During community share, students can bring to the attention of the whole class any words that they found especially interesting. These words can then be added to the word wall.

- NOTE: You may want to limit the number of words that students add to their lists each day. Two to three words per day is enough. One Book Club teacher found that without limits students sometimes fill up their sheet on the first day—but neglect to finish their reading.

Lesson 5

GOAL:
To provide a visual strategy for students to use when developing a concept

ASSIGNED READING:
3:16 P.M.–4:01 P.M.
(pages 54–63)

Comprehension:
Word Web Around the Concept of Pain

- Tell students that pain is an important concept in today's reading. Tell them that this exercise will help them better understand and identify with Jonathan's experience in this section of the book.

- If necessary, use the chalkboard to model for students how to start a word web. Have students give examples of words to place on the web and discuss how they relate to the concept of pain.

WRITING PROMPT:

Add words and phrases from your reading to your word web for "pain."

- Ask students to work in small groups to create a web of words and phrases that they associate with both emotional and physical pain. Students may use general terms often associated with pain, or they may include words that refer to their own experiences, the experiences of friends and family, or incidents described in books, movies, or newspapers.

- As a class, share the word webs, stories, and examples of pain. You may want to place expressive words on the word wall, or create a class word web.

Lesson 6

GOAL:
To check students' comprehension of story content and to teach students to summarize a story effectively

ASSIGNED READING:
4:10 P.M.–5:30 P.M.
(pages 64–75)

WRITING PROMPT:
Free choice

Comprehension:
Summarizing and Reviewing Story Content

- The process of summarizing a story—restating the major events in one's own words—can help a reader understand the story better. As the reader creates the summary, he or she may see the events of the story in a new light, or discover that he or she does not, in fact, really know what is happening in the story. Summaries are also useful for retelling a story to another person, and they can provide practice in clear, concise writing.

- Have students complete the day's reading assignment and respond to the writing prompt **before** you begin the lesson. Before students hold their book club discussions, talk with the whole class about why summaries and summarizing are valuable.

- Have students work in groups to list four or five important events or ideas from the section that they've just read. Possible events and ideas include: the Hessians appear to be lost or uncertain about what to do; Jonathan wonders about how to communicate with the Hessians; Jonathan worries that he hasn't been thinking about escape and about how he has failed all the people who are important to him; one of the soldiers sees something in the woods and Jonathan is sure that it was the Corporal; the Hessians find a house.

- As a class, review the events and ideas students listed. Help students distinguish between big events and smaller details. How do these big events help students understand what it might have been like to be an

continued on next page

continued from previous page

inexperienced soldier in the Revolutionary War? Do the smaller details help the students understand more?

- Working with the five most important events discussed by the class, model the writing of a summary using the overhead projector and thinking aloud as you write. As you model writing the summary, discuss also the details that you are **not** including and the reasons why you are not including them.

- Students can discuss their free-choice writing in their book clubs.

Lesson 7

GOAL:

To focus students' attention on the story's point of view, and to help them under stand the effect point of view has on the way a story is told

ASSIGNED READING:

5:40 P.M.–6:35 P.M.
(pages 76–88)

WRITING PROMPT:

Pick any character in the story (other than Jonathan) and retell the story so far from his or her point of view.

Literary Elements: Point of View

- Explain to students the different points of view in which stories are typically written—*first person* and *third person.* Tell students that in a story written in the first person, the narrator uses words such as *I* and *we* and may participate in or directly observe the action of the story. In a story written in the third person, the narrator uses words such as *he, she, it,* and *they* and is usually on the outside of the story's action.

- Tell students that in some stories the narrator's point of view is limited, meaning that the narrator can reveal only the private thoughts and feelings of herself or himself or of a single character. In other stories the narrator's point of view is omniscient, meaning that he or she can reveal the private thoughts and feelings of any character.

- Ask students to describe the point of view of *The Fighting Ground* or of another book that they have read. Is it first person? third person? Is the narrator's point of view limited or omniscient? Ask them to identify the clues that help them answer these questions.

- Discuss with students the ways in which *The Fighting Ground* or another book that they know would be different if it were told from the point of view of a different character. What information would the reader no longer have? What additional information would the reader gain?

- In community share, continue the discussion about point of view, asking students how the story changed for them when seen from another character's point of view.

Lesson 8

GOAL:
To encourage students to use other books and movies with which they are familiar to aid in their understanding of the book that they're currently reading

ASSIGNED READING:
6:45 P.M.–7:40 P.M. (pages 89–99)

WRITING PROMPT:
Connect this book to any other books or movies you've read or seen about the Revolutionary War. Feel free to compare and contrast if that is helpful.

Comprehension:
Intertextual Connections

- NOTE: Intertextuality allows students to compare and contrast other books or movies with the book they are currently reading. Students should be able to explain the comparison that they are making. A think sheet such as Comparing/Contrasting or Venn Diagram might help students organize their thoughts. A Response Choice Sheet with the Intertextuality response type described on it can also aid students' thinking. Sample forms are available in the Blackline Masters: Think Sheets section following page 261.

- If necessary, introduce the term *intertextuality* to your students. Discuss how most books or movies remind readers of other books and movies and that making connections between different stories can help them better understand themes and characters.

- If you're using *The Fighting Ground* in a theme unit with other books about war or about young people learning important lessons through difficult experiences, or if you're using a thematically related read-aloud book, help students make intertextual connections with one of these. You can also choose another short book or picture book to read aloud for the purpose of encouraging students to make intertextual connections.

- Use a Venn diagram to record similarities and differences between *The Fighting Ground* and another book. There are several ways to focus the students' intertextual comments. You may want to have students focus on story elements such as characters, theme, plot, setting, conflict, or perhaps vocabulary, illustration (if present), or author's point of view.

- Sample student log pages that show intertextuality and comparing/contrasting appear on page 134. Other samples appear in the lesson plan for *Hatchet*, on pages 184–185.

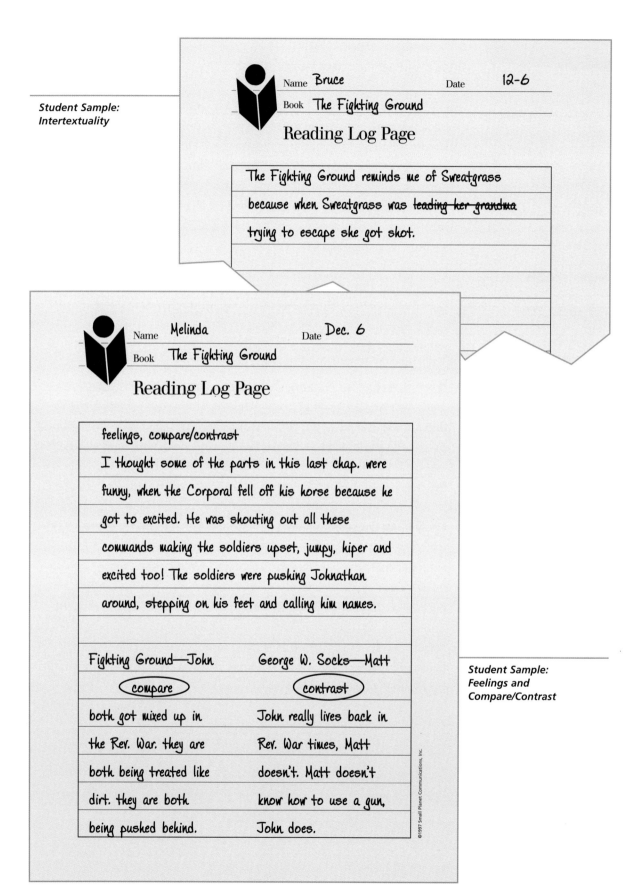

Student Sample:
Intertextuality

Name Bruce   Date 12-6

Book The Fighting Ground

Reading Log Page

The Fighting Ground reminds me of Sweatgrass

because when Sweatgrass was ~~leading her grandma~~

trying to escape she got shot.

Name Melinda   Date Dec. 6

Book The Fighting Ground

Reading Log Page

feelings, compare/contrast

I thought some of the parts in this last chap. were

funny, when the Corporal fell off his horse because he

got to excited. He was shouting out all these

commands making the soldiers upset, jumpy, hiper and

excited too! The soldiers were pushing Johnathan

around, stepping on his feet and calling him names.

Fighting Ground—John	George W. Socks—Matt
(compare)	(contrast)
both got mixed up in	John really lives back in
the Rev. War. they are	Rev. War times, Matt
both being treated like	doesn't. Matt doesn't
dirt. they are both	know how to use a gun,
being pushed behind.	John does.

Student Sample:
Feelings and
Compare/Contrast

©1997 Small Planet Communications, Inc.

Lesson 9

GOAL:
To help students become
fluent readers and recognize
fluency in other readers

ASSIGNED READING:
8:15 P.M.–11:25 P.M.
(pages 100–112)

WRITING PROMPT:
Free choice

Language Conventions:
Fluency Review

- Explain to students that a fluent speaker is one who speaks clearly, smoothly, and expressively. In a chart, help the class list all the elements of fluent speech, including the use of inflection, or changes in tone and pitch; a smooth and polished sound; and a careful observation of punctuation and pauses in a reading. You might want to model how a good speaker uses inflection to show end punctuation, such as a period, exclamation point, or question mark. For example, write a question on the board and read it in a completely flat tone. Then read it with inflection, and make sure students hear the difference.

- Have students work in pairs. Each student should read a section from *The Fighting Ground* (a section that they have already read) to his or her partner. Remind them that as they read and as they listen to their partners read, they should keep in mind the elements of fluent speech recorded on the chart. Encourage partners to offer each other constructive, helpful suggestions after reading. If necessary, model or role-play making constructive comments.

- Walk from pair to pair with a clipboard or notebook and make notes about the fluency of each child. Look for the elements that you and the class recorded in the chart, as well as their use of decoding skills and their ability to correct miscues in their own speech and reading. We've found that using a checklist is an easy and efficient way to record this data. (A sample Fluency Checklist is provided in the Blackline Masters: Assessment section following page 281.)

Teaching Tip

This activity is an excellent assessment opportunity. However, it is very difficult to observe and take notes on an entire class during one class period. You may want to focus on 10–15 students during today's lesson and then repeat the activity next week to observe the rest of the class.

Lesson 10

GOAL:
To use the author's details to draw conclusions about the story that are not specifically stated in the text

ASSIGNED READING:
11:35 P.M.
(pages 112–121)

WRITING PROMPT:
Has Jonathan's attitude toward the war changed at all at this point in the novel? How do you know?

Comprehension:
Drawing Conclusions

- Have students read the assigned reading **before** you conduct the lesson.

- Ask students to think about what has happened in this section of the novel (pages 112–121). Ask them to draw conclusions about what Jonathan is realizing about the Corporal and about war.

- Ask students to use clues that Avi has provided to make sense of what is happening now in the story. Remind students to support their ideas with examples from the text. You can guide them with the following questions.

  – What strikes Jonathan as strange about the Corporal's reaction to his story? How do you know that Jonathan feels uneasy?

  – What do you think is the monstrous idea that formed in Jonathan's mind?

- Write students' answers to the questions and any conclusions that they have drawn on the chalkboard or on chart paper. Underneath each conclusion, write specific details from the story that support it.

Lesson 11

GOAL:
To understand the techniques an author uses to build suspense in a story

ASSIGNED READING:
11:50 P.M.–5:30 A.M.
(pages 121–134)

WRITING PROMPT:
Describe how Avi builds the story to this point. Consider <u>critiquing</u> as well as reporting on this.

Literary Elements:
Building a Plot to a Suspenseful Climax

- Explain to students that suspense is a reader's feeling of curiosity or anticipation about what will happen next in a story. A writer increases suspense by creating a mood of excitement or anticipation.

- Discuss with students any questions that the story has raised in their minds. Make a list of these questions on the chalkboard or on chart paper. Ask students the following questions and record their answers.

  – What words or phrases used by the author contribute to the feeling of suspense in the book?

  – Do the time segments add to the suspense? If so, how?

– How is Jonathan feeling after he returns to the American soldiers? How do you know?

– Do Jonathan's fears add to the suspense of the story? Explain your answer, supporting it with details from the story.

• Discuss the suspense that Avi has built into the plot and how the book would be different if the reader never had any questions about its outcome.

Lesson 12

GOAL:
To increase students' understanding of the roles that the French, the Tories, and the Whigs played in the Revolutionary War

ASSIGNED READING:
5:35 A.M.–6:10 A.M. (pages 135–146)

WRITING PROMPT:
• Have you ever been in a situation like Jonathan's, in which you had to do something you didn't want to do? Describe it. Be sure to include your feelings in your description.
• Write about the different people involved in the Revolutionary War.

Comprehension:
The Roles of the French and the Tories in the Revolutionary War

• Because the book makes many references to Hessian soldiers and Tories, you might want to share with students the following background information.

The Tories and the Whigs, two political groups formed in England in 1679, were among the first great political parties in history. During the period of the Revolutionary War, Whigs were colonists who no longer wanted to be part of Great Britain. They supported the revolution. The Tories were colonists who defended the English king and were against the revolution. Colonists became serious about breaking from Great Britain when King George III began his 60-year reign over England and its colonies in 1760. During this time, he put his own Tory friends in power and his government placed new taxes on the American colonies. Many of the colonists were outraged. They believed that Great Britain had no right to tax them without their consent. Great Britain sent troops including Hessian, or German, mercenaries to enforce the taxes, and the colonists fought back.

Loyalists, or Tories, were also outraged, but at the thought of secession. About 500,000 people were public about their loyalist feelings. Many others were quiet supporters of the crown and the king of England. All these people were in great danger during the Revolutionary War. They were abused and put in prison, their property was taken, and sometimes they were killed. At least 100,000 left the colonies and headed back to England, north to Canada, or south to Florida. The fact that there were so many people

continued on next page

continued from previous page

loyal to the crown makes the Revolutionary War a civil war as well as a fight for independence. People on both sides felt that they were fighting for the future of their country and home.

On July 4, 1776, the Declaration of Independence was created. Two years later, French troops and ships entered the war on the side of the colonists, helping them tremendously. One sympathetic French politician and general was George Washington's friend Marquis de Lafayette, who believed strongly in the War for Independence and fought under General Washington in the Battle of Brandywine and at Valley Forge. With the help of the French, the Americans won their independence, and the Treaty of Paris officially ended the war.

Lesson 13

GOAL:
To encourage students to use their prediction skills to help them understand the story

ASSIGNED READING:
6:13 A.M.–10:30 A.M.
(pages 146–152)

WRITING PROMPT:
Free choice

Comprehension:
Predicting Outcomes

- When you near the end of the book, it is helpful and interesting to have students predict how the story might end. Ask questions such as the following: Where are we in the story currently? What do we know about story grammar, or structure, that can help us predict the ending? What clues is the author giving us?

- Brainstorm a list of possible endings or pieces of the ending. Have the class discuss each idea presented, looking for continuity in style and with the events of the story. Talk about why each proposed ending seems plausible or implausible. Review the kinds of clues that the author has given to Jonathan's character. Ask students to think about the things that Jonathan would or wouldn't do and how his character traits might affect the ending.

- Remind students to think about these predictions as they read and respond to the end of the book in book club discussions.

- An example of a student's reading log entry with predictions about the end of the book as well as questions for her group is shown on page 139.

Teacher Comment:

"This student has combined two response types. Integrated with her own predictions are the questions she will ask her book club members to find out what they predicted."

Name **Alyssa**   Date **Dec 21**

Book **The Fighting Ground**

Reading Log Page

Prediction & Questions
I think the Caorpral will get killed by the Hssianss.
Do you? Do you think Jonathan will go home soon?
And what do you think his parents will say? Yes I
think Jonathan will go home soon. I also think his
parents will be very happy he got home ok and that
he was safe but they'll probably punish him! What
would you do if you were his parent? I would say if
you don't want to follow my rules or listen to me
then you don't have to live under my roof, so pack up
and move out!! Since you want to fight so bad then
see ya latter!!!!!!!!!!!!!!!! But when I grow up and
have kids I would not do that.

Lesson 14

GOAL:
To encourage students to think about the story as a whole and to discuss any remaining issues or questions about the story that they might have

ASSIGNED READING:
None

WRITING PROMPT:
Choose one of the following topics.

- It is twenty years later. How does Jonathan describe this day to his children?
- The war continues and Jonathan is once again called to battle. How will he handle this situation?
- You are Jonathan on the morning the bell tolled. What is your reaction?

Response to Literature:
Analyze the Ending and the Story as a Whole

- Discuss with students the ending of the story and the story as a whole. Have students bring up any questions or issues they might have. What did they enjoy most about the book? What did they enjoy least? How did they feel at the story's end?

- You may want to map out the major events in the story with the class. Reviewing the events might help students recognize things that they would like to know more about or would like to discuss in the community share setting. A partial example of a story map is shown below.

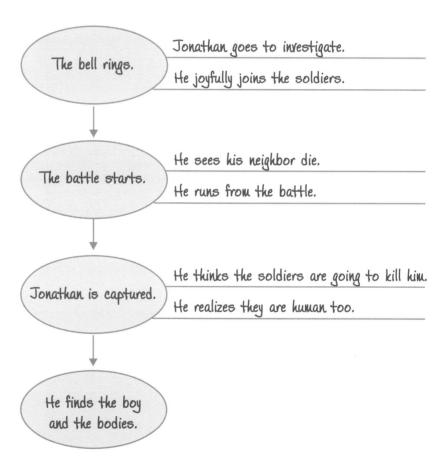

- You might discuss some of the alternate endings that students came up with during Lesson 13. Talk about how the actual ending differed from, or concurred with, their expectations.

141

Lesson 15

GOAL:
To introduce students to the concept of Reader's Theater and the planning and writing of a script

ASSIGNED READING:
None

WRITING PROMPT:
With your book club group, select a favorite scene in the book and plan how you will present it in Reader's Theater. Begin writing the script.

Language Conventions:
Reader's Theater—Planning and Writing a Script

- Explain to students that they are going to have the opportunity to choose a favorite scene from *The Fighting Ground* to present for their classmates.

- If necessary, explain that Reader's Theater is an adaptation of a part of a book so that it can be read as a script. The presenters read the script and do not have to memorize their lines. Props and costumes, if they are used, are very simple. A Reader's Theater presentation is short, no longer than 5–7 minutes.

- Talk to students about which parts of *The Fighting Ground* are appropriate for Reader's Theater. Note that the first section of the book might not make a good Reader's Theater because most of it consists of Jonathan's thoughts, while the scene at the tavern might be more interesting. Remind students that they will want to decide as a group whether everyone will be a presenter or if some members of the group will be in charge of scripts and/or props.

- Have students work in their book club groups to choose a favorite scene from *The Fighting Ground*. When each group has selected a piece of text from the novel, have students begin drafting their scripts. You might want to demonstrate for the class how to adapt the text so that it reads as a script.

Teaching Tip

If your students are writing a script for the first time, you may need to give them more than a day to finish. Some additional resources that you can consult for more information about Reader's Theater are listed below.

- *Presenting Reader's Theater: Plays and Poems to Read Aloud* by Caroline Feller Bauer (H. W. Wilson, 1987)
- *Stories on Stage: Scripts for Reader's Theater* by Aaron Shepard (H. W. Wilson, 1993)
- *Multicultural Folktales for the Feltboard and Readers' Theater* by Judy Sierra (Oryx, 1996)

Lesson 16

GOAL:
To encourage students in small groups to work together to complete a script and to learn the elements of a good presentation

ASSIGNED READING:
None

WRITING PROMPT:
Finish writing the script and practice the scene with your group.

Language Conventions:
Reader's Theater—Elements of a Good Presentation

- Scripts from Lesson 15 are required for this lesson.

- After the scripts are prepared, talk with students about good presentation skills, such as making eye contact, controlling tone and volume, and pronouncing words clearly.

- Give students time to practice reading their scripts in their groups. You might want to walk from group to group offering advice and assistance, particularly if it appears that a group's script is running long.

Lesson 17

GOAL:
To help students learn to perform before a group and to teach them how to be good audience members

ASSIGNED READING:
None

WRITING PROMPT:
Critique your Reader's Theater performance.

Response to Literature:
Performing Reader's Theater

- Before students perform their scripts, talk to them about how they can be attentive audience members. You might guide them with the following tips.

  – Do not make noise or talk while performers are on stage. Everyone is nervous when he or she performs, and a loud audience can cause actors to make mistakes.

  – Listen carefully. When the words are not right in front of you, you have to make an extra effort to hear and understand the actors.

  – Pay careful attention. Try not to look around the room or daydream as other students perform. Show them that you appreciate their hard work.

  – Show support for your classmates by clapping when they have finished performing.

- Give all groups the opportunity to perform.

Lesson 18

GOAL:
To draw on both historical information from the social studies curriculum and fictionalized information from *The Fighting Ground* to identify some "big ideas" about war in general

ASSIGNED READING:
None

WRITING PROMPT:
War often affects the lives of innocent people. What examples does *The Fighting Ground* present to support this statement? Write an essay tying together what you learned about this idea in social studies with the fictional story by Avi.

Comprehension: Synthesis

- Tell students that history books and works of historical fiction both present information from which we can draw larger conclusions. In other words, Jonathan's experiences in *The Fighting Ground* provide more than just an exciting story—they can tell us something about war in general. Similarly, the events of the Revolutionary War that students have read about in their textbooks have something in common with wars that have taken place throughout history and all over the world.

- Remind students of the basic elements of an essay. An essay is a form of nonfiction writing that begins with a thesis statement—the main idea of the essay. The body of the essay contains examples that support the thesis. The essay ends with a conclusion that ties together all of the examples cited in the body and restates the thesis.

- Tell students that the writing prompt for today asks them to write an essay. The thesis of the essay is "War often affects the lives of innocent people." Their essays should be about one-half to three-quarters of a page long and should provide examples from *The Fighting Ground* as well as from their social studies reading that support this thesis.

Lesson 19

GOAL:
For students to think about their classroom experiences during *The Fighting Ground* and to fill out an evaluation form to share their impressions with the teacher

ASSIGNED READING:
None

WRITING PROMPT:
Fill out the self-assessment form.

Student Self-Assessment

- Remind students of the importance of assessment—both self-assessment and evaluation by another person. Self-assessment provides time to step back and reflect on the work one has done, to think about what has gone well and what needs improvement. A person who never pauses for self-assessment may find himself or herself repeating behaviors that are not helping—and may in fact be preventing—the person's growth. Evaluation from an outside source, such as a respected teacher or friend, provides another perspective that a person may not be able to see for herself or himself.

- Distribute self-assessment forms (a sample Book Club Self-Assessment form is provided in the Blackline Masters: Assessment section following page 281) and ask students to read them carefully before they begin writing. Answer any questions they may have about the content of the forms and the procedure for filling them out.

Lesson 20

Teacher Evaluation

GOAL:
To discuss the grades you've given each student, and to help students set personal goals for the next Book Club unit

ASSIGNED READING:
None

WRITING PROMPT:
After reviewing your self-assessment form and your grade, write some goals for the next Book Club.

- Teacher assessment and evaluation during Book Club can take several forms, as outlined in the introductory chapters to this guide. Your goals and your convenience are the criteria that determine the means of assessment and evaluation. Below are several suggestions for ways to communicate your evaluation to students. (Sample teacher evaluation forms are provided in the Blackline Masters: Assessment section following page 281.)

- Option 1: Talk to the students about the trends you see across the class— such as how you saw many students using a wide variety of response choices and how proud you are. Or that you noticed an increase in the use of spelling strategies in students' logs. After the general discussion, pass back each student's evaluation sheet(s), along with the self-assessment sheet, and give students time to read, reflect, and ask questions. Walk around the classroom and answer individual questions as necessary. After students have had time to read through your notes, pass out the Reaction and Goal-Setting Sheet where students can reflect and comment on their grades and then set goals for the next Book Club.

- Option 2: Meet with each student individually and share your evaluation and grades. If appropriate, review the goals that the student set at the end of the last Book Club and discuss how well the student has done in meeting those goals. Then give the student a form on which to record his or her reactions to your conference and to set some concrete goals for the next Book Club. NOTE: Individual conferences are time-consuming. You may want to use this method at the end of semesters or quarters. The Book Club evaluation can be rolled into a general evaluation conference where grades and perhaps portfolios are discussed for all curriculum areas.

- Option 3: Meet with each book club group and talk about the different discussion strategies that you observed them using. Then pass out individual evaluation forms, and give students time to read them and ask any questions. Students can then set goals for the next unit and discuss goals for improving group discussion and management. NOTE: This kind of evaluation can take place over several days toward the end of the book. You can use the time set aside for book clubs while other groups conduct their normal book club discussions.

A Wrinkle in Time
by Madeleine L'Engle

Introducing the Book

A Wrinkle in Time, combining science fiction
and fantasy, has been a children's favorite for many years. Readers will
identify with the characters' hopes and dreams throughout the book.
However, the vocabulary and technical concepts—even though many
are pure fantasy—can challenge some readers.

One Book Club teacher found this to be true
for her fifth graders, even when she used the book at the end of year.
To identify points that were confusing for her students (so that she
could provide appropriate instructional support), she did regular comprehension checks during a community share at the end of each Book Club session. Based on her
comprehension checks, we've identified topics that may challenge your students and require some
instructional support. These topics are indicated at the end of each lesson provided here.

Some confusions were attributed to vocabulary in the text. Thus, a second
support we suggest is the use of vocabulary think sheets. (A sample form is provided in the Blackline
Masters: Think Sheets section following page 261.) Teachers who have used *A Wrinkle in Time* suggest that students may want to add one or two words a day to their vocabulary think sheets. During
closing community share, a brief amount of time can be devoted to talking about these words and
adding them to the word wall. (See Lesson 7 for *Bridge to Terabithia*, page 112, for a full discussion of
word walls.) We've indicated this vocabulary emphasis as one of the writing prompt choices. Note
that while you might emphasize vocabulary, it should be the students' choice, depending upon
whether or not they find words that they feel are worth exploring.

NOTE: The teacher who developed this lesson plan mapped her writing
prompts onto the response types her students knew how to use. Throughout the lessons, therefore,
you'll see labels such as "Me & the Book," "Vocabulary," and "Compare/Contrast" on most of the
writing prompts. The labels can provide cues about when you might want to introduce or review a

Paperback Edition, Bantam Doubleday Dell Books for Young Readers, ©1962 by Madeleine L'Engle Franklin.
ISBN: 0-440-49805-8.

certain response type with your class. (All of the response types are listed and described on the four Response Choice Sheets in the Blackline Masters: Think Sheets section following page 261.)

You'll also notice that there are usually two or three different writing prompts for each day in this lesson plan. This is because *A Wrinkle in Time* is a challenging book that you'll probably be teaching near the end of the year, when your students will be doing several response types in their journals each day. You may want to remind students at the beginning of this unit that "free choice" is always an option for their writing, even though it is not explicitly listed under the writing prompts.

Summary Meg Murry and her brilliant but eccentric younger brother, Charles Wallace, share adventures traveling through time and space as they try to rescue their father, a scientist. Their father had been working on "tessering," a form of space and time travel, when he disappeared years ago. With the help of three strange beings—Mrs. Who, Mrs. Whatsit, and Mrs. Which—and a stranger, Calvin O'Keefe, they "tesser" to the planet of Camazotz. There the children's father is imprisoned behind the Black Thing, an evil force in the universe. The Black Thing is helped by the power of IT, a disembodied brain that controls all the people of Camazotz.

On Camazotz, Meg, Charles Wallace, and Calvin fight against the power of IT. Charles Wallace voluntarily succumbs to IT in order to obtain information, while Meg works to free her father. Meg succeeds. Her father then tessers Meg and Calvin off the planet to protect them from IT. Unfortunately, Charles Wallace is left behind. After narrowly escaping the cold power of IT in her first encounter, Meg faces the enormous physical and moral challenge of returning to Camazotz to save Charles Wallace. Because of her love for her brother, she goes, and through expressing this love, she is able to free him.

Through Meg's voice, author Madeleine L'Engle weaves a powerful narrative. L'Engle combines the realism of Meg's emotional journey with the fantastic world of tessering, IT, and the Black Thing.

Themes Two themes in this book are the struggle between good and evil and the imperfection of people. Meg, Charles Wallace, and Calvin are called to put themselves in danger in order to help Mr. Murry fight evil in the universe. They discover the pure evil of the Black Thing and a shadow of evil over their own planet, Earth. They learn of the grand battle that has been going on for eons between the forces of good and evil. In the course of their adventure, the characters face their own imperfections but continue to strive in spite of them. Both themes can provide ample topics for discussion in book clubs.

Special Classroom Library Madeleine L'Engle has written several other books featuring the Murry children, including *A Wind in the Door* (Farrar, Straus and Giroux, 1973), *A Swiftly Tilting Planet* (Dell, 1981), and *Many Waters* (Farrar, Straus and Giroux, 1986). All are books that students who find *A Wrinkle in Time* intriguing will want to have available. Other books that students might find interesting are in the genre of science fiction or fantasy and may involve the topic of time travel. Some suggested titles are listed below.

Title	Author	Publisher, Date
The Trolley to Yesterday	John Bellairs	Dial Books for Young Readers, 1989
The Children of Green Knowe	Lucy M. Boston	Harcourt, Brace, 1989
The Halloween Tree	Ray Bradbury	Knopf, 1988
Switching Well	Peni R. Griffin	Puffin Books, 1994
The Phantom Tollbooth	Norton Juster	Knopf, 1988
The Lion, the Witch, and the Wardrobe	C. S. Lewis	HarperCollins Children's Books, 1994
The Giver	Lois Lowry	Houghton Mifflin, 1993
The Princess in the Pigpen	Jane R. Thomas	Clarion Books, 1989
Jeremy Visick	David Wiseman	Houghton Mifflin, 1990

Lesson 1

GOAL:
To familiarize students with the elements of fantasy and to encourage them to begin thinking about *A Wrinkle in Time*

ASSIGNED READING:
Chapter 1
(pages 3–21)

Literary Elements:
Elements of Fantasy

• Introduce or review the elements of fantasy, depending upon your students' needs. Fantasy is filled with highly imaginative, improbable, or even unrealistic characters and events. However, fantasy may also mix realistic characters and events with the imaginative ones. A story may begin—as *A Wrinkle in Time* does—with such routine events as not being able to sleep, getting up to make some cocoa, and meeting your brother in the kitchen. To give another example, in *Tuck Everlasting*, a child goes for a walk in the woods and comes across a natural spring. However, in fantasy, such routine events lead to other experiences that could not possibly happen in real life, such as instantaneous travel across space and time.

continued on next page

continued from previous page

WRITING PROMPT:
Choose at least two of
the following:

- Me & the Book: Write
  about your own experi-
  ence with weather and
  storms.
- Vocabulary
- Write about the IQ testing that Meg and Charles
  Wallace had. Do you
  think IQ tests are good,
  bad, or both?
- What events in Chapter
  1 are realistic? What
  events give you clues that
  this is a fantasy story?
  Do you have any more
  predictions about what
  will happen?

- This would be a good time to remind students that categories such as fantasy are called "genres," and to differentiate fantasy from other genres they may have already studied, such as contemporary realistic fiction (e.g., *Hatchet*) or historical fiction (e.g., *The Fighting Ground*). Invite students to share other fantasies they may have read or movies they have seen, and help them compare features that help to define the genre.

- After students have had time to look over the book—the front and back covers, chapter titles, and so forth—ask them to make predictions. To extend the activity, you might want to read the first half of Chapter 1 and then ask for more predictions. Book Club teachers who have done this have found this second round of predictions to be more elaborate and detailed than those based solely on the covers and chapter titles.

- The word *tesseract* is a key concept throughout the book. Since it is introduced in Chapter 1, you may want to spend some time discussing the word during the closing community share. Important points include not only what the word means but also how Meg and Charles Wallace's mother, Mrs. Murry, reacted when she heard it.

Lesson 2

GOAL:
To review with students
the ways in which authors
reveal their characters

ASSIGNED READING:
Chapter 2
(pages 22–37)

WRITING PROMPT:
Discuss in detail one of
the characters you've met
so far.

Literary Elements:
Author's Craft—Character Development

- You might begin this lesson by reminding students that thinking about author's craft can help them understand the story better. For example, looking closely at the way an author reveals a character can help a reader appreciate subtle details about the character. Focusing on author's craft can also help students when they do their own writing.

- Review with students the different techniques authors use to introduce their characters to readers, reminding them that they should pay close attention to descriptions of characters; the way characters talk, behave, and interact with others; and the private thoughts and feelings of characters. (For a full treatment of the topic of characterization, see Lesson 2 for *Bridge to Terabithia*, page 107.)

- Invite students to talk specifically about the characters they have met so far in the book. What techniques of characterization does L'Engle use, and where specifically does she use these techniques?

- As a comprehension check, you'll want to observe and informally assess students' book club discussions. As you walk through the class and listen in on these discussions, be sure that students are able to discuss the events and characters of the book. Offer your help whenever a group seems to be misunderstanding some aspect of the story.

Teaching Tip

One Book Club teacher describes her informal assessment process as follows: "I wander from group to group listening for interesting conversations, misconceptions, or managerial problems. Sometimes I use a checklist to see if everyone is sharing. However, most notes I take are in narrative form on mailing labels, with a child's name on each label. Later I put these labels in a folder for each child, or in my journal for my own reference."

- In community share, you might want to work with students to create character webs on chart paper. Ask them to name and describe characters to whom they have been introduced so far and then describe how these characters are related to each other.

- Another comprehension aid that you might use in community share is a sequence chart of the events of the first two chapters. This can be done on the chalkboard, or on chart paper if you plan to refer back to the chart as students continue reading.

Lesson 3

GOAL:
To focus on book club groups and how students can discuss a fantasy story in their book clubs

ASSIGNED READING:
Chapter 3
(pages 38–55)

WRITING PROMPT:
Choose at least two of the following:
- Author's Craft: Describe the unusual ways of speaking that Mrs. Who, Mrs. Which, and Mrs. Whatsit have. You might try to imitate them in your speech or in your own writing.
- Wonderful Words or Vocabulary
- Compare/Contrast: Compare or contrast yourself with Meg, Calvin, or Charles Wallace.

Language Conventions: Book Club Talk

- If you think it is necessary, spend some time reviewing how book club groups should work. Remind students that good book club conversations don't just happen—everyone in the group has to participate and follow the guidelines for good book club discussions. (See pages 37–38 of the Teaching Tips chapter for a list of suggested guidelines.) If a group's discussions are not going well, the group members have to think about what's going wrong and set goals for improvement.

- You might want to talk specifically about the discussion of fantasy stories and ask students if discussing fantasy is different from discussing other kinds of stories. Have they been able to ask each other questions about the story that promote discussion? Do they find discussing this story more challenging than discussing other stories? Ask them to give reasons for their opinions.

- Ask students to describe how they might improve their group. What goals can they set for future book club discussions? Ask them to monitor the group's progress each day, either in their reading logs or on a self-assessment form. (A sample Book Club Self-Assessment sheet is provided in the Blackline Masters: Assessment section following page 281.)

- In community share, ask students to describe how their groups did today. Did they achieve their goals? Why, or why not?

- You might also invite students to talk about Mrs. Whatsit, Mrs. Who, and Mrs. Which. What is strange about the way these women speak? Refer back to the author's craft discussion from yesterday as you ask them to describe these characters.

Lesson 4

Literary Elements:
Author's Craft—Descriptive Language

GOAL:
To understand how an author uses descriptive language to paint pictures in the reader's mind

ASSIGNED READING:
Chapter 4
(pages 56–73)

WRITING PROMPT:
Choose at least two of the following:
- Picture: Draw a picture inspired by something you've read in the novel.
- Summary: What happened in "the trip"?
- Vocabulary: Record and explore the meaning of "wonderful words" from the chapter.

- Review with students the importance of descriptive language in writing. What techniques do authors use to paint pictures in our minds? Be sure that students understand what sensory details are—details that appeal to the senses of sight, hearing, touch, smell, and taste—and why they are essential to descriptive writing.

- Students can describe specific pictures that L'Engle has created in their minds so far. Then ask them to read today's assignment to discover new pictures created by L'Engle.

- You might ask students to get into pairs to do today's assigned reading. One student in each pair can read aloud the first half of the chapter, and the other can read the second half. Encourage students to listen carefully as their partners read and appreciate how the descriptive language *sounds* as it's read aloud. Can they form pictures in their minds as they listen?

- In community share, ask students to share any story summaries they have written in their logs. You might also ask them to describe the idea of the "wrinkle in time," or to explain what they think the chapter title "The Black Thing" means.

- This is a good lesson with which to informally assess students' comprehension. Pay close attention to their summaries and to their discussions of story events, both in book clubs and in community share.

Teaching Tip

In general, story summaries do not make the best log entries or topics for book club discussion. Summarizing is a relatively low-level thinking skill, and summaries read aloud do not tend to generate lively conversations. However, with a challenging and complex book such as *A Wrinkle in Time*, summarizing becomes important both as a thinking tool and as a way to check students' comprehension. You should use your judgment of a book's difficulty and of your students' abilities to determine when to encourage or discourage the use of summaries for Book Club.

Lesson 5

GOAL:
To review the elements of fantasy and to help students recognize these elements in the book

ASSIGNED READING:
Chapter 5
(pages 74–90)

WRITING PROMPT:
Choose at least two of the following:
- Author's Craft: How does L'Engle use the illustrations on pages 76 and 77 to add to the story?
- Intertextuality: How is this book like other fantasy books you've read?
- What do you think of time travel? Why?

Literary Elements:
Elements of Fantasy, Revisited

- Ask students to think again about the elements of a fantasy story. Then ask them to give evidence that *A Wrinkle in Time* is a fantasy story. Students might mention Charles Wallace's ability to "read" people and situations, the first appearance of Mrs. Which and her decision not to completely "materialize," and, of course, the events of Chapter 4— including their trip to Uriel, the mention of the word *tesser* and the idea of time travel, and the appearance of the Black Thing.

- Ask students if there are also realistic scenes in the book. Students might mention that except for Charles Wallace and the three elderly women, the characters seem realistic and average. The family's home and the school are realistic, and the situation concerning their missing father seems strange but not necessarily unrealistic at first. Ask them if the fact that the author starts the story realistically—by introducing real children with whom readers might identify—helps to draw them into the story. How would they have felt if the story had started with the events of Chapter 4?

- In community share, you might invite students to discuss the issue of good versus evil in the world, and then relate this topic to the story and to the students' own lives. What kinds of good do students see in their everyday lives? What kinds of good do Meg and Calvin see? What examples of evil do we face? How do we overcome evil?

Lesson 6

GOAL:
To use illustrations in the book and the students' own writing as a springboard for a discussion about time travel

ASSIGNED READING:
Chapter 6,
pages 91–102 only

Comprehension:
Fifth Dimension and Time Travel

- This point in the novel is a good time to check students' comprehension. You might want to reassure them that no one is likely to have a perfect understanding of the fourth and fifth dimensions and how they relate to time travel. These are very abstract concepts, and readers don't need to know a lot about physics to follow the story.

- Using the illustrations on pages 76 and 77 of *A Wrinkle in Time* and the students' writing from yesterday, discuss the idea of time travel. What do students think about this idea? If they do believe it can happen, how might it work? Do they believe that there is a "fifth dimension"?

WRITING PROMPT:
- Title Explanation: Who is "The Happy Medium"?
- Comprehension Check: What have we learned about the past of Mrs. Whatsit?

- Invite students to discuss various ways of looking at time travel and creative ways of explaining how it might work in a fantasy story. Have they ever read any other books or watched any movies that involved time travel?

- In community share, discuss the adventure the children have begun on Camazotz. Also, community share might be a good place in which to discuss the pun this chapter's title makes with the phrase *happy medium*. Make sure that students understand what this phrase usually means and why the expression might be funny or ironic in the chapter title. If some students explored this topic in their reading logs, focus on their writing.

- Students are now nearly halfway through the novel. You might use this as another point at which to informally assess student comprehension and progress. Continue working your way through book club groups, making notes about each student's contributions to the conversation. It might take you several days to get a thorough understanding of how each child is handling the story and the discussions.

Teaching Tip

If, while gathering data for your informal assessment, you notice that some students are struggling, try the following strategies.

- Help students "jump-start" their book club discussions by asking a few probing questions to prompt their thinking.

- With the whole class or with individual groups, review the guidelines for dynamic, focused book club discussions. (See the Teaching Tips chapter, pages 37–38.)

- Spend more time in community share, asking students to identify parts of any chapter that are tricky for them.

- Read aloud part of the assigned reading for a particular day.

Lesson 7

GOAL:
To encourage students to think about their own community by comparing and contrasting it with Camazotz

ASSIGNED READING:
Chapter 6,
pages 103–113

WRITING PROMPT:
Choose at least two of the following:
- Compare/Contrast: Compare the town of Camazotz to your own town.
- Feelings: Describe Charles's feelings about Camazotz. How do you feel about the town? How are Charles's feelings different from Meg's or yours?
- Picture: Draw a picture of Camazotz.

Comprehension:
Describing Our Town

- In this lesson, students will use comparison and contrast to reach a better understanding of two communities: their own and Camazotz. You might point out to the class that by comparing and contrasting something in a book with something from real life, a reader can shed light on both subjects.

- Ask students to brainstorm a class list of details about their community. How does the community function? What are some of the routines and traditions of the community?

- Ask students to describe what a visitor might notice about their community. As they try to look at their town or city through the eyes of someone seeing it for the first time, what stands out as particularly unique and interesting? Explain to students that in their reading assignment today, they—along with Meg, Charles, and Calvin—will be visitors to a very unusual community.

- In community share, you might want to have students collaborate to create an illustration or a map of the community of Camazotz. Visualizing will aid their understanding, and you can use this activity to assess their level of comprehension.

Lesson 8

GOAL:
To review the advice and gifts given to the children, and to predict how these gifts might help them in Camazotz

ASSIGNED READING:
Chapter 7
(pages 114–132)

Comprehension:
Reviewing Content and Making Predictions

- Predicting what will happen next in a story is a good way for readers to check whether they've understood what has happened already. It can also build suspense, as readers keep turning pages to find out if their predictions will come true.

- Ask students to describe the advice and gifts given to the children by Mrs. Who, Mrs. Which, and Mrs. Whatsit. Allow them to review the first half of Chapter 6 in order to come up with concrete responses. For example, students will remember that Mrs. Whatsit strengthens Calvin's gift for communication, gives Charles Wallace childhood resilience, and gives Meg her faults—fear, anger, and impatience. She warns that the

WRITING PROMPT:
Choose at least two of the
following:
- Prediction Revisited:
How well did we predict?
Where will the story
go now?
- If I Were in the Story:
What would you do now
if you were in the chil-
dren's predicament?
- Title Explanation: Who is
"The Man with the
Red Eyes"?

danger is greatest for Charles Wallace because of his pride and arro-
gance, that Calvin must look after Meg, and that Meg must stay angry
because her anger will help her get through the difficult times. Above
all, the three children are warned that they must stay together.

- Then tell students to predict how each gift and piece of advice might
help the children on Camazotz. What situations might the ladies be
predicting?

- Suggest that from this point on, students make notes in their reading
logs every time some advice or gift from the ladies helps the children.
(You may want to model one example for the class.) Then they can discuss these situations in their book clubs and in community share.

- You can use the class's time in community share today to check students'
comprehension. Ask them where Charles has gone. Then discuss further the idea of time travel and the fifth dimension. What might have
happened to Charles? Invite students who responded to the "If I Were in
the Story" writing prompt to share their ideas for getting out of the children's predicament.

Lesson 9

GOAL:
To review with students the
concept of fluency and to
informally assess students'
oral reading fluency

ASSIGNED READING:
Chapter 8
(pages 133–143)

WRITING PROMPT:
- Write a description of IT.
(You may choose to do a
character map, an illustration, or both.)
- Me & the Book: Imagine
that someone in your
own family is trapped
somewhere and you must
rescue him or her.
How would you feel?

Language Conventions:
Fluency Review

- A fluent speaker is one who speaks clearly, smoothly, and expressively.
Becoming fluent oral readers can help students speak clearly and learn
how to project their voices when they are engaged in public speaking.
Observing students reading aloud can also give you clues as to what
strategies students are using to correct miscues. This in turn informs
your reading instruction.

- Ask students if they remember the elements of fluent speech, including
use of inflection, or changes in tone and pitch; good intonation; smooth
and polished sound; and careful observation of punctuation and pauses.
Read a short section of Chapter 7 aloud and have students make observations about your reading fluency. You may want to "throw in" a few
errors for which students can give you constructive criticism, or model
how to self-correct a miscue (including telling how you knew it was
necessary to self-correct).

continued on next page

continued from previous page

- Have each student select a favorite passage (about one to one and a half pages in length) from Chapter 7 and practice reading it aloud. Since all students will be reading aloud at once, remind everyone to keep their voices low. After about five minutes, have students form pairs and practice reading their passages aloud to their partners. Remind students that as they read and as they listen to their partners read, they should keep in mind the elements of fluent speech. Encourage partners to offer each other constructive, helpful suggestions after reading. You might want to remind students of possible constructive comments by modeling or role-playing making these comments.

- While students are reading, you can administer a fluency assessment. Lesson 9 for *The Fighting Ground*, on page 135, provides a complete model for administering this assessment. See also the Fluency Checklist in the Blackline Masters: Assessment section following page 281.

- Have students read Chapter 8 silently, respond to their choice of writing prompts, and conduct discussion in book groups.

- In community share, have a discussion about Father. What has happened to him? How did he get to Camazotz? What is his relationship to IT? Ask students to brainstorm and start putting the pieces of the plot puzzle together. They should mention details from the book to support what they think are the main facts about Father's situation. You may want to create a quick character map of Father to record students' ideas and help them visualize the information that they have collected.

Lesson 10

GOAL:
To review with students the major events of the story by creating a class sequence chart

ASSIGNED READING:
Chapter 9
(pages 144–162)

WRITING PROMPT:
- If I Were in the Story: You are a citizen of

Comprehension:
Sequencing

- Remind students that thinking about the sequence of events in a book can help them remember details and understand the story more completely. Tell them that creating a sequence chart is a good strategy for organizing events in a novel like *A Wrinkle in Time* and can also be used with nonfiction texts.

- Review/summarize the major events of the novel so far. With students, create a sequence chart of major events. (For a full treatment of sequence charts, turn to Lesson 10 of *Last Summer with Maizon*, page

Camazotz. What is it like to be a member of this community?

- Character Map: Focus on one character in the book. Draw a picture of this character, make a character chart, or write a description of this character.
- Map/Illustration: Add to or revise your interpretation of IT.
- Write about tessering. How is it done? What does it feel like? Why do you suppose it feels that way?

75.) As students contribute to the sequence chart, you can assess their understanding of the novel.

- Discuss any problems or confusion the students might be experiencing with the novel. Then ask them to name their favorite characters and ideas in the novel so far.

- In community share, revisit the concept of the "tesseract." What do students say it is? Discuss how this concept has influenced the story. You might want to create a class concept web around the idea of a tesseract, including details that readers know at this point in the story that they didn't know when the term was first introduced (in Chapter 1). The web should also include any synonyms such as *time travel* and *wrinkle* that were discussed earlier.

Lesson 11

GOAL:
To encourage students to make predictions about events in a story based on a chapter title

ASSIGNED READING:
Chapter 10
(pages 163–175)

WRITING PROMPT:
Choose at least two of the following:
- Title Explanation: What does "Absolute Zero" mean?
- Picture: Draw a picture of the three beasts that approach Meg, Calvin, and Mr. Murry.
- Me & the Book: Compare Meg's relationship with her father to your relationship with your own parents. Do you understand her feelings?

Comprehension:
Using Text Features and Prior Knowledge to Make Predictions

- Talk to students about the fact that good readers are constantly making predictions and revising their predictions about a book as they read. It can be as simple as asking oneself, "What do I think is going to happen next?" or "What does this detail mean about the story?" and then reading on to find out.

- Tell students that the title of the next chapter is "Absolute Zero." What do students think this title could mean? What images does the title create in their minds? One Book Club teacher found that students often came up with words and phrases having to do with freezing and cold.

- With the class, predict what the title "Absolute Zero" might mean for the story. Ask students to talk about any other clues (from text features or content) that point to the contents of Chapter 10. Then invite them to read their assignment to find out.

- In community share, spend extra time talking about students' log responses. During the course of this discussion, you can find out if the students have a clear picture in their minds of the unusual beings who appear in this chapter, and you can further find out if students

continued on next page

continued from previous page

understand the relationship between the children and their father. Ask students to discuss why the group has arrived in this strange place, what the meaning and connotation of *absolute zero* is, and the different images of stillness, cold, and pain that appear in the chapter. Some students might also want to discuss why Meg feels anger, disappointment, and frustration toward her father in this chapter. How does her father respond to these feelings?

Lesson 12

GOAL:
For students to discuss the character of Aunt Beast based on what they know about fantasy, time travel, and the other characters in the story so far

ASSIGNED READING:
Chapter 11
(pages 176–191)

WRITING PROMPT:
Choose at least two of the following:
- Problem Solving: How will Meg, Calvin, and Father get Charles Wallace back and return to Earth?
- Continue the discussion about Aunt Beast that we started in the lesson.
- Intertextuality: Talk about how your experiences with other books and movies about time travel have influenced your experience with this book.

Comprehension:
Using Background Knowledge to Analyze Characters

- Discuss how what students know about a book and its characters can help them predict what a new character in the book might be like. Have students identify other books in which they have encountered new characters but have already known what they might be like.

- Revisit your previous discussions about fantasy, time travel, and characters such as Mrs. Which and the Happy Medium. Discuss with students the kind of universe that Madeleine L'Engle has created. What kinds of characters have students met in the book so far? What did these characters' names reveal about them? Tell students that they are about to meet a character named Aunt Beast, after whom Chapter 11 is named.

- Ask students to discuss the following questions: If we believe in this world that L'Engle has created, what kind of character might Aunt Beast be? What kind of connotation does her name have? Do you think she will be good or evil? How do you think the encounter with Aunt Beast will affect the rest of the story? Write key words and phrases from the students' discussion on the chalkboard or chart paper.

- Have students read the assigned reading with these questions in mind.

- At the beginning of community share, return to the notes made during the initial discussion and have students compare how they described Aunt Beast before reading the chapter with how they would describe Aunt Beast now. Review the kinds of clues that students used before they read the chapter—for example, prior knowledge of L'Engle's characters, the author's purpose, and events in previous chapters.

- You might also revisit Lesson 4 and your discussion about descriptive language. What sensory details does L'Engle use in Chapter 11? How does Meg's conversation with Aunt Beast (pages 181–182) reveal how much she relies on her sense of sight? What sensory details are the most important on the planet Ixchel?

- Then return to the class concept web for *tesseract* that was created in Lesson 10. Add to and revise the web as necessary to reflect today's lesson and students' writing. For example, students will have more details to add about time travel and about creatures and activities in other dimensions.

Lesson 13

GOAL:
To encourage students to discuss their ideas about what Madeleine L'Engle is trying to tell readers with her story

ASSIGNED READING:
Chapter 12
(pages 192–211)

WRITING PROMPT:
Choose at least two of the following:
- Author's Purpose: Write your thoughts about Madeleine L'Engle's purposes in writing this book, using today's lesson and conversations from previous days to support your ideas.
- Drawing Conclusions: L'Engle leaves a lot of blanks for us to fill in (like how it's been back on Earth and what the Dark Thing looks like now). Write about one of these "blanks," making your own guesses and predictions.

Response to Literature: Author's Purpose

- Have a discussion of author's purpose. Remind students that an author usually has a reason, or purpose, for writing a particular story. An author usually wants readers to take away from the story certain impressions, ideas, or messages. Relate author's purpose to students' own writing. What kinds of ideas or impressions have they tried to convey with their writings?

- Do students think L'Engle is trying to tell readers something with *A Wrinkle in Time*? What might she be trying to tell us? Ask students to support their responses with details from the story. Past Book Club students have mentioned that the book addresses the themes of good versus evil, control and abuse of power, and love between friends and family. The book also asks readers to look with sensitivity and new understanding on people and families considered "outcasts," and it encourages readers to use their imaginations to consider worlds outside their own.

- Spend time talking about these issues. Then tell students to read the final chapter to discover more details and clues about the author's purpose. Tell them that they will have an opportunity to discuss their ideas further after they have read the chapter, written in their logs, and met with their book clubs.

- In community share, bring the discussion back to the story's purpose. Explore the message "Love can conquer all." Is this message supported

continued on next page

continued from previous page

- Feelings: Discuss your feelings and thoughts about the book's ending and about the book as a whole.

in the story? Do students see this message supported in real life? What other lessons do students find in this book? Invite students who wrote about author's purpose to share their writings.

- Ask students how they might use this story in their own lives. Has it taught them lessons that might help them to get along with others and to look at their world with new respect and interest? Ask them to explain.

Lesson 14

GOAL:
To review with students the elements of fantasy and to identify common lessons that appear in books of this genre

ASSIGNED READING:
None

WRITING PROMPT:
Begin writing a fantasy story of your own. You may get ideas for your story by thinking about the characters and events of *A Wrinkle in Time* and other fantasy books that you've read.

Literary Elements:
Genre—Fantasy

- Review with students the elements of fantasy writing. What makes a good fantasy story? Talk to students about what they like about fantasy stories. In what way does *A Wrinkle in Time* fit the description of a fantasy story? If you plan to integrate process writing with this lesson, have students start thinking about how they could write a good fantasy story.

- Ask students to think about other fantasy stories that they've read. Do they notice that there seem to be certain lessons and themes that appear in most stories of this genre? If your students have read *Tuck Everlasting*, another fantasy story, you can focus on comparing its themes to themes in *A Wrinkle in Time*. (A lesson plan for *Tuck Everlasting* begins on page 81.) For example, in comparing these two books, students might notice that both stories discuss the idea that it is dangerous and wrong to try to control nature so that nothing changes and/or people are all alike. Both stories send the message that although nature is not perfect, it's a mistake to tamper with what is natural and genuine. Conformity and sameness do not improve the world. Students might notice that this theme is especially common in fantasy stories. Students might also notice that good versus evil is another common theme in fantasy stories.

- If you want students to write their own fantasy stories, encourage them to draw on what they have learned during the process of reading and discussing *A Wrinkle in Time*. You might also want to review the steps in the writing process before students begin. Give students ample time to share rough drafts of their original fantasy stories with their book club groups. You might wish to walk through the class and offer your own assistance as students share their pieces. NOTE: Students will probably need several days to finish their stories and to go through a sharing and revision process. After today, their pieces should be worked on during another time of the day—preferably during writing instruction or writing workshop.

Lesson 15

GOAL:
To explore with students the process of adapting a book into a movie script

ASSIGNED READING:
None

WRITING PROMPT:
List the parts of *A Wrinkle in Time* that would have to change in order for it to be made into a movie. Then write how each part would change if you were the screenwriter.

Response to Literature:
Developing a Movie Script Based on a Book

- Remind students that there are many different ways to convey information. Talk about the way that drawings, music, writing, and movies can all communicate a story. Ask students if stories communicated through each of these mediums are the same, different, or not as good as others. Discuss how different mediums are equally valid, but people have to choose the best way to convey a certain story.

- If you have shown students movie versions of any of the books they've read, ask them to think about these movies. If you have not, ask them if they have ever seen a movie or television show that has been made from a book they've read. What did they think of the movie or TV show? Did they notice any changes made to the story? What kinds of changes were made? How did they feel about the changes? Was the story better, worse, or just different?

- If students are having difficulty describing how they feel about the changes, tell them that people often feel that a book version of a story is more interesting and complete than a movie or television version of the same story. Ask them: Why might this be so?

- Discuss the reasons why certain aspects of stories might need to be changed for theaters or television. You might mention that some things need to be changed to add theatrical excitement and that some things are simply not physically possible.

- If necessary, mention that the people who write or rewrite books when they are being made into movies are called screenwriters. The screenwriters are the people who "visualize" the story for television or movies.

- Students can work individually, in pairs, or in their book club groups to complete the writing assignment.

continued on next page

continued from previous page

- During community share, spend time reviewing the lists and changes that students have created. One Book Club teacher noticed that this activity drew a great deal of interest and excitement from her class. The students went so far as to list actors to play each role, suggest possible locations for the scenes on other planets, and begin writing scripts. The activity engaged students' imaginations and gave them an outlet for creative response.

Lesson 16

Student Self-Assessment

GOAL:
For students to assess their own performance during the *Wrinkle in Time* unit

ASSIGNED READING:
None

WRITING PROMPT:
Complete the End-of-Book Self-Assessment sheet I've handed out.

- A sample End-of-Book Self-Assessment sheet is provided in the Blackline Masters: Assessment section following page 281. Hand out a copy of this sheet or a similar one of your own creation to each student.

- Encourage students to think carefully about their answers to the questions on the sheet. Remind them that they should provide as much detail as possible; an answer such as "The book was good" doesn't tell you much.

- For a fully developed lesson on student self-assessment, see Lesson 12 of *Last Summer with Maizon,* page 80.

Lesson 17

Teacher Evaluation

GOAL:
For you to share your grades and comments with the students and give them a chance to respond

ASSIGNED READING:
None

WRITING PROMPT:
Fill out the Reaction and Goal-Setting Sheet I've handed out.

- Before Book Club, write students' grades on a form that allows them to react to their grades and set goals for improvement. (A sample Reaction and Goal-Setting Sheet is provided in the Blackline Masters: Assessment section.) Pass out these forms to the class.

- Encourage students to consider the grades you've given them and to think about whether the grades match their own assessment of their performance during this unit. Then they should write well thought-out responses to the questions on the form.

- For more ideas about conducting a teacher evaluation lesson, see Lesson 13 of *Last Summer with Maizon,* page 80.

Hatchet
by Gary Paulsen

Introducing the Book

Gary Paulsen's adventure novel *Hatchet* has been a perennial favorite with Book Club teachers and students. It's most often used with fifth- or sixth-graders. Our lessons for *Hatchet* include several that focus on the "building blocks" of the Book Club program, such as share sheets, response choices, qualities of a good book club, self-assessment sheets, and qualities of a good share sheet. These lessons can be adapted for use with any book, and they will probably form an essential part of your Book Club curriculum, no matter which books you decide to use.

NOTE: The daily reading assignments in this lesson plan are very short—generally eight to twelve pages. Depending on your class, you may decide to combine some reading assignments and teach fewer than twenty-six lessons.

Summary Thirteen-year-old Brian Robeson is in a small plane flying over the Canadian wilderness when the pilot suddenly has a heart attack and dies. Brian manages to survive the plane crash but finds himself alone and lost to civilization. His only possession is a hatchet that his mother gave him before he boarded the plane. Although Brian is still plagued by painful memories of "The Secret" he knows about his parents' divorce, he quickly sees that he must focus all his thoughts and energy on his own survival. He learns, mostly by making mistakes, how to shelter himself, make fire, and find food. He encounters swarms of rapacious mosquitoes, a porcupine, a bear, a wolf, a skunk, a moose, and a tornado—and learns something from each encounter. By the time Brian is able to recover the plane's survival pack, he knows how to take care of himself. That afternoon another plane responds to Brian's radio signal, and his fifty-four days in the wilderness are over. Paulsen's well-told story brings to mind modern people's distance from the natural world and conveys a respect for nature as well as human resourcefulness.

Paperback Edition, Aladdin Paperbacks, ©1987 by Gary Paulsen. ISBN 0-689-80882-8.

Themes *Hatchet* brings up issues including what is essential to human life, how people deal with painful secrets, people's relationship to nature, and how experiencing failure often leads to learning. The main character is a boy who is both admirable and believable; he responds to difficult and frightening situations in ways that make sense to young readers. Thus, the book provides sufficient material for students to discuss, debate, form opinions, change their minds, and make connections to other ideas. The theme of survival in *Hatchet* raises profound questions that are relevant to students' study of science and nature as well as to their reading of other literature. By drawing students' attention to universal themes like these, they will learn to make intertextual links and relate what they learn in school to the real world.

Special Classroom Library Your special classroom library for *Hatchet* might include the two sequels that Gary Paulsen has written. In *The River* (Dell, 1993), a survival expert is interested in learning how Brian survived in the wilderness, so Brian takes him back to the place by raft. The adventure turns into another survival story when the man is hit by lightning and Brian has to get him back for medical attention. The other sequel, called *Brian's Winter* (Bantam Doubleday Dell, 1996), pursues a different ending for *Hatchet,* telling what would have happened if Brian hadn't been rescued by the airplane and had to survive through the winter.

Other books on the theme of survival include: *Jayhawker* by Patricia Beatty (William Morrow, 1991), *The Incredible Journey* by Sheila Burnford (Bantam Doubleday Dell, 1996), *The Lake* by John P. Cooke (Avon Books, 1989), *Monkey Island* by Paula Fox (Orchard Books, 1991), *Julie of the Wolves* by Jean Craighead George (HarperCollins, 1996), *The Mangrove Summer* by Jack Lasenby (Oxford University Press, 1988), *Island of the Blue Dolphins* by Scott O'Dell (Dell, 1994), *The Voyage of the Frog* by Gary Paulsen (Orchard Books, 1989), and *Maniac Magee* by Jerry Spinelli (HarperTrophy, 1990). Any of these could be used for read aloud, for the special classroom library, or for book clubs.

Lesson 1

Comprehension:
Elements of Survival

GOAL:
To draw upon students' prior knowledge and build background for reading the novel

ASSIGNED READING:
Chapter 1
(pages 1–12)

- *Hatchet* is the story of a boy who finds himself in a very unusual situation, and the only thing that can save his life is the knowledge he already has. The story is realistic and believable because Brian uses knowledge that most thirteen-year-olds would actually have. You could introduce the book to students by sharing this insight with them. Then tell them that readers also draw upon prior knowledge to understand a new book. Since they are about to read a survival story, they will begin with a class discussion of what they already know about survival.

WRITING PROMPT:
Describe what happens
to the pilot and Brian's
reaction.

- On chart paper, make a chart with four sections. Label the sections as follows: tropical island, large city, Canadian wilderness, and desert.

- Have students work in cooperative groups to list what they would need to survive in each of these very different environments. They could be given the following prompt: If you were left all alone in this place, what would you need to survive? Suggest that students first list basic human needs in any environment—such as water, food, shelter, and so on—and then talk about how they could find or create these things in each place.

- As a class, choose the most important elements of survival for each of these four locations. Discuss the difference between "wants" and "needs." Prioritize the most important items in all areas, and record them in the chart. Be sure to save this chart for future reference (See Lesson 18, page 180).

- Focus on the Canadian wilderness and discuss in more depth what one would need to survive. Use this as an opportunity to bring out what students already know about survival and the Canadian wilderness before they begin reading the book.

- In community share, after students have read and discussed Chapter 1, you might ask students to share their responses to the writing prompt. Ask them what Brian's immediate survival needs are, now that the pilot is unconscious and the plane is still in the air.

Lesson 2

GOAL:
To introduce students to a
new format for written
responses, the share sheet

ASSIGNED READING:
Chapter 2
(pages 13–25)

WRITING PROMPT:
Brian has to make a
decision about landing the
plane. What do you think
he will do? Why?

Response to Literature:
Use of Share Sheets

- NOTE: This lesson assumes that students have been doing Book Club for a while and have built up a repertoire of different response types that they feel comfortable using. See the discussion of share sheets in the Teaching Tips chapter, page 39, for more about when and why you might want to introduce share sheets. If you decide to introduce this reading log option to your class, proceed with the following lesson.

- Tell the children that they've become very good at responding to literature, and that many of them are writing three or four entries in their logs every day. Because of this, you're going to introduce a new format

continued on next page

continued from previous page

for the response log that will make it easier to organize and share their responses. It's called a share sheet.

- Explain that a share sheet allows students to record several different responses to the same reading assignment on one log page. This way, during book club discussions or community share, they won't have to keep flipping through their logs to find the ideas they've written in separate entries—all the ideas will be on a single page.

- On the chalkboard or on chart paper, model how a share sheet might look. A teacher model is provided below.

Teacher Model of a Share Sheet

Intertextuality
This book reminds me of another book I read called <u>My Side of the Mountain.</u> That book has a boy character who has to survive on his own too.

Prediction
I think it will be a good book. I think Brian will have to survive in the wilderness with only his hatchet, and he will hunt and fish to live.

Chapter 1
January 10

Favorite Part
My favorite part was when the pilot died. That was really gross. I liked it because it was exciting and had action.

Questions for Group
What do you think Brian will do about the dead pilot?

Do you think Brian is going to make it?

Would you be scared sitting next to a dead guy?

- Ask children to practice the share sheet format when they make their responses today. To remind them of the response types they have to choose from, you can refer students to a Response Choice Sheet ("What can I do in my reading log?"). Examples are contained in the Blackline Masters: Think Sheets section following page 261. You should also point out that responding to today's writing prompt can fill one of the "spokes" on their share sheets.

GOAL:
To remind students of the different ways they have learned to respond to literature, and to provide them with response choice sheets that will help them to create rich and varied share sheets

ASSIGNED READING:
Chapter 3
(pages 26–30)

WRITING PROMPT:
Describe the plane crash.

Response to Literature: Use of Response Choice Sheets

- NOTE: This lesson assumes that students received a first Response Choice Sheet earlier in the year—perhaps in October or November. This sheet would probably describe about six to ten response choices. Samples are provided in the Blackline Masters: Think Sheets section following page 261, including a blank form that you can use to design your own choice sheet depending on the specific response types you want to teach. Teachers in lower grades have made sheets that offer only five choices at a time; others pick and choose which response types are appropriate for their class.

- Response Choice Sheets serve to remind students of all the different ways they can respond to their reading. Book Club teachers have found that students can fall into the habit of repeating one type of response— such as summarizing—if there is no mechanism to remind them to vary their responses. As the year goes on and students learn more and more response types, you should keep up with this progress by introducing new Response Choice Sheets.

- Ask children to look at the Response Choice Sheet they've been using so far this year. Ask them if they have responded in ways other than those listed on the sheet. Write the response types they mention on chart paper or the chalkboard. Encourage or prompt them to remember all the ones you've taught, and to include any that they've made up themselves.

- Pass out a new Response Choice Sheet and make sure all students know how to write each kind of response. Answer questions as necessary. Tell children that when they are stuck for a way to respond, they should remember to look at both Response Choice Sheets for suggestions.

- During community share, after students have read and discussed Chapter 3, you might ask students to share their log entries to show how they used their Response Choice Sheets to create good share sheets. Which response types were used by many students, and which were used by only a few or none of the students? How many students chose to respond to the writing prompt? Does the writing prompt coincide with any of the other response types?

Lesson 4

GOAL:
To use the author's details to draw conclusions about the story that are not specifically stated in the text

ASSIGNED READING:
Chapter 4
(pages 31–42)

WRITING PROMPT:
How is "the divorce" affecting Brian? What makes you think this?

Comprehension:
Drawing Conclusions

- Since the purpose of this lesson is to teach or review the process of drawing conclusions from a text, it should take place after students have read Chapter 4, written in their logs, and discussed the reading with their book club groups.

- Refresh students' memories by reading the first section of Chapter 4 (pages 31–32) aloud to the class. Ask students to draw some conclusions about what Brian is remembering about his mother.

- Brainstorm a list of possibilities, and write students' suggestions on the chalkboard or chart paper.

- Discuss the choppy style of text used by the author in this section, and help students draw conclusions about why it is written in this style. You might guide students with questions like the following.

  – What emotions do you think Brian was feeling when he saw his mother in the station wagon?

  – What kind of mood does the choppy writing create? How do you feel when you hear this passage or read it yourself?

  – How does the mood created by the writing help you to draw conclusions about what Brian saw that day?

  – Does the description of Brian's memory seem realistic? Do you have any memories that include small, vivid details such as the time shown on a clock or the wheel of your bicycle spinning in front of you?

- Students who responded to the writing prompt in their logs might discuss with the class any conclusions they needed to draw in order to answer the question.

Lesson 5

GOAL:
To help students focus on positive and negative behaviors for small-group discussion, and to identify some goals they can work toward to improve their book club participation

ASSIGNED READING:
Chapter 5
(pages 43–55)

WRITING PROMPT:
Describe Brian's injuries. How are they affecting him?

- Depending on where you are in the school year and how you feel your students are doing in their small groups, you may want to conduct a lesson about what makes a good book club group. This will serve to remind students of what they already know about good book club behaviors, and give them an opportunity to assess whether their groups are living up to these guidelines.

- On the chalkboard or on chart paper, make a two-column chart with the headings "Qualities of a good group" and "Qualities to avoid in groups." Ask the students to brainstorm ideas for the chart. A sample chart is provided below.

Qualities of a good group	Qualities to avoid in groups
everyone talks	only one or two people talk
talk stays on the topic	talk strays from topic
members are polite to each other	members are rude to each other
members ask lots of questions	no one asks questions
members respond to each other's ideas	members ignore each other's comments
voices stay at conversational level	voices become loud

- Have students identify three areas they want to improve and write these goals in their logs. You can refer back to these goals during future lessons, prompting students to discuss how their goals have changed and to adjust the goals accordingly. In Lesson 7 (page 170), students will learn how to use a Book Club Self-Assessment sheet to record goals for future reference.

- Another option for this lesson is to have students role play some of the positive and negative behaviors they have mentioned in the chart. The class can then critique the role plays and offer suggestions to improve the interactions.

Lesson 6

GOAL:
To check comprehension of the story so far, and to review the strategy of summarizing

ASSIGNED READING:
Chapter 6
(pages 56–66)

WRITING PROMPT:
The mosquitoes have attacked Brian twice now. Offer suggestions for solving this problem.

Comprehension:
Summarizing

- Before you begin this lesson, you might want to point out to students that summarizing what they have read—either in their minds or on paper—is a good strategy for checking their own understanding of a story. It can be used as a quick self-assessment while they are reading *Hatchet* or any other text.

- After students have read Chapter 6 and written in their logs, have them work in their groups to list the five most important events in the chapter.

- As a class, decide on the five most important events, distinguishing between big events and small details.

- Have a discussion about why summaries are important and when they are helpful. Some of the points that have come up in our classrooms are that summaries help in understanding the story, help when retelling the story, and help students' own writing to be more concise.

- Model for the class the writing of a summary, using the overhead projector and thinking aloud as you write.

- As the last part of community share, you might ask students to share what they wrote in their reading logs today. Since book clubs were used for practice in summarizing, the students may have some questions and issues about Chapter 6 that they'd like to discuss with the class before moving on to the next chapter.

Lesson 7

GOAL:
For students to learn or review how to use a self-assessment sheet to assess their own performance in book club groups and set goals for improvement

Language Conventions:
Use of a Self-Assessment Sheet

- Self-assessment is an essential part of any learning process. You might discuss with your students why it is important to assess one's own progress while learning to do something new, such as participate in a book discussion. You might also explain that setting goals helps to provide "markers" of progress along the way: Each time a person stops to self-assess, he or she can ask, "Have I met the goal I set for myself last time?"

ASSIGNED READING:
Chapter 7
(pages 67–78)

WRITING PROMPT:
What did Brian learn
from his encounter with
the bear?

- Ask students to recall the list they created in Lesson 5 of positive and negative book club behaviors. Then introduce the Book Club Self-Assessment sheet (or a similar sheet of your own design), available in the Blackline Masters: Assessment section following page 281. Read the three questions with your students, and explain your expectations for completing the sheet. We suggest the following guidelines: they should do it immediately after the group conversations (before community share); they should use the chart for reminders of good group behaviors; and they should be very honest.

- After the reading, writing, and book club groups, remind students once more of your expectations regarding the self-assessment sheet. Allow them several minutes to complete the self-assessment, and then collect the sheets.

- NOTE: These self-assessment sheets can be used as a dialogue between teacher and student. As you read through the sheets later in the day, you can write comments and words of encouragement, and you can motivate the children to achieve the personal goals they have recorded. In our classrooms, this has worked well to shape students' view of a good group and to help them participate appropriately. See page 34 for an example of a student-teacher dialogue on a self-assessment sheet.

- During community share, encourage students to discuss how their book club conversations went today. Ask them what they talked about (including their responses to the writing prompt) and how well they met the guidelines for positive book club behaviors.

Lesson 8

Language Conventions:
Qualities of a Good Share Sheet

GOAL:
To help students discuss
examples of good share
sheets

ASSIGNED READING:
Chapter 8
(pages 79–86)

WRITING PROMPT:
Free choice

- This lesson plan assumes that you have decided to use share sheets with your class. Analyzing good share sheets will give students who may still be struggling with the format some concrete examples of what you expect from them.

- Select a few examples of good share sheets that students have done previously. Project these on an overhead projector and discuss with the class what makes them good examples. Be sure to select a variety of

continued on next page

continued from previous page

styles so the children will understand that there are many acceptable ways to approach share sheets.

- It's a good idea to set some guidelines regarding the amount of writing you expect students to do in their logs each day. You might specify, for example, that you expect children to choose three different response types for each daily share sheet entry. As part of your discussion of good share sheets, remind students of your quantitative expectations for log entries.

- You may want to discuss with students the meaning of a "free choice" for writing in their journals. This means that there is no set writing prompt for the day; they can write about whatever strikes them in the assigned reading. For example, they might develop a list of questions about important things that happen in Chapter 8. Then they could write their own responses to these questions in their journals, or save some questions for their book club discussions. Also remind them to refer to their response choice sheets (see Lesson 3, page 167) for ideas about what to write in their journals.

Lesson 9

GOAL:
To encourage students to look for interesting vocabulary by creating a word wall for the story

ASSIGNED READING:
Chapter 9
(pages 87–93)

WRITING PROMPT:
- How do you think Brian's life will change now that he has fire? Why?
- Choose some interesting words from today's reading to add to your vocabulary sheet.

Comprehension:
Vocabulary—Word Wall

- NOTE: This lesson assumes that students have been using vocabulary think sheets to record interesting or unknown words from their reading. (A sample is provided in the Blackline Masters: Think Sheets section following page 261. Students should begin a new vocabulary sheet for each book.) In this lesson, you'll introduce the "word wall" as a space where the whole class can record the most interesting words from their individual lists. For a detailed description of word walls, see Lesson 9 for *Last Summer with Maizon*, page 73.

- Prepare a large sheet of chart paper on a wall or board in your room, labeled with the title of the book and the author's name. Tell students that this space will be the class's word wall for *Hatchet*.

- Ask children to take out their vocabulary sheets and share some of the words they've identified during the story. Place them on the chart paper, modeling the format of date/word/page number (as it is on the students' vocabulary sheets). Talk about the words and determine their meanings, using either context clues, someone else who knows, or a dictionary. Include the meanings on the chart.

- Tell children you will be adding interesting vocabulary words to the word wall chart periodically throughout the story. Remind them that if they encounter one of these words in their reading, they can look up at the chart to check its meaning.

Lesson 10

GOAL:
To model intertextual connections, and to improve comparison and contrast vocabulary

ASSIGNED READING:
Chapter 10
(pages 94–102)

WRITING PROMPT:
Compare/contrast *Hatchet* with another survival story.

Comprehension:
Intertextuality

- If students are not already familiar with the term *intertextuality*, explain that it refers to finding things that are similar and different between two or more texts. You might also discuss why making intertextual links is important and how it enriches a reader's experience of a book.

- If you're using *Hatchet* in a themed unit with other survival books such as *Island of the Blue Dolphins* (O'Dell, 1960) or *Maniac Magee* (Spinelli, 1990), or if you are using a thematically related read-aloud book, model making intertextual connections with one of these. You could also choose a picture book to read aloud for the purpose of making inter-textual connections related to survival. Use a Venn diagram to record similarities and differences between *Hatchet* and another survival book. Below are sample Venn diagrams for comparing and contrasting two or three books.

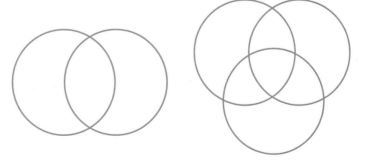

- You might discuss the vocabulary used to compare and contrast. If needed, focus on elements of the story—such as setting, characterization, theme, plot, climax, and conflict—as reference points for making the intertextual connections.

continued on next page

continued from previous page

- After students have completed their reading, writing, and book club discussions, you might focus community share on the comparing and contrasting students did in their reading logs. What elements of *Hatchet* did students compare and contrast with other texts? Did any of them compare and contrast *Hatchet* with a movie or television program? Did they create any new formats, besides the Venn diagram, for comparing and contrasting?

Lesson 11

GOAL:
To analyze how an author shows changes in a character over time

ASSIGNED READING:
Chapter 11
(pages 103–109)

WRITING PROMPT:
Focus on how Brian is changing.

Literary Elements: Character Development

- You might begin this lesson by asking students whether they think characters are more interesting if they stay the same throughout a story or if they change over time. Which kind of character would be more realistic? Explain that authors have ways of showing that characters are changing and growing, and that good readers are alert to these changes.

- As a class, discuss ways in which people change over time. You can prompt students by asking them how they are different today than they were two years ago, and how they expect to be different two years from now. Point out that changes can be grouped in categories like physical changes and psychological changes.

- Share with students the chart shown on page 175. Tell students that it is one example of a chart that can show how a character is changing over time. The first section of the chart might contain words and phrases, including brief quotes from the book, that describe Brian's frame of mind in the beginning of the story. The first overlapping area could be filled with descriptions of the events that change how Brian sees life. The middle section could then describe Brian after these events, and so on. You might choose to complete a chart like this in community share, or you might have students create charts individually, in pairs, or with their book club groups.

- After you have introduced the chart, students are ready to read today's assignment, write in their logs, and hold book club discussions. Encourage them to respond to the writing prompt as one of their share sheet "spokes." After book clubs, focus community share on the idea of character development and how Gary Paulsen shows that Brian is changing. If students created charts in their reading logs, ask them to share their work and compare the insights each student or small group had about the changes in Brian.

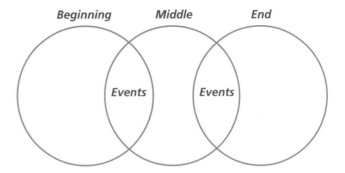

Lesson 12

GOAL:
To help students understand that good readers "picture" or visualize the story in their minds, and to give them practice in using this strategy

ASSIGNED READING:
Chapter 12
(pages 110–118)

WRITING PROMPT:
- Discuss the signal fire, the chance for rescue, and Brian's devastation when he misses that chance.
- Draw a picture of another scene from Chapter 12.

Comprehension:
Visualizing

- Visualizing is an important skill for all readers. Reading requires the active use of one's imagination, and creating mental images of what is being described in a text is crucial to understanding the text. You might tell students that visualizing not only increases their enjoyment of reading, but also serves as a comprehension check. If they aren't able to visualize a scene in a book, they should stop to reread the scene until it becomes clear in their minds.

- Before students begin their independent reading of Chapter 12, read aloud the description of Brian fishing with a spear (pages 110–112). Then reread the section while students draw their interpretations of the scene.

- Discuss students' drawings, pointing out similarities and differences. Remember to stress that the differences are good, and that these differences reflect the different background knowledge that each reader brings to a story. Discuss how the different visualizations add to the diversity of book club discussions. Display the drawings in the classroom.

- Remind students to continue visualizing the action as they read Chapter 12. Later, in community share, you might ask students to share and discuss any pictures they drew in their reading logs.

Lesson 13

GOAL:
To focus students on the setting of the story, and to help them understand its impact on the development of the story itself

ASSIGNED READING:
Chapter 13
(pages 119–127)

WRITING PROMPT:
Discuss the setting of this chapter. What clues does the author provide to help you understand the passing of time?

Literary Elements:
Setting

• Review with students the importance of understanding setting in a story. Ask them what is the setting of *Hatchet*. Focus on both place and time.

• Ask students how long Brian has been stranded. How do we know? What clues does the author give us? Ask students to predict how long he will be stranded.

• Create tension for reading Chapter 13 by telling students that something in the setting will change in this chapter. Ask them to focus on that change in their responses today.

• After students have completed the reading, writing, and book club portions of today's lesson, bring the class together for community share and ask students to describe what change occurred in the setting in Chapter 13. Why do they think Gary Paulsen showed the passage of time in this way—why did he not continue to describe each day of Brian's life, as in the first twelve chapters?

• At this point, you might also want to ask students to refer back to their Book Club Self-Assessment sheets. Ask them to think about how well they are accomplishing the goals they set for themselves earlier.

Lesson 14

GOAL:
To review the journal entry "Me & the Book," and to focus students on the importance of affective responses and connecting the book to their lives

ASSIGNED READING:
Chapter 14
(pages 128–136)

Response to Literature:
Affective Responses (Me & the Book)

• Before students read this chapter, review the entry "Me & the Book," which is described on the Response Choice Sheets in the Blackline Masters: Think Sheets section following page 261. Ask students to find something in Chapter 14 that they can relate to their own lives. (The idea of mistakes comes up repeatedly in this chapter.)

• During writing time, place a prompt on the board or overhead that focuses on relating the book to their lives. (The writing prompt on page 177 is one example.)

• During community share, focus the discussion on the connections stu-

WRITING PROMPT:

Mistakes. Brian has made a lot of them. How does he use his mistakes to learn? What has he learned? Are you like this?

dents described in their logs and book club discussions, emphasizing that the book will become much more meaningful if they relate it to their lives. In particular, you can ask students to share stories from their own lives in which they made mistakes and learned from them. You might have students explain the adage "Experience is the best teacher," relate it to Brian's experiences and their own, and tell whether they think it is true.

- To extend the discussion, students could compare and contrast the knowledge Brian has from past reading (which helps him but is usually vague and partial) with the knowledge he gains during his survival experience (which is vivid and immediately relevant to his life). Ask them whether they think they know enough from books they have already read to survive in the wilderness as Brian does.

Lesson 15

GOAL:
To provide a visual strategy for students to use when learning a new concept or vocabulary word

ASSIGNED READING:
Chapter 15
(pages 137–146)

WRITING PROMPT:
Describe the impact the skunk had on Brian and his life.

Comprehension:
Vocabulary—Concept Web

- Remind students that they have been learning a lot of new words while reading *Hatchet*. Their vocabulary think sheets and the word wall chart are two tools they are using to learn these new words. Today the class will look at another way to understand a concept more fully and thus understand the story better—a concept web.

- Begin a concept web on the chalkboard or on chart paper with the word *skunk* in the middle. Have children brainstorm and share ideas they have about a skunk. Ideas that aren't shared by everyone can be identified by either a different color marker, underlining, or a question mark.

- Tell students that they can make webs of some of the interesting vocabulary words they identify in the stories they read, and they can include these webs in their response choices.

- Tell them that you selected *skunk* for a special reason. They will need that knowledge to understand today's reading assignment. After students have read Chapter 15, written in their logs, and met in their book clubs, you can initiate a community share discussion about how the concept web helped them understand the scene with the skunk.

Lesson 16

GOAL:
To help students see all the possibilities for share sheets

ASSIGNED READING:
Chapter 16
(pages 147–160)

WRITING PROMPT:
Describe the tornado and the changes it caused.

Response to Literature:
Share Sheet Options

- Ask students to brainstorm all the different types of responses they can include on share sheets. On chart paper, make a list of all the possible spokes for share sheets that they mention.

- Be sure to ask students to share some of the original response types that they've developed. Students who have come up with their own ideas for log entries can explain to their classmates how they work and why they're helpful during book club discussions. (You might post examples of these original response formats in a special place in the classroom, or distribute a Response Choice Sheet with these new response formats listed.)

- Increase your expectation for writing—for example, to four response types per student per day, or more detailed and better quality responses. Remind students that they should not pre-select what types of responses they will do on a given day. Instead, it should be free choice based on what they read and feel each day.

Lesson 17

GOAL:
To help students use sequencing as a strategy for checking their comprehension of a story

ASSIGNED READING:
Chapter 17
(pages 161–172)

WRITING PROMPT:
- If you were Brian, would you try to get the survival pack out of the plane? Why or why not? If so, how would you do it?
- Create a sequence of story events using one of the formats we discussed.

Comprehension:
Sequencing

- Depending on how much sequencing you have done already this year, you can use this lesson to introduce the skill or to review it. Sequencing is one of the response types listed on the Response Choice Sheets in the Blackline Masters: Think Sheets section following page 261.

- Refer to an experience that the entire class has shared. It might be a picture book, novel, poem, movie, field trip, or the daily class routine. The current read-aloud book often provides a good example.

- Ask the class to generate a list of four or five big events from the experience. Help the class to distinguish between a big event and a small detail.

- Ask the class to arrange the events in the order in which they happened. Tell students that this is called a sequence of events. The sequence shows the order in which events occurred.

- Discuss why sequencing is important. Guide students to see that it helps them to understand a story, it helps them to write their own stories, and it is useful for retelling or discussing a story.

- Have students generate several ways to visually represent their sequences in their logs, adding ones that you feel are important. (Several formats are suggested below.)

- Ask students to practice sequencing by creating a sequence of story events in their response logs today.

1.	2.	3.
4.	5.	6.

1. _____
2. _____
3. _____
4. _____
5. _____
6. _____

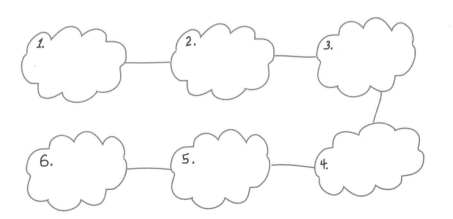

Lesson 18

GOAL:
To review what students have learned, along with Brian, about survival

ASSIGNED READING:
Chapter 18
(pages 173–183)

WRITING PROMPT:
Predict the ending of the story.

Comprehension:
Elements of Survival, Revisited

- Remind students of the chart they made about survival in various environments (Lesson 1, page 164). Ask them to review what they wrote in the section for the Canadian wilderness, and to review any relevant notes they may have taken in their logs.

- Have students discuss whether the chart they made earlier was complete and/or accurate. Did they leave out any items that Brian found he needed to survive? Did they include any items that they believed were essential but that Brian managed to do without? Students can revise the chart as appropriate.

- In Chapter 18, Brian finally rescues the survival pack from the plane. Have students predict what Brian will find in the pack. Then ask students to use what they have learned from Brian's adventure to plan their own survival packs. What objects would they include in the pack, and what information or instructions? What extra things might they include to satisfy a few simple "wants"?

- After students have completed their reading, writing, and book club discussions, initiate a community share discussion of students' predictions about the ending of the story. Did the students have good discussions about their predictions in their small groups? What were some of the most interesting or controversial predictions? As a class, what do they think is the most likely outcome of the story? NOTE: You will return to this discussion of students' predictions in tomorrow's lesson and talk about using story grammar to predict how a story will end.

Lesson 19

GOAL:
To encourage students to use their prediction skills to help them understand the story

Comprehension:
Predicting

- Predicting what will happen next in a story, and how the story might end, provides an opportunity for readers to check how well they are understanding the story. If a reader has identified the story's main conflict, he or she will probably have some ideas about how the conflict will be resolved.

ASSIGNED READING:
Chapter 19
(pages 184–191)

WRITING PROMPT:

- On page 187 the text says that the survival pack "gave him up and down feelings." What do you think this means?

- Did your predictions about the end of the story come true? What, if anything, surprised you about the ending?

- You might begin this lesson by asking students what major conflict or problem Brian has been facing throughout the story. Then ask them to share their predictions about how the story might end from yesterday's lesson. You can guide the discussion with questions such as *Where are we in the story currently? What do we know about story grammar that will help us to predict the ending? What clues is the author giving us?* You might also suggest that students think about other survival stories they know to help them predict how *Hatchet* might end.

- Brainstorm a list of possible endings, or parts of the ending. Have the class discuss and critique each idea presented.

- Remind students to think about these predictions as they read and respond to the end of the book.

Lesson 20

GOAL:
To think about the author's purpose for writing an epilogue, and to use that to interpret the meaning of the story

ASSIGNED READING:
Epilogue
(pages 192–195)

WRITING PROMPT:

- How has Brian's life been changed permanently by this experience?

- What did the epilogue tell you, if anything, about Paulsen's purpose for writing this book?

Literary Elements:
Author's Purpose

- Remind students that authors usually have a purpose for writing stories. Have them think back to some of the other books they've read this year. For example, why did Scott O'Dell write *Sing Down the Moon* or Avi *The Fighting Ground*? Then ask them why they think Gary Paulsen wrote *Hatchet*. Gather several responses.

- Ask students: How did other authors we've read help us to understand their purposes? (Students may mention devices such as an epilogue, an afterword, a preface, an author's note, etc.) As they are reading Paulsen's epilogue today, ask them to consider his purpose for telling us this story.

- After students have read the epilogue, written in their logs, and talked with their book club groups, return to the class discussion of author's purpose. You might begin a list on the chalkboard or on chart paper of students' various ideas about Paulsen's purpose. Did talking about the author's purpose in their small groups help students to form clear ideas about it?

- To wrap up this community share discussion, you may want to remind students that an author's purpose for writing a story is almost never cut and dry. It's important to think about the author's purpose, but that

continued on next page

continued from previous page

purpose can't always be boiled down into a simple statement. And since each person who reads a story brings his or her own background experience and personal responses to it, a story can serve a different purpose for each reader—even some purposes the author didn't intend. You can use this opportunity to emphasize the value of each individual's response to a story.

Lesson 21

GOAL:
To discuss ideas for a sequel to *Hatchet*, and to motivate students to read Paulsen's actual sequels, *The River* and *Brian's Winter*

ASSIGNED READING:
None

WRITING PROMPT:
Choose one of the following to answer in a full page.
- Why do you think this book is called *Hatchet*?
- Rewrite the ending as if the plane had not come and Brian had had to live through the winter.
- Pretend you are Brian in fifty years. What story might he tell his grandchildren about his survival in the wilderness?

Response to Literature: Developing Ideas for Sequels

- Sometimes a reader may finish a book with a strong desire to know more about what was described in the text. This may be a result of especially intriguing characters or situations, or it may show that the reader feels frustrated over not fully understanding the book. By asking students to describe what they'd like to see in a sequel to *Hatchet*, you can gain some insight into how much the book engaged them and how well they understood it.

- Students can begin today's Book Club time by responding to the writing prompts in their logs. Then, when students are ready to meet with their book clubs, give them the following discussion prompt: If you were Gary Paulsen and you were interested in writing another book about Brian, what would be some possible story lines that you could choose? Book club groups can each make a brainstorm list as they talk. Have each group try to narrow their ideas to a single story line.

- Record the groups' best story lines on a class chart and have the groups order them from most interesting to least interesting. From this discussion, you can learn a great deal about what the students did and did not understand about the book, and which ideas and issues were left unresolved.

- As an extension activity, you could encourage students to use their process writing time to rewrite Chapter 19, or add a Chapter 20, so that the book ends in the way they would like. Introduce the two sequels that already exist: *The River* and *Brian's Winter.* These are possible choices for future book clubs, or they could be read-aloud selections or special classroom library titles.

Lesson 22

GOAL:
To think about questioning and the reasons for asking questions, and to focus on letter writing

ASSIGNED READING:
None

WRITING PROMPT:
Generate questions you would like to ask Gary Paulsen. Write a letter to him incorporating these questions.

Response to Literature: Questioning; Letter Writing

- Review with students the kinds of questions we ask in Book Club (i.e., ones that require an answer that is not limited to one word, *yes* or *no*, or a numerical answer; ones that we truly don't understand or want to know about). Then review the purposes for asking questions, such as clarifying, understanding, and encouraging discussion or response.

- Tell students that they will be putting these ideas into an authentic situation today as they form questions that they can ask Gary Paulsen in a friendly letter.

- NOTE: You may want to include a lesson on the parts of a friendly letter, and model how to write one.

Lesson 23

GOAL:
To compare and contrast book and movie versions of the same story

ASSIGNMENT:
View the movie *A Cry in the Wild,* based on the book *Hatchet.*

WRITING PROMPT:
Compare/contrast the book and the movie.

Comprehension: Compare and Contrast

- Before they watch the movie, ask students what is different about watching a story told in a movie as opposed to reading a story.

- Review the use of Venn diagrams to compare and contrast two or more things. Suggest that as they watch the movie, they look for things that are similar and different between it and the book *Hatchet.* They may take notes in a Venn diagram while they view the film. Some examples of student share sheets involving comparison and contrast appear on pages 184–185.

- After the movie, you may wish to have students meet in their book club groups to discuss how it was similar to and different from the book. Then have a community share with the whole class. Ask students to think about why certain things were different in the movie. (For example, the part about the moose was missing because you couldn't get a moose to act that way for the camera.)

- In community share, have students recall the purpose they identified for Paulsen's writing *Hatchet.* Ask them whether they think this purpose was accomplished as well, not as well, or better in the movie version.

continued on next page

continued from previous page

Student Example #1:
Venn Diagram Think Sheet

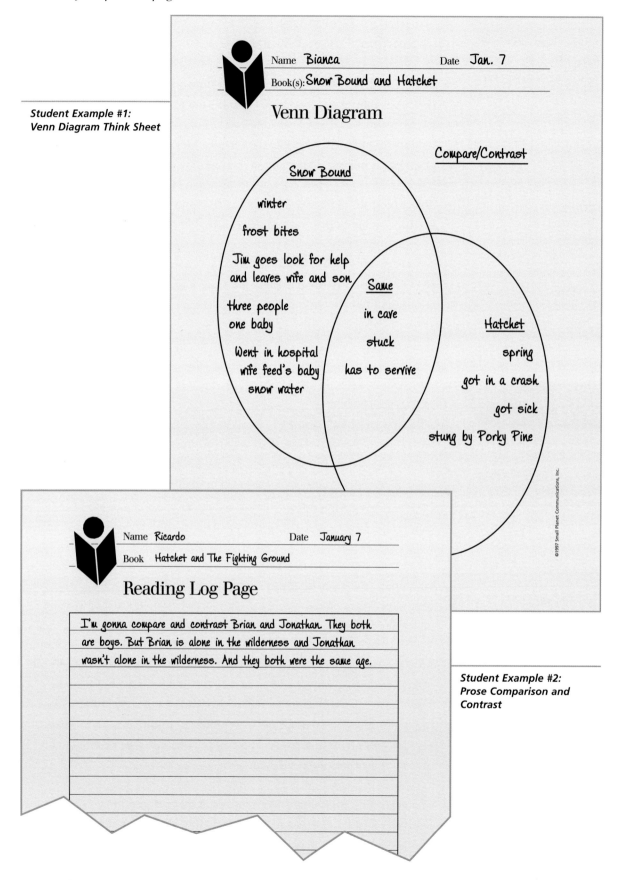

Name Bianca   Date Jan. 7

Book(s): Snow Bound and Hatchet

Venn Diagram

Compare/Contrast

Snow Bound

winter

frost bites

Jim goes look for help
and leaves wife and son

three people
one baby

Went in hospital
wife feed's baby
snow water

Same

in care

stuck

has to servive

Hatchet

spring

got in a crash

got sick

stung by Porky Pine

©1997 Small Planet Communications, Inc.

Name Ricardo   Date January 7

Book Hatchet and The Fighting Ground

Reading Log Page

I'm gonna compare and contrast Brian and Jonathan. They both
are boys. But Brian is alone in the wilderness and Jonathan
wasn't alone in the wilderness. And they both were the same age.

Student Example #2:
Prose Comparison and
Contrast

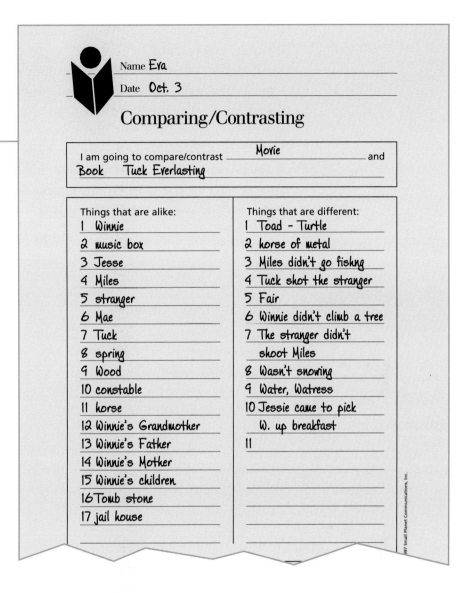

Student Example #3:
Comparing/Contrasting
Think Sheet

Name Eva

Date Oct. 3

Comparing/Contrasting

I am going to compare/contrast _____ Movie _____ and
Book   Tuck Everlasting

Things that are alike:	Things that are different:
1 Winnie	1 Toad - Turtle
2 music box	2 horse of metal
3 Jesse	3 Miles didn't go fishing
4 Miles	4 Tuck shot the stranger
5 stranger	5 Fair
6 Mae	6 Winnie didn't climb a tree
7 Tuck	7 The stranger didn't
8 spring	shoot Miles
9 Wood	8 Wasn't snowing
10 constable	9 Water, Watress
11 horse	10 Jessie came to pick
12 Winnie's Grandmother	W. up breakfast
13 Winnie's Father	11
14 Winnie's Mother	
15 Winnie's children	
16 Tomb stone	
17 jail house	

97 Small Planet Communications, Inc.

Lesson 24

GOAL:
For students to discuss what
they have learned about
survival and survival stories
from reading *Hatchet*, and
to write their own survival
stories

ASSIGNED READING:
None

Response to Literature:
Process Writing—An Original Survival Story

- Now that students have just finished reading and discussing a realistic survival story, it is a good time for them to try their hands at writing an original story in the same genre.

- Ask students to discuss what they liked and didn't like about the book *Hatchet.* You might prompt them with questions such as: Did the story make you feel excited? What parts were the most exciting? What did you learn from reading the story? Did the story make you want to read other survival stories?

continued on next page

continued from previous page

continued from previous page

WRITING PROMPT:
Begin a process writing project: create your own survival story.

- Have students recall their previous discussions about the elements of survival (Lessons 1 and 18, pages 164 and 180). They can refer to the charts and any other notes they created during these discussions. Have students work individually to brainstorm ideas for their own survival stories. Suggest that they first pick a setting for a story, and then think of a character or characters who must survive in that place.

- Students may choose to write survival stories during process writing time. Remind them that if they want to write realistic stories, they may have to do some research before they write.

Lesson 25 — Student Self-Assessment

GOAL:
For students to assess their own performance during the *Hatchet* unit

ASSIGNED READING:
None

WRITING PROMPT:
Fill out the self-assessment forms I've handed out.

- See Lesson 19 of *The Fighting Ground*, page 143, for a fully developed self-assessment lesson.

- Distribute copies of the End-of-Book Self-Assessment sheet, or a similar sheet of your own design. (A blackline master is available in the Blackline Masters: Assessment section following page 281.) Tell students what your expectations are regarding their completion of the sheet, and give them time to write thoughtful answers.

Lesson 26 — Teacher Evaluation

GOAL:
To inform students about the grades they've received for *Hatchet*, and to give them a chance to respond

ASSIGNED READING:
None

WRITING PROMPT:
Read over your grades and the comments I've written. Then fill out a Reactions and Goal-Setting sheet.

- See Lesson 20 of *The Fighting Ground*, page 144, for a fully developed teacher evaluation lesson.

- Distribute copies of your grades and any other comments. You can use the Book Club Evaluation forms in the Blackline Masters: Assessment section. Then allow students time to read your evaluation and to fill out a Reactions and Goal-Setting sheet, also available in the Blackline Masters: Assessment section. You can respond to students' comments as you're reading the Reactions form later on. An example of a student-teacher dialogue on a self-assessment sheet is provided on page 34.

Walk Two Moons
by Sharon Creech

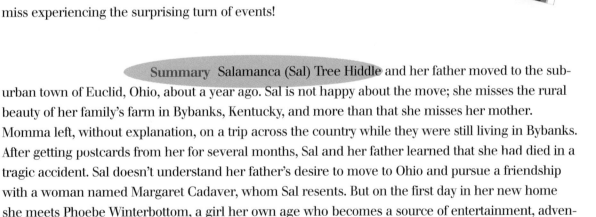

Introducing the Book

Walk Two Moons has become an instant favorite with the Book Club students who have read and discussed it. The teacher who developed this lesson plan found that her students were eager to read ahead and unravel the mysteries in the skillfully interwoven tales of two thirteen-year-old girls and their families. *Walk Two Moons* is author Sharon Creech's first novel for children, and it was awarded the Newbery Medal for 1995. It is most appropriate for grades five and six. NOTE: We recommend that you read the entire book *before* reading our summary (below). You won't want to miss experiencing the surprising turn of events!

Summary Salamanca (Sal) Tree Hiddle and her father moved to the suburban town of Euclid, Ohio, about a year ago. Sal is not happy about the move; she misses the rural beauty of her family's farm in Bybanks, Kentucky, and more than that she misses her mother. Momma left, without explanation, on a trip across the country while they were still living in Bybanks. After getting postcards from her for several months, Sal and her father learned that she had died in a tragic accident. Sal doesn't understand her father's desire to move to Ohio and pursue a friendship with a woman named Margaret Cadaver, whom Sal resents. But on the first day in her new home she meets Phoebe Winterbottom, a girl her own age who becomes a source of entertainment, adventure, annoyance, friendship—and ultimately healing.

When the novel begins, Sal has joined her grandparents on a six-day trip across the country—from Ohio to Idaho—on the same route Sal's mother took when she left Kentucky. To pass the time as they travel, Sal tells her grandparents about the previous year's outrageous adventures with Phoebe. At that point *Walk Two Moons* becomes two stories—Sal's journey with Gram and Gramps woven together with Phoebe's story, which is in itself a type of journey. Phoebe's unusual story begins with poetic messages left on her family's front steps and the appearance of a mysterious stranger. Then Phoebe's mother disappears. Despite the evidence that Mrs.

Paperback Edition, HarperTrophy, © 1994 by Sharon Creech. ISBN 0-06-440517-6.

Winterbottom left intentionally, Phoebe becomes convinced that her mother was kidnapped and enlists Sal's help in trying to crack the case. Phoebe's mother finally does return to reveal a surprising secret to her family—a son, born before her marriage to Mr. Winterbottom, whom she was forced to give up for adoption. This now teenage son turns out to be the mysterious stranger, solving just one of the many mysteries that have been obsessing Phoebe and Sal.

As Sal tells Phoebe's story, she finds it to be in part a reflection of her own story. Her journey with her grandparents leads her not only to unfamiliar states and beautiful national parks, but to a long-overdue realization that her own mother will never return to her. Sal visits the site of the accident that took her mother's life and begins to allow herself to heal. Although Sal will never know why her mother felt compelled to leave in the first place, she finds comfort in the fact that perhaps, like Phoebe's mother, she had a very good reason and would eventually have returned if the accident had not happened. *Walk Two Moons*, a beautifully written novel that examines human relationships, manages to be all at once sad, warm, and humorous.

Themes *Walk Two Moons* is an exploration of how an intelligent, sensitive child sorts out her feelings after the loss of a beloved parent. It is a journey through shock, pain, denial, and finally acceptance. The book is also about family and the complex web of emotions—both positive and negative—that ties families together. Sal's relationship with her eccentric, loving grandparents provides sweetness and humor to counterbalance the painful and confusing experiences she's had to endure. The themes you may want to explore with your class while reading this book include loss or death, family, journeys, and friendship.

Special Classroom Library Sharon Creech has written three other books for children that students may want to explore during or after they read *Walk Two Moons*. *Absolutely Normal Chaos* (HarperCollins, 1995) is a companion novel to *Walk Two Moons* centered around the character Mary Lou Finney. *Pleasing the Ghost* (HarperCollins, 1996) is about a nine-year-old boy whose father and uncle have died and who keeps encountering "ghosts" in his bedroom. These ghosts are a lively and interesting cast of characters who help him deal with his loss in unexpected ways. *Chasing Redbird* (HarperCollins, 1997) is about a thirteen-year-old girl who uncovers family secrets while clearing a mysterious old trail leading from her family's farm in Kentucky. Other books that deal with the themes of loss, families, and journeys are listed below.

Title	Author	Publisher, Date
Bridge to Terabithia	Katherine Paterson	HarperTrophy, 1977
Racing the Sun	Paul Pitts	Avon Books, 1988
Missing May	Cynthia Rylant	Dell Publishing Co., 1993

Lesson 1

GOAL:
To introduce *Walk Two Moons* as a story within a story and to have students explore the word *journey* through a class concept web

ASSIGNED READING:
Chapters 1–2
(pages 1–9)

WRITING PROMPT:
- Write about the layering of stories in *Walk Two Moons*. What two stories are you going to be told as you read? How does the author introduce these two stories? Why might the author want to put these two stories together in one novel?
- Begin a character chart to keep track of the book's many characters, their relationships to one another, and where they live. What are your first impressions of some of the characters?

Literary Elements:
Author's Craft—Story Structure

- Giving students information about the structure of *Walk Two Moons* before they begin reading will pique their interest and keep them from becoming confused in the book's opening chapters. Creating a class concept web will get students thinking about types of journeys, both literal and figurative, and prepare them for the journeys featured in the novel.

- Explain to students that *Walk Two Moons* actually tells two stories about two different families. You might tell them that Sal, the narrator, shares the personal journey of her friend Phoebe while Sal and her grandparents are making a special journey of their own. You might ask students if they have ever read a story or seen a movie that had a story-within-a-story format. If so, ask them to explain how the stories were structured. How were the two different stories introduced? In what ways were the two stories related?

- Create a class concept web around the word *journey*. Ask students to brainstorm and share ideas they have about different types of journeys and the feelings they associate with journeys, such as fear, anticipation, or excitement. They should be able to come up with ideas related to literal journeys, but they should also understand that a journey can be a passage through any challenging experience.

- Tell students that understanding the word *journey* and keeping in mind that *Walk Two Moons* is about journeys will help them as they read.

Lesson 2

GOAL:
To review with students the elements of a good book club discussion

ASSIGNED READING:
Chapters 3–4
(pages 10–24)

Language Conventions:
Elements of a Good Book Club Discussion

- It is important to ask students to name, based on their past experiences with Book Club, the attributes of a quality student-led discussion. They will benefit from having this information fresh in their minds as they begin discussing *Walk Two Moons*.

- Brainstorm with students a list of the qualities of a good book club discussion. List student responses where everyone can see them, on the chalkboard or using an overhead projector. (For a list of suggested

continued on next page

continued from previous page

WRITING PROMPT:
What things frighten you? Do you consider yourself to be a brave person? Describe a situation in which you or someone you know did something brave. How does this situation compare to Sal's handling of the spider in her class?

guidelines for good book club discussions, see Lesson 5 for *Hatchet*, page 169, and the Teaching Tips chapter, pages 37–38.) You might also ask students to share some of their favorite book club experiences.

- After students meet in their book club groups on this day, ask them to self-assess their discussion. (See student samples on page 191.) They can do this by writing in their reading logs or by using the Book Club Self-Assessment sheet provided in the Blackline Masters: Assessment section following page 281. Students can share their ideas when the class meets for community share. You can informally and regularly assess the functioning of your class's book clubs by walking through the class and listening in on discussions.

Teaching Tip

To provide students with a way to manage what they are learning about characters and relationships in the novel, you may want to introduce some visual strategies. Turn students' attention back to the story and make a geographic chart and/or family tree diagram on the chalkboard or overhead projector. (Examples of these types of charts are provided on page 192.) Students might find the variety of characters confusing, and these charts and diagrams will keep the names of people and places straight in their minds. As a class, you can also look at a U.S. map so that students can see where the places mentioned in the book are located.

Lesson 3

GOAL:
To help students begin to understand and compare/contrast the novel's main characters and to analyze their relationships to one another

ASSIGNED READING:
Chapters 5–6
(pages 25–35)

Comprehension:
Learning About Characters

- NOTE: Sharon Creech is an author who is exceptionally skilled at character development. *Walk Two Moons* is comprised of a series of character-driven and interwoven story lines. Throughout these lessons, we highlight the different ways that character plays a role in understanding and appreciating the story. Starting with this lesson (or Lesson 2 if you chose to teach the visual strategies), we have students explore character development by the author, examine characters' actions to comprehend the story, and respond to the story by writing and talking about character relationships. This book really invites and demands this emphasis through the excellent writing of Sharon Creech.

continued on page 193

Name **Stefanie**   Date **November 12**

Book   **Walk Two Moons**

Reading Log Page

Grade [A—]

Good: We did good because we did almost all of these but we did not huddle.

better: We could do better by huddling and Have better realilistic speech and questions and pay more attenchen to the person who is talking and not playing with things.

Name **Paul**   Date **November 12**

Book   **Walk Two Moons**

Reading Log Page

Grade [A+]

because I should be always talking about the book, and I'd Have lots of Ideas. I'll keep on task, and try to keep every one else on task to. I will always. I will ask questions when I need Help on some thing. I shouldent get an E because I'm a vary good worker and I will do all of the above.

Teacher Comment:

"I asked my students to give themselves a grade for their book club discussion on this day, and then to explain why they thought they deserved that grade. Some students focused more on their individual performance, while others talked about how the group did as a whole. By 'huddle' (mentioned in the first sample), Stefanie is referring to what a group looks like while they discuss their books."

Sample Geographic Chart

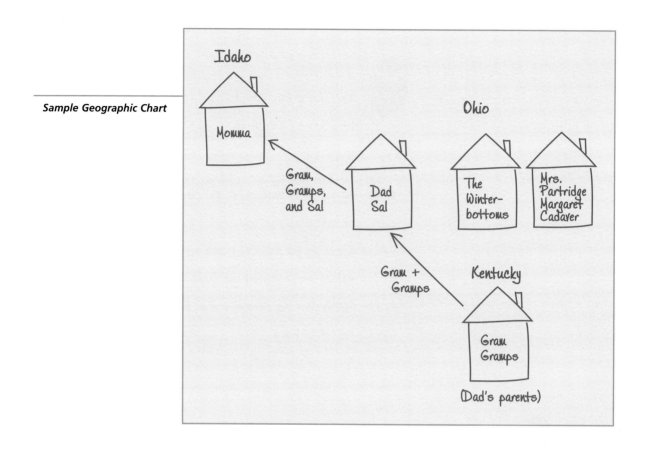

Sample Family Trees

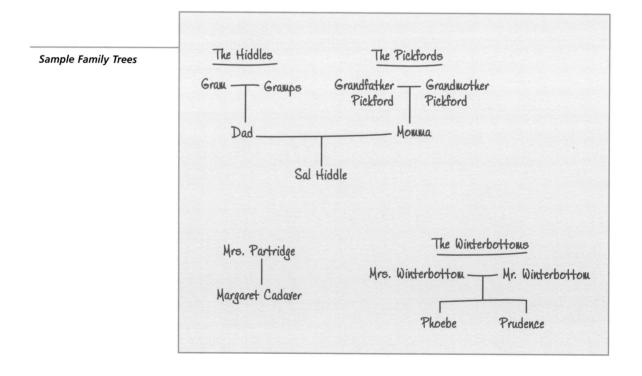

continued from page 190

continued from page 190

WRITING PROMPT:

- Choose one character and make a detailed character map, or make a character map for each main character.
- What are you learning about Sal's personality through the actions and descriptions of other characters?
- Compare how Mrs. Winterbottom appears to each of the other characters with how she actually seems to feel about herself and her life. Why do you think Sal is the only one to notice that she seems sad?

• Talk to students about the different ways in which they can learn about characters as the story progresses. Mention that readers learn about the personality traits of characters by reading direct descriptions by the author and by observing how characters behave, what they say, and how they interact with one another. Give as an example the growing relationship between Sal and Phoebe. Sal is accepting and patient toward Phoebe despite the fact that Phoebe can be difficult and has some unusual habits. What do students think this says about Sal as a person? Ask them to support their responses with examples from the book.

• Create with the class a Venn diagram comparing and contrasting the Hiddles and the Winterbottoms. In the diagram, refer to specific characters in each family. How do students think the author helps readers understand these characters? How do descriptions of the actions of some characters help readers understand the personality traits of other characters?

Lesson 4

GOAL:
To check students' understanding of the format of the book

ASSIGNED READING:
Chapters 7–8
(pages 36–45)

WRITING PROMPT:

- Are you enjoying the "story within a story" format of *Walk Two Moons* at this point in your reading? Why do you think the author chose to tell the stories in this way?
- What do you think of Phoebe's imagination? Do you think her ideas about characters and events are accurate?

Literary Elements:
Author's Craft—Story Structure, Revisited

• Now that students are several chapters into the story, it is a good time to do a comprehension check to be sure that they clearly understand the format of the book. The activities that follow deal with the sequence of the story and the role of the book's format in the story line. Both activities will inform your instruction and help you clear up any confusion that students may be experiencing.

• Ask students if the story's setup is clear to them. You might ask them to explain the sequence of events so far in the book, and list briefly this sequence of events on the chalkboard.

• Find out if students can tell when the author is switching story lines. Clues about a change in the story line include a switch in characters, new chapters, and the use of blank lines, italics, and indentations. Students should also be able to tell from the context of their reading.

• In community share, encourage students who chose the third writing prompt to share their stories about people in their own lives who are similar to Gram and Gramps. One Book Club teacher found that students

continued on next page

continued from previous page

- What do you think of Gram and Gramps? Do they remind you of anyone you know?

enjoyed sharing wonderful stories about elderly relatives and neighbors. You could begin the discussion by sharing a story of your own.

Lesson 5

GOAL:

To help students assess their own progress in writing appropriate, meaningful log entries

ASSIGNED READING:

Chapters 9–10 (pages 46–58)

WRITING PROMPT:

- What do you think the message "Don't judge a man until you've walked two moons in his moccasins" means? Can you think of examples from your own life to support your explanation of the message?
- What do you think "huzza, huzza" means? Have you found any other "wonderful words" in your reading?
- Describe a time when you had feelings of panic similar to the ones Sal has when she cannot find Gram.

Language Conventions:
Book Club Log Entries

- It is important to check periodically to see that students understand how to write good log entries, since these entries are the basis for book club discussions and are key to helping the students to broaden their thinking about their reading assignments.

- Explain to students that writing in their logs should be used as a thinking tool. Good reading log entries should be more than just summaries of what they read—they should reflect students' thoughtful responses to the reading. Tell them that sometimes just starting to write will help them clarify their thoughts and feelings about what they've read. They might start out writing about one thing and find that a lot of other related ideas come out on the page.

- Using the chalkboard or an overhead projector, list different ways of creating good reading log entries. This list might include the following, but should also include ideas from your students:

  – Connect many ideas to one central idea.

  – Connect the book in some way to your own life.

  – Make intertextual connections between the events and characters in this story and those in other books or movies. For example, you might compare Sal to the character of Winnie in *Tuck Everlasting*.

  – As you write, try to solve problems and answer questions about what you are reading. This includes asking questions about characters, situations, and vocabulary.

  – Think of new ideas to share with your book club.

  – Challenge the ideas of characters in the story or people in your book club.

- Immediately after holding this discussion, you might want to give students time to self-assess a previous day's written entry according to the criteria for good log entries that the class developed. They can write their self-assessments in their reading logs.

- When the class is finished, discuss their self-assessments. Then ask each of them to come up with three ways that they might improve their written entries so that their writing is truly being used as a thinking tool. Some students might want to share their goals with the class.

- After students have completed the day's reading, writing, and book club discussion, ask volunteers to share their responses to the writing prompts with the whole class. Students will have an opportunity to assess these log entries in Lesson 6, using the criteria established today.

Lesson 6

GOAL:

To review and revise the goals that were set for log entries in Lesson 5, and to have students self-assess the previous day's written responses using these goals

ASSIGNED READING:

Chapter 11
(pages 59–69)

WRITING PROMPT:

- What do you think the second message means? Who do you think is sending the messages, and why?
- Who do you think "the lunatic" is?
- What do you think of the relationship between Ben and Sal?
- How do you feel about Mrs. Cadaver?

Language Conventions:
Assessing Book Club Log Entries

- Continuing with the theme of yesterday's lesson will reinforce good habits when students create their log entries.

- Ask students to self-assess their written responses to yesterday's writing prompts. They should use the three goals that they set for themselves yesterday as guidelines. Remind them to think about how their log entries helped them to think about their reading and how the entries aided their book club discussions.

- When students have finished assessing their work, they should revise their individual goals. To help them do this, ask them to think about what they were able to improve and what still needs improvement. They should also decide if they notice any other areas in need of improvement. Encourage students to share their ideas about their own writing with the rest of the class.

- Review the list that was generated by the class yesterday and encourage the students to discuss and make any necessary changes. Allow them to add new items to the list, if they want to.

Lesson 7

GOAL:
To give students information about the Native American tradition of passing a pipe so they can understand its significance in Chapter 12

ASSIGNED READING:
Chapters 12–13
(pages 70–83)

WRITING PROMPT:
- Do you know any family stories that have been passed down through the years like the story of Gram and Gramps and their marriage bed? Why are stories like this fun to tell?
- Have you ever had a teacher like Mr. Birkway? Why might he want the class to write in journals?
- Write about the pipe that Sal shares with her grandparents. How do you feel about this tradition?

Comprehension:
Background Knowledge—The Native American Peace Pipe

- Background information about the Native American tradition of sharing a pipe will be useful for students as they read and discuss this section of the book. You might choose to give this lesson *after* students have had a chance to read the selection, since it will hold more meaning for them at that point.

- Tell students that the ceremonial pipe of many North American Indians is called a calumet. It is usually a long pipe made out of a reed, which is a stiff, slender type of grass. At the end of the pipe is a stone bowl, where tobacco is placed. The pipe is often ornamented with eagle feathers. You might show them a picture of such a pipe from a dictionary or other reference book, so that they can visualize the pipe being shared by Sal and her grandparents. Explain to students that this pipe, often called a peace pipe, is shared on special occasions as a token of peace, companionship, and good will. The pipe also has religious significance to some Native American groups.

- You might ask students to think about rituals and traditions that they honor in their own lives, either at family or community events or at religious ceremonies or services. Are any of their own rituals or traditions similar in meaning to the pipe tradition?

- After students have had a chance to read the selection, spend time in community share discussing this tradition and how students feel about Sal's participation in it. One Book Club teacher found that students reacted negatively to Sal's smoking the pipe, because in their lives they had been so well informed about the dangers of tobacco and cigarette addiction. The way that you approach this issue will depend on the ages and maturity level of your own students, but you should be able to point out that cigarette addiction in modern American culture is different from the ceremonial custom that is described in the book. Invite students to share their ideas and concerns about this subject.

Lesson 8

Comprehension:
Character Development; Wonderful Words;
Background Knowledge—Snake Bites

GOAL:
To revisit the idea of character development; to encourage students to record in their reading logs some of the book's colorful language; to inform students about the proper first-aid treatment for snake bites

ASSIGNED READING:
Chapters 14–15 (pages 84–97)

WRITING PROMPT:
• Record more "wonderful words" in your journal as you read. Explain why you like the words you chose.
• What is your own theory about Mrs. Cadaver? Explain and provide evidence from your reading.
• Predict what you think will happen next in the story.
• What is your impression of the stranger who takes Gramps's wallet and then helps Gram on the way to the hospital?
• Have you ever been in an emergency situation like Gram's? Were you the one in need of help, or did you have to help someone else? Explain the situation and how you felt throughout it.
• Write about what you learned about Gram, Gramps, and Sal. Were you surprised at how the scene at the river turned out?

Teaching Tip

This lesson has three distinct sections. Each is important to the students' understanding of the novel. You may want to teach the lesson in two parts, covering character development and "wonderful words" on one day and having a discussion about snake bites the next day. It would be equally appropriate to teach character development and "wonderful words" in the pre-reading lesson and then discuss the background information about snake bites in community share.

• Encouraging students to keep track of words that they find interesting and fun will help them expand their vocabularies and appreciate language in the books that they read.

• Remind students that in their reading logs they can record "wonderful words"—words they've come across in their reading that they find new, crazy, or descriptive. When they record a word, they should include a sentence or two about why they chose it and the page number so that they can find it again. For a comprehensive lesson on "wonderful words," see Lesson 9 for *Last Summer with Maizon*, page 73.

• Discuss with the class several of the colorful words the author has used so far in the book. *Manna* (page 81), *figure* (page 76), and *ornery* (page 76) are examples of words that students might find intriguing. You might ask students to explain why these words stand out to them.

• After students have done today's reading, revisit the concepts of character development and characterization introduced in Lessons 2 and 3. Remind students that understanding a character and noticing how the character is developing will help them understand the novel.

• Discuss the encounter that Gram, Gramps, and Sal have with the boy on the riverbank. What does the reader learn about Gramps and Gram through this encounter? Talk to students about Gramps's bravery when the boy threatens them, Gram's bravery when she is bitten by the snake,

continued on next page

continued from previous page

and how her faith in the goodness of people is supported when the boy helps them instead of robbing them. Ask students to comment on how this encounter helped them understand Gram, Gramps, and the way that Sal might feel about her grandparents.

- You might want to hold a discussion about the proper first-aid treatment of a snake bite. This subject comes up in Chapter 15 when Gram is bitten by a snake, and students might have questions about how the bite was initially treated by Gramps and the boy. Explain to students that at one time people treated snake bites by cutting the flesh around the fang marks, sucking the venom from the wound, and spitting the venom out. This method, however, is no longer considered to be safe or effective. Cutting into the wound, if you are not a medical professional, can cause more damage than is already there. Also, the person sucking the venom can become infected with the venom (or any blood-borne infections that the victim might have) and can contaminate the wound with germs. Instead, the American Red Cross advocates taking the following steps:

  – Wash the affected area with soap and water.

  – Keep the bitten area still and below the heart.

  – Get the victim medical attention as quickly as possible.

  – If you cannot get to a hospital within thirty minutes, you can try to slow the venom by wrapping a bandage two to four inches above the wound. You should never completely cut off the flow of blood to a limb. If you have a snake bite kit, you might find a suctioning device that can be used to draw venom from the wound. These must be used carefully and according to their instructions.

- One Book Club teacher found that her students enjoyed this discussion, even though they found some of the details of snake bite treatment "gross." It is important information to pass along, and you can adjust the information to fit the needs and maturity level of your own students.

Lesson 9

GOAL:

To encourage students to recall and discuss expressions and sayings that people in their own families use, and to analyze why people use these expressions

ASSIGNED READING:

Chapters 16–18
(pages 98–113)

WRITING PROMPT:

- Write about family sayings and expressions used in your family or among your friends. Explain what the expressions mean and why you think people use them.
- In what way is your family like or unlike the Winterbottom family? the Hiddle family?
- What do you think Mrs. Cadaver has to do with Sal's story?

Response to Literature:
Personal Response—Family Sayings and Expressions

- Encouraging students to discuss sayings and expressions used regularly by their own families will help them identify with the people in *Walk Two Moons.* They will realize that some of their family expressions or sayings might sound strange to other people, just as some of the ones used by Gram and Gramps might sound strange to them.

- Begin a class discussion about sayings and expressions that students hear members of their families, or other people in their lives such as friends and neighbors, use on a regular basis. Where do these expressions come from? Are they completely unique, or are they expressions that most people would recognize? Which ones do students like and dislike, and why? List the expressions on the chalkboard or use an overhead projector.

- Point out that the author of *Walk Two Moons* has her characters use some interesting and unique expressions. Ask students why the author might have chosen to do this. Does it make scenes seem more realistic to them? Do these expressions make the characters seem more endearing? Why, or why not?

Lesson 10

GOAL:

To have students think about and define unfamiliar words and expressions, and to have students revisit the variety of relationships in the book and identify how these relationships have changed over time

ASSIGNED READING:

Chapters 19–20
(pages 114–128)

Comprehension:
Vocabulary; Character Relationships

- Encouraging students to identify and discuss words that are unfamiliar to them will help them to enjoy their reading more. At this point in the novel you might also want to check students' understanding of the various relationships in the book and how they have changed over time.

- To begin the lesson, ask students to identify words in the chapters they have read that they do not see very often. As an example, call students' attention to the word *flinch,* which is introduced in Chapter 11 and appears again in Chapter 20. Have they seen this word before? You

continued on next page

continued from previous page

WRITING PROMPT:

- Why do you think Sal flinches when she is touched? Why did she not flinch when Ben touched her hand in Chapter 20?

- Can you think of a time in your own life when you have flinched or seen someone else flinch? Why do you think this happened?

- Do you ever feel as if you're trying to "catch fish in the air"? Write about a specific experience in your own life.

- What do you think is *really* happening in Phoebe's family, and why is it happening?

might ask students who are familiar with the word to demonstrate what it means. Invite students to identify and discuss other unusual or new words used in the book.

- Introduce the expression "fish in the air," which is the title of Chapter 19. Tell students that this expression is a figure of speech, meaning that it has more than a literal, word-for-word meaning. By using this expression, Sal's father is comparing Sal, who he believes is making up stories in an attempt to scare him away from Mrs. Cadaver, to someone who is trying to catch fish in the air. Invite students to analyze what this expression might mean in this context. Would a person be able to catch fish in the air? What would be the result of this person's efforts? What might Sal's father be saying about her efforts to turn him against Mrs. Cadaver?

- Open a discussion about the different family relationships in the novel. What relationships do students find most interesting? What changes have some of the relationships undergone?

Lesson 11

GOAL:
To encourage students to create and share their own "soul drawings," as the children in the book do

ASSIGNED READING:
Chapters 21–22
(pages 129–141)

WRITING PROMPT:

- Compare and contrast your soul drawing with the drawings of some of your classmates. Write a response to what you see.

Response to Literature:
Personal Response—Soul Drawings

- Students will probably enjoy creating "soul drawings" like those described in Chapter 21. Doing this activity before they read will help them visualize what the characters are doing in their classroom. The activity will also work well if it is done after students complete the day's reading assignment. (Some examples of soul drawings done by children in a Book Club classroom are shown on page 201.)

- Tell students that you are going to ask them to draw, in a short amount of time, pictures of their souls. If they have already read Chapter 21, they will have a context for this activity. If they have not yet read the chapter, you might tell them these will be simple drawings that express something about how they are feeling or who they are.

- Ask students to turn to a blank page in their logs. Then give them a short amount of time to draw their souls. In the book, Mr. Birkway gives his students 15 seconds to complete this exercise. The amount of time you

• Write about the evidence that Phoebe finds. What do you think it proves or does not prove about Mrs. Winterbottom's disappearance?

allow is up to you, but keep in mind that the drawings are supposed to be spontaneous and simple.

• When they have finished, invite willing students to hold up their drawings for others in the class to see. Tell students that they can take more time to share and explain their drawings in their book club groups.

• In community share after book clubs have met, ask students to talk about the drawings of the souls that were shared in their groups. What similarities and differences do they see between their drawings and those of Mr. Birkway's class?

Sample "Soul Drawings"

Teacher Comment:

"I called this activity a 'drawing party.' I gave my students more time than Mr. Birkway in the book—almost a full minute."

Lesson 12

GOAL:
To have students use drawing pictures as a tool for gaining a better understanding of characters and events in the story

ASSIGNED READING:
Chapters 23–24
(pages 142–156)

WRITING PROMPT:
- How do you think the tragedy of the baby's death affected the Hiddle family?
- Have you ever felt like the "birds of sadness" were flying around your head? Write about this experience. You could also draw a picture about the experience.

Response to Literature:
Creative Response—Drawing Pictures

- By drawing pictures of their favorite scenes from the book, students will see how the author creates pictures in their minds with language. You may want to begin by modeling out loud how you would visualize a scene. This will help students to *see* pictures that the text evokes.

- Individually, students should choose one scene or event, from anywhere in the book up until this point in their reading, that stands out in their memories. Then they should draw pictures of their special scenes.

- After drawing their pictures, students should write about what they drew and why they were attracted to the scenes they chose. Invite them to share their work with the rest of the class.

- After students have read Chapters 23–24 and have met with their book clubs, invite them to share their responses to the writing prompts with the whole class.

Lesson 13

GOAL:
To help students understand how the author reveals the feelings of her characters through their actions and related dreams

ASSIGNED READING:
Chapters 25–26
(pages 157–169)

WRITING PROMPT:
- What is really going on in Phoebe's mind? Why is she acting the way she is toward people? Can you relate to the experience of having difficult feelings affect how you treat other people? Have you ever had to try to deal with a difficult person?

Literary Elements:
Author's Craft—Characterization Through Actions and Dreams

- This lesson will help students identify with the feelings of Phoebe and Sal. Students will then be asked to notice the subtle ways in which an author shows how characters are feeling.

- Ask students the following questions: Have you ever had a time when you felt terrible and because of this acted badly toward yourself and others? How did people deal with you? Have you ever had a sibling or friend who acted in this way? How did you deal with it? You might give students a few minutes to respond to these questions in writing first, and then invite them to discuss what they've written. In the discussion, ask them to describe the different clues people give, sometimes without realizing it, that let others know they are feeling sad or angry.

- Then ask students if they have ever had dreams that seemed to be related to things that were going on in their lives or that seemed strange at

- Respond to Sal's dream in Chapter 26. What do you think it means? How does it relate to the story and how Sal is feeling?

first but that later made sense to them. Ask students who feel comfortable doing so to share these dreams.

- Tell students that as they read Chapters 25 and 26 they should try to notice how the feelings of the characters affect how they act toward themselves and others. As they read, they might keep the following questions in mind: How do both Phoebe and Sal respond to the problems in their lives? What does Sal understand about Phoebe's behavior? Why does the author choose to describe Sal's dream at the end of Chapter 26?

- One student's response to the first writing prompt is shown below.

Student Sample: Me & the Book

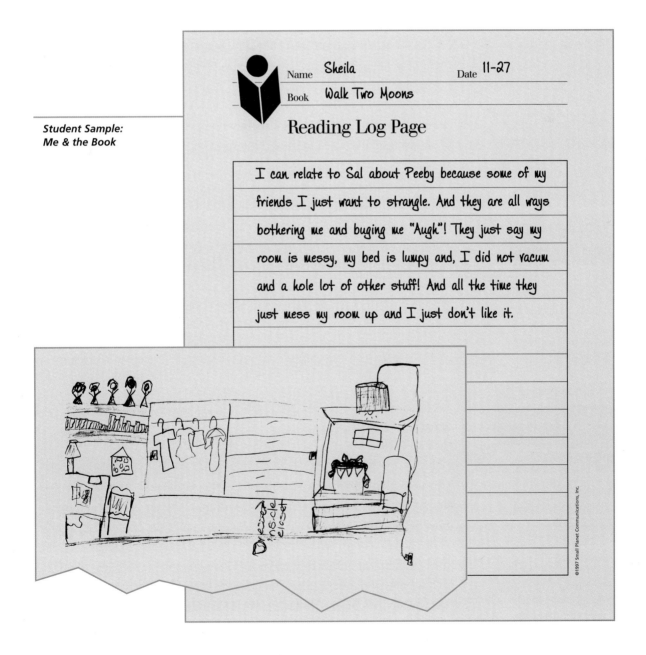

Name Sheila   Date 11-27

Book Walk Two Moons

Reading Log Page

I can relate to Sal about Peeby because some of my friends I just want to strangle. And they are all ways bothering me and buging me "Augh"! They just say my room is messy, my bed is lumpy and, I did not vacum and a hole lot of other stuff! And all the time they just mess my room up and I just don't like it.

Lesson 14

GOAL:
To encourage students to create new ways of responding to literature in their reading logs

ASSIGNED READING:
Chapters 27–29
(pages 170–188)

WRITING PROMPT:
- Spend extra time free writing about anything related to the story.
- Think about all of the messages that Phoebe has received. Taken as a whole, what do you suppose they mean?
- After community share, write about the different interpretations that people in your class have of Phoebe's messages.

Language Conventions:
Creating New Types of Reading Log Entries

- NOTE: This is a two-part lesson. You may choose to do both parts on the same day, do only one of the two parts, or teach the lesson over the course of two days.

- This lesson first gives students a chance to use their own creativity and experience with reading logs to add to the class list of response types. Students will enjoy collaborating and helping one another as they experiment with new log entries. In the second part of the lesson, students will have a chance to discuss and practice poetry interpretation.

- First, explain to students that after they read today they will be given extra time for free writing. As they write, they should see if they can invent new reading log response types. When the class is finished writing, ask them to share their logs—either in book clubs or in community share—and help each other come up with new ways of responding to the literature. Discuss and record the new response types as a class.

- In the second part of the lesson, ask students to discuss poetry interpretation. Tell them that people often interpret the same poems in different ways, based on their own personal experiences. How do students feel about the messages, which together form a type of poem, that Phoebe has received? What do they think these messages mean?

- After the discussion, ask students to write about the different interpretations of the poem that were discussed. What do they think of them?

Lesson 15

GOAL:
To direct students toward understanding the points of view presented in the story and toward thinking about the points of view that are not presented

Literary Elements:
Point of View

- This lesson will allow students to look at the same story from another character's point of view. This will give them a deeper understanding of the story and show them that point of view shapes the way a story is told.

- Turn students' attention to the Point of View response type, described on the third Response Choice Sheet in the section following page 261. Discuss this response type with them. Do students sometimes think that

ASSIGNED READING:
Chapters 30–31
(pages 189–204)

WRITING PROMPT:
- Write about an incident in the story from another character's point of view (besides Sal's).
- Have you ever done anything that you consider to be daring? Have you ever seen someone do something daring?
- What do you think the lunatic has to do with the story? Why was he in the picture with Sergeant Bickle? Predict what you think will happen next with this character.

the author does not consider some ideas that are important to understanding a particular character? Which characters have expressed their points of view so far in the story? Which points of view do students not know about, but would like to understand? Why do students want to understand more about these characters? Tell students that they will have a chance to supply some of this "missing" information if they respond to the first writing prompt for today.

- NOTE: You can help students prepare for subsequent events in the book by asking if they have ever done anything daring that they felt was a good idea at the time they were doing it. Did it turn out later that it wasn't such a good idea? Why, or why not? Explain that this subject will come up in the chapters that they are about to read.

Lesson 16

GOAL:
To encourage students to put themselves in the places of characters in the book and decide how they would feel if their own personal writings were shared against their wishes

ASSIGNED READING:
Chapters 32–33
(pages 205–221)

WRITING PROMPT:
Write about how you would feel if something you wrote that was personal was read aloud without your permission.

Response to Literature:
Personal Journals

- This lesson, which must follow the day's reading assignment, will broaden students' understanding of the children in the book and of Mr. Birkway by asking them to connect events in the reading with their own lives.

- Begin a discussion about what happened in Mr. Birkway's classroom. How do students feel about the way Mr. Birkway handled student journal writing? How would they feel if a teacher read aloud some of their personal writing, without their permission? Students might choose to read aloud what they wrote in their reading logs about this subject.

- Ask students to then think about the situation from Mr. Birkway's point of view. Do they think that Mr. Birkway is trying to be mean or cruel, or do they think he just doesn't know any better? Ask students to give reasons for their opinions.

Lesson 17

GOAL:
To enhance student understanding and appreciation of the story by allowing ample and unrestricted free writing time

ASSIGNED READING:
Chapters 34–36
(pages 222–235)

WRITING PROMPT:
Free write about any characters or aspects of the story that are becoming clearer to you at this point.

Response to Literature:
Free Writing

- The Book Club teacher who developed this lesson plan found that at this point in the novel, students benefited most from having extra free writing time in place of structured lessons. She felt that lessons were more likely to restrict student thinking at this time than enhance it. You might choose to split the class time between free writing and book club groups or community share. Although it is not commonly done, you might choose to allow students to spend the entire time reading and writing individually.

Lesson 18

GOAL:
To be sure students have a grasp of the important events that are unfolding at this point in the story and how characters and events are linked together

ASSIGNED READING:
Chapters 37–39
(pages 236–250)

WRITING PROMPT:
Free write about what you've read today, or about any responses that you have to the story so far.

Response to Literature:
Free Writing and Checking Comprehension

- Allow students ample time to free write. As in Lesson 17, you might choose to have students meet in book club groups or community share for discussion, or you might choose to allow them to free write for the entire period.

- You can get a good overview of how the class is responding to and understanding the novel by reviewing students' log entries for yesterday and today. Look for evidence that students understand the relationship of Mike Bickle to Mrs. Winterbottom, that they understand why Phoebe is angry with her family and her mother, and that they realize the importance of the changing relationship between Sal and Ben. You can also use the information that you gather in this way to inform your instruction, so that you can support students in understanding the twists and turns in the plot during the last chapters of the book.

Lesson 19

GOAL:
To allow students time to finish the book and think about how the story might end and how conflicts might be resolved

ASSIGNED READING:
Chapters 40–44
(pages 251–280)

WRITING PROMPT:
Free write about the story's ending.

Comprehension:
Predicting the Story's Ending

- The teacher who developed this lesson plan found that, at this point in the novel, students were eager to finish the book in one day. Therefore she allowed her class to read the last five chapters in one sitting. Depending on your class, however, you may choose to spread the reading assignment over two days.

- Before students read, have them make predictions about the ending in their reading logs.

- You might check in with students periodically as they are reading to see if there is anything they would like to discuss along the way. Following the reading, students should free write about the book's ending.

- Allow time for book club or community share discussions to flow around the students' reactions to the end of the story. Revisit, or have students revisit, the predictions they made prior to reading. Students should be encouraged to discuss how they feel about the ending and how conflicts were or were not resolved by the ending. Is the ending very different from the predictions they made? Why?

Teaching Tip

Reading five chapters in one session may be difficult for your class. One Book Club teacher found that reading a chapter or two aloud and then having the class read the rest was a good compromise.

Lesson 20

GOAL:
To have students examine what they liked and disliked about the book by developing a class critique

ASSIGNED READING:
None

Response to Literature:
Writing a Book Critique

- Developing a class critique will give students the chance to look at the novel as a whole, examine their own feelings about it, and then hear the ideas of their classmates.

- Explain to students that a critique is a written evaluation of a story. People writing a critique of a novel should look at the different parts of

continued on next page

continued from previous page

continued from previous page

WRITING PROMPT:
Write about what you liked and disliked about *Walk Two Moons.* Prepare to bring your ideas about the book to your group.

the novel with a critical eye and examine what works and what does not work for them as readers.

- Tell students that they will be putting together a class critique that will include the ideas of each member of the class.

- First, allow the students to spend time writing individually. After each student has had a chance to examine his or her own ideas, students should meet in their book club groups. Each book club should come up with two or three positive and negative aspects of the book. Then the class should meet in community share to combine the ideas of the book club groups and to add any other ideas that might have been left out. Give students time to discuss as a class the different opinions that were presented.

- Pull together the ideas that students agree are the best or most important in their class critique, and write these on chart paper to be displayed in the classroom.

Lesson 21

Self–Assessment

GOAL:
To have each student assess his or her work over the course of the unit

ASSIGNED READING:
None

WRITING PROMPT:
Think about the work you've done in Book Club for *Walk Two Moons.* Pick out a log entry that represents your best work, and write why you think so. Write about your overall performance in this unit, and give yourself an honest grade.

- This final lesson gives students a chance to look over the work they have done during the course of the unit and to find a piece that makes them feel proud. This activity gives them valuable practice in self-assessment.

- Tell students to look over the work they completed during the unit, both individually and in book club groups. Each student should find his or her best log entry and be able to explain why it is the best. Then the student should give the entry a grade. He or she should be able to explain why the grade chosen is appropriate.

- Self-assessment procedures are up to you. Students can base their assessments on a standard grading system, or they can fill out the End-of-Book Self-Assessment sheet from the Blackline Masters: Assessment section following page 281.

Maniac Magee
by Jerry Spinelli

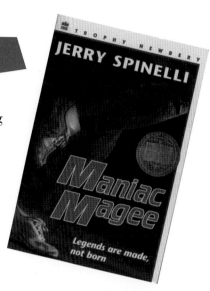

Introducing the Book

One Book Club student wrote after reading *Maniac Magee*, "This book is great! The beginning, middle, and end were all awesomely excellent." While it may be too much to expect that all of your students will have such an enthusiastic response to any single book, *Maniac Magee* has been very popular in our classrooms. The novel is quite complex, with many characters and changes in setting, and its vocabulary is sophisticated. Therefore we recommend it for fifth- and sixth-grade classes.

Summary After his parents die in a trolley accident in Bridgeport, three-year-old Jeffrey Magee is sent to live with his aunt and uncle two hundred miles away. They do not talk to each other and have two of everything except Jeffrey. After eight years, Jeffrey snaps during a school concert and runs away. A year later, Jeffrey is back in the Bridgeport area. He startles the population of Two Mills with his ability to run, jump, spin, dance, and outthink everybody he meets. He can also untie incredibly tangled knots. For all of these astounding feats, he earns the reputation of being a "maniac."

Thus the legend of Maniac Magee is born. There are, however, two things that Maniac Magee can't do. He can't find a permanent address, and he can't understand why it is that white people stay on the west end of town and black people stay on the east. In fact, he doesn't even see how people can call themselves black or white when they are obviously many different colors. Then someone makes the distinction clear to him—through racist graffiti and vandalism against the black family with whom he's been staying. He realizes that he has made enemies in both the East End and the West End, and that he must leave the closest thing to a home that he's ever found.

Maniac forms a friendship with an old man who works in a local zoo and stays with him for a while. When his friend dies and no one but Maniac turns up at the funeral or

Paperback Edition, HarperTrophy, © 1990 by Jerry Spinelli. ISBN 0-06-440424-2.

seems to care about the man's life, Maniac runs away again. After a period of wandering, Maniac winds up staying with a white family in the West End. Things come to a crisis when he is asked to rescue one of the boys in this family after the boy wanders out onto the bridge where Maniac's parents were killed. Maniac can't do it, but one of his "enemies" from the East End does. This first contact between East End and West End finally leads to Maniac Magee's being called home by the black family he loves the most of all his new friends. The now-complete legend of Maniac Magee, created throughout his sojourn in Two Mills, brings readers full circle to the first scene in the book, in which East End *and* West End children are playing jump rope together.

Themes *Maniac Magee* explores the issue of racism through the eyes of a main character who is at once naive and wise. Jeffrey's generosity of spirit makes him blind to the hatred that surrounds him in the segregated town of Two Mills, but ultimately he is forced to face the reality and then to try to bridge the gulf between black and white. The novel can also be used to support themes such as people who are misunderstood, intergenerational friendships, families, belonging, death, grief, and survival.

Special Classroom Library Jerry Spinelli has written so many excellent books for young readers that you'll probably want to stock your classroom library with more titles by him. Suggestions include *Who Put That Hair in My Toothbrush?* (Little, Brown, 1994), *Dump Days* (Little, Brown, 1988), *There's a Girl in My Hammerlock* (Simon & Schuster, 1993), and *Crash* (Random House, 1996).

You may also select thematically related titles for the special classroom library. Other books relating to the theme of racism include *The Watsons Go to Birmingham—1963* by Christopher Paul Curtis (Delacorte, 1995) and the works of Mildred Taylor, some of which are featured in an author study on pages 225–240. Another powerful story by Mildred Taylor is *The Well: David's Story* (Dial, 1995). Books on the themes of homelessness, belonging, and society's treatment of outsiders include *Monkey Island* by Paula Fox (Orchard Books, 1991) and *The Midwife's Apprentice* by Karen Cushman (HarperCollins, 1996). To explore the themes of loss, grief, and survival, you might try the nonfiction book *Part of Me Died, Too: Stories of Creative Survival Among Bereaved Children and Teenagers* by Virginia Lynn Fry (Dutton, 1995).

Lesson 1

GOAL:
To get students thinking about point of view and the concept of a legend, and to review ideas for reading log entries

ASSIGNED READING:
Chapters 1–6
(pages 5–21)

WRITING PROMPT:
- Describe some of the legendary feats of Maniac Magee.
- Do you know anyone personally whom you would call a "legend"? What makes this person a legend?
- What do you think Maniac did during the year he traveled the 200 miles from Hollidaysburg to Two Mills?
- Write about something else in the first six chapters that catches your interest or makes you want to read more.

Literary Elements:
Point of View

- The humor and humanity of this novel spring largely from the contrast between two points of view: that of Jeffrey versus that of the Two Mills children who turn him into a "legend." To make sure that students see this contrast from the beginning, you might start your teaching of *Maniac Magee* with a focus on legends and a discussion of point of view. Depending on the needs of your class, you might also decide to review reading log options.

- Before you begin the lesson, have students read the first section of the book, "Before the Story." You can ask them to read this section independently, or you can read it aloud to the class.

- After they finish "Before the Story," students will know that Maniac Magee is a legend in the town of Two Mills. Ask students to describe what it means to be a legend. (As students brainstorm, you might create a web diagram on the chalkboard.) Do they know any legends? Invite students to describe some legends they might have read in books or heard in their own families or communities. Explain that legends are stories that are often based at least partially on facts but that grow and change as they are passed from generation to generation.

- Ask students to set up a "Legendary Feats" page in their reading logs. On this page, students can begin making notes about some of the legendary feats of Maniac Magee. Alternatively, they might create a time line to keep track of Maniac's feats and travels.

- If necessary, review with students the various types of reading log entries that they can do. You might pass out a new Response Choice Sheet that describes all of the response types they know at this point in the year. (Blackline masters are provided in the Blackline Masters: Think Sheets section following page 261.) For more ideas about teaching a lesson on reading logs, turn to Lesson 1 for *Tuck Everlasting*, page 83.

- Begin community share by sharing the major ideas that came up in book clubs. Then focus students' attention on point of view, reviewing the concept with them as necessary. (For more ideas about teaching point of view, turn to Lesson 12 for *Tuck Everlasting*, page 96.) Ask them to describe how Jeffrey sees the world. How does he interact with other people? What seems to be important to him? Then ask how the people

continued on next page

continued from previous page

of Two Mills see Jeffrey. How do they react to the things he does? What do they think of him? Tell students that point of view—how various characters perceive the world—is something to keep in mind as they continue reading the book.

Lesson 2

GOAL:

To help students notice and understand the various elements of a story by helping them to begin a story map

ASSIGNED READING:

Chapters 7–11 (pages 22–40)

WRITING PROMPT:

- Compare and contrast Maniac and Mars Bar.
- Jeffrey is having trouble fitting in with some of the other children in Two Mills. How do you explain this?
- Based on what you know so far, what do you think will happen when Amanda brings Jeffrey home?

Literary Elements:
The Elements of a Story

- Pointing out the different elements of a story will help students to better understand and appreciate the way in which these elements work together to make a story unique and interesting.

- Explain to students that most stories are made up of several different elements. You might list on the chalkboard the following elements: setting, mood, conflict, plot, resolution, characters, and theme. Ask students to define the terms that they know, and explain to them any terms that are unfamiliar to them, using examples from other stories the class has read.

- You might begin a story map on chart paper so that the class can work together to keep track of the story elements in *Maniac Magee.* The story map should include all of the elements you've discussed in the lesson. Begin by filling in what students know from Chapters 1–6.

- After students have done today's reading, written in their logs, and met with their book clubs, return to the story map and fill in new information through Chapter 11. A sample story map is shown on page 213.

- Ask students to share what they discussed in their book clubs and what they wrote in their logs. Any new themes that students mention should be added to the class story map.

- In the section of the book that students read today, they have faced (along with Maniac) the segregation and racism that exist in the town of Two Mills. The deep division of this community is an important theme in the book, and you should make sure that students are aware of it. Students may have noticed and want to talk about the term *fishbelly,* an insulting name for a white person used by the character Mars Bar.

Maniac Magee	
Setting:	Hollidaysburg (one year ago), Two Mills (present)
Characters:	Jeffrey "Maniac" Magee, Aunt Dot and Uncle Dan, Amanda Beale, Brian Deneky and James "Hands" Down, Finsterwald, the Pickwells, John McNab, Mars Bar Thompson
Conflict:	Maniac has made John McNab and Mars Bar Thompson angry, and they're both after him.
Plot:	Maniac came to Two Mills and borrowed Amanda's book. He performed amazing feats on the football field, at Finsterwald's, on the railroad tracks, and on the baseball diamond. John McNab chased him into the East End, where Mars Bar started threatening him. Amanda saved him and offered to take him to her house.
Mood:	sometimes funny, sometimes scary or nervous
Themes:	What makes a legend? Jeffrey wants a home. Two Mills is segregated black/white.
Resolution:	

Sample Story Map for Maniac Magee

Lesson 3

Response to Literature:
Empathizing with a Character

GOAL:
To help students explore their empathy with the main character and see how this adds to their enjoyment of the story

ASSIGNED READING:
Chapters 12–15
(pages 41–56)

• Empathizing with a character helps readers engage more deeply with a story and understand it better. The section of *Maniac Magee* that students will read today shows a change in the mood of the story, reflecting a change in how the main character feels about his life. It is a good point at which to encourage students to explore their empathy with Maniac.

• Remind students of the story element *mood,* and review what has already been recorded on the class story map under this category. Ask students to keep the mood of the story in mind as they read Chapters 12–15.

continued on next page

continued from previous page

WRITING PROMPT:

- Would you feel at home and comfortable at the Beales' house? In what ways are they like your own family?
- What little everyday things about family life had Maniac been missing?
- How has Maniac's point of view changed?
- Why do you think Maniac responds the way he does when Mrs. Beale slaps him?

- During community share, encourage students to share some of the ideas and feelings that came up in their writing and in their book club discussions. Ask them to identify the mood of the section they read today. How did it change from Chapter 11? How does Maniac feel now that he is staying with the Beales, and how did that affect how the students felt as they read?

- Ask students whether they feel empathy with Maniac. If necessary, explain that *empathy* means sharing the feelings of another person or a story character. What things do they have in common with Maniac that allow them to feel empathy with him? Does feeling empathy with a character make them enjoy a story more? Does it teach them anything about themselves?

Teaching Tip

In Chapter 14 (page 51), Maniac expresses confusion over the way people in the East End call themselves "black," since he sees many different shades of skin but none that looks like licorice. One Book Club teacher brings this point home for her class by having her students stand in a circle and put all of their hands in the middle. They can all see easily that there is a spectrum of skin colors—none of which is really "white" or "black"—and they can discuss how silly it is to divide people into two distinct and opposite categories.

Lesson 4

Literary Elements:
Theme and Plot

GOAL:
To further explore the themes and plot of the book

ASSIGNED READING:
Chapters 16–21
(pages 57–76)

WRITING PROMPT:
- How does Maniac feel when he realizes that some people in the East End don't like him because he's white? Have you ever been treated badly for no apparent reason? How did you feel?
- Explain Amanda's reaction when Maniac wants to leave after the graffiti incident.
- Pick a section in the reading and draw a picture of it. Explain why you drew it and tell what words Jerry Spinelli used to create the picture in your mind.
- Why do you think Maniac left town? Was this really best for the Beales? What would you have done in his position?
- Predict what Jeffrey will do next. What are your reasons for making this prediction?

- If you taught Lesson 2 on story elements, you have already touched on the topics of theme and plot with your class. This lesson will allow you to further explore some of the major themes of the book as well as to discuss how the plot is developing.

- Tell students that this section of the reading is very important to the themes and plot of the book. If you created a story map earlier, you may want to refer back to it and ask students if they have anything to add.

- During community share, focus the discussion on Maniac's sudden realization that some people in the East End don't like him because he's white. How do the events of the story—the black man calling him "Whitey" and telling him to "go back to his own kind"; the racist graffiti on the Beales' house; Amanda's encyclopedia being stolen and torn to shreds—develop the themes? Of the themes that students have added to the class story map, which ones seem to be the most important? At this point, students may want to revise the story map to reflect what they now know about the central problem(s) or conflict(s) in the story.

- You might also ask students to discuss how they feel about the plot so far. Are they enjoying the story? Do the events seem realistic or believable? Are they eager to find out what will happen next? By asking them to share their impressions of the plot at this stage, you will prepare them to discuss rising action, climax, falling action, and resolution in Lesson 9 (page 221).

Teaching Tip

You may want to focus an extension activity for this section of *Maniac Magee* on Jerry Spinelli's vivid, poetic language at the beginning of Chapter 17 (page 59). The author uses a parallel structure (repetition of the phrase *so hot*) and a series of striking sensory images to describe a particular day in August. Ask students to imitate this style to describe something from their own experience, in either poetic or prose form.

Lesson 5

Literary Elements:
Characterization; Point of View (Revisited)

GOAL:
To focus students' attention on the author's craft of characterization and to revisit point of view

ASSIGNED READING:
Chapters 22–26
(pages 79–99)

WRITING PROMPT:
- Do you know someone who tells wonderful stories like Grayson? Write about that person and what you've learned from his or her stories.
- Has Maniac forgotten about the Beales? How do you think he feels about them? How do you know?
- How does Grayson view people from the East End? Why do think this is so?
- Create a character map for Grayson to show what you know about him. What questions do you have about him?

- This lesson provides an opportunity to discuss how Jerry Spinelli artfully reveals the feelings and personalities of his characters and to build on your discussion of point of view in Lesson 1.

- Before students begin the reading for today, you might review some of the themes that have emerged in Part I and add them to the class story map. Ask students why they think the author divided the book into three parts, and what they think Part II might be about. If necessary, review character maps with the class so they will be prepared to make one for Grayson if they choose. (Lesson 3 for *Last Summer with Maizon*, page 63, provides more ideas for teaching character maps.)

- During community share, invite students to discuss what they wrote in their logs and what they talked about in their book clubs. You might ask any students who did character maps of Grayson to share and compare their work. Ask them what they think of Grayson's questions about African Americans (pages 87–89). How does the scene in the diner affect their opinion of Grayson?

- Encourage students to discuss the ways in which Jerry Spinelli reveals how Maniac is feeling. What do details such as his remembering the baths with Hester and Lester and the icing on Mrs. Beale's finger show? Why does Maniac refuse to live at the Y with Grayson? Would the story have been better or worse if Spinelli had simply written, "Maniac missed the Beales, and he was afraid to get too close to Grayson for fear of being hurt again"?

- The unusual opening to Chapter 22 (pages 79–80) provides a good opportunity for you to revisit your discussion of point of view. Ask students from what point of view this part of the story is told. Why do they think the author chose to write from the point of view of the baby buffalo? Did they find this technique interesting? confusing? imaginative? How does the reader know when the story switches to Grayson's point of view?

Lesson 6

GOAL:
To review share sheet format and to help students analyze the developing relationship between Maniac and Grayson

ASSIGNED READING:
Chapters 27–32
(pages 100–118)

WRITING PROMPT:
- Make a time line or a sequence chart showing how the relationship between Maniac and Grayson is changing over time.
- Why was it so important to Maniac to paint a number on the door of the baseball room?
- Have you ever lost someone you were very close to? Can you relate to how Maniac feels?
- What will happen to Maniac now that Grayson is gone? Make some predictions.

Language Conventions:
Review of Share Sheets

- Depending on your class, you may want to review the share sheet format and encourage students to use it in their reading logs.

- If necessary, review with students how to create share sheets. Tell them that because they are becoming very good at Book Club, they should be writing several different types of responses to their reading each day. Share sheets allow them to combine several responses on one page so that they will have easy access to all of their ideas when they meet with their book clubs. (For more information about share sheets, turn to page 39 in the Teaching Tips chapter. An example of a student share sheet for *Maniac Magee* appears on page 218.)

- You may want to go over the list of response types that students know at this point and ask them to share any new formats they've invented. It helps to give students clear guidelines for what you expect them to do in their logs—e.g., four different response types per day.

- The section of the book that students will read today describes the growing closeness between Maniac and Grayson—and Maniac's feelings of desperation when his friend dies. This provides a good context for students to think about how relationships grow and change over time, how people deal with the death of a loved one, and how these events relate to the larger themes in *Maniac Magee*.

- During community share, you may want to focus on the time lines and sequence charts that students created to show how Maniac and Grayson's relationship changed from the time when Maniac politely refused to live with Grayson at the Y to the time when they celebrated Christmas together in the baseball room. Other topics that you may want to explore are the teaching and learning that are exchanged between the two, and Maniac's feelings when Grayson dies.

- Now that the students have completed Part II of the novel, they should be able to discuss how the major themes are being developed in the story. Some themes that you may wish to bring up with your students are Maniac's homelessness and his need to belong somewhere, what makes two or more people a family, and what effect painful losses can have on a person's life.

continued on next page

continued from previous page

Teaching Tip

One Book Club teacher found this to be a good time to conduct an oral reading assessment. She had her students rehearse reading Chapters 27–30 (pages 100–111) independently; then the students worked in pairs to read the section aloud to each other. While they read aloud, she walked around the classroom with a clipboard and took notes on their fluency. A Fluency Checklist is available in the Blackline Masters: Assessment section following page 281.

Sample Share Sheet
for Lesson 7

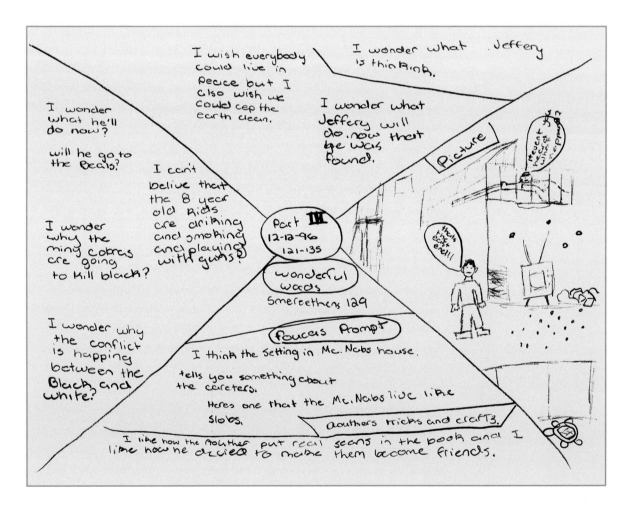

Lesson 7

GOAL:
To focus students' attention on setting and how the author uses it to develop his characters

ASSIGNED READING:
Chapters 33–36
(pages 121–140)

WRITING PROMPT:
How do certain settings in the book inform the reader about characters?

Literary Elements:
Setting

- At the end of yesterday's reading, Maniac was seen running away from Grayson's funeral. You might set up today's lesson by asking students to share any predictions they made about where Maniac will go next. Tell them that setting is an important story element at the beginning of Part III, and suggest that they pay special attention to where Maniac is and how that reflects what his life is like now.

- Either before or after students read, you might want to build background about Valley Forge, which is one of the settings in Chapters 33–34. Ask the class to share what they know about this place. If necessary, tell them that Valley Forge was the campground where George Washington and about 11,000 of his soldiers spent a miserable, cold winter in 1777–1778. The troops suffered from severe shortages of food, clothing, and shelter, and the Valley Forge National Historic Park pays tribute to their endurance and heroism.

- After students have done the reading, responded in their logs, and met with their book clubs, focus community share on the various settings they have encountered in the book so far. Begin with Valley Forge, and ask students to comment on what that setting was like and what the author might have been saying about Maniac by placing him in that setting. You might then make a chart on the chalkboard like the one shown below and fill it in with students' descriptions of each setting, including the mood that each one creates. You can also update your class story map with any new setting information.

Beales' house	101 Band Shell Blvd.
Pickwells' house	McNabs' house

- An example of a student's share sheet from this day in the lesson plan is shown on page 218.

continued on next page

continued from previous page

Teaching Tip

Here's an idea for an extension activity based on the "Picture Dialogue" activity in *Literature and Cooperative Learning: Pathway to Literacy,* by Nancy Whistler and Judy Williams (Literature Cooperative, 1990). Have students think about the mysterious scene between Maniac and Finsterwald on pages 139–140. Ask them to picture in their minds the conversation that might have taken place and write this dialogue in their logs. When they've finished writing, invite students to share their dialogues with other members of the class. Encourage them to compare and contrast the dialogues that were written. You might also have students work in pairs to act out the dialogues.

Lesson 8

GOAL:
To review the comprehension strategies of sequencing and summarizing the main events of a story

ASSIGNED READING:
Chapters 37–40
(pages 141–157)

Comprehension:
Sequencing and Summarizing

- As the novel becomes more complex in terms of events, characters, and settings, skills such as sequencing and summarizing become more important to students' comprehension. In this lesson students will have a chance to review these skills.

- Depending on the needs of your class, review with them how to make a sequence chart, map, or list to keep track of the main events of the story (in chronological order). In *Maniac Magee,* one reason it's important to keep the order of events straight is that Maniac's understanding of racism is growing with each experience he has. You might recall with students the first time Maniac realized that some people disliked him because he was white—when the old man in the East End called him "Whitey." Since then, he's encountered Grayson's naive ignorance about African Americans ("Them black people, they eat mashed potatoes, too?") and the virulent racism of the McNabs, who are preparing for an uprising of the East End "rebels." Maniac's attitude has gone from confusion to hurt to disgust, and tension is building toward a climax of the story.

- Tell the class that everyone should respond to the first writing prompt and make a sequence chart of the events in Chapters 37–40 today. You may choose to extend this writing prompt into a summary writing activity at the end of the Book Club session.

WRITING PROMPT:

- Create a sequence chart of the main events in Chapters 37–40. (Everyone should do this.)
- Have you or someone you know ever performed any heroic feats? Write about this.
- What was significant about the race with Mars Bar? Should Maniac have let him win? What would have happened if he had?
- Describe or draw a picture of the McNabs' pillbox. Why are they building it? How does Maniac feel about them now?

- After students have read the assignment, written in their logs, and met with their book clubs, focus community share on the issues that came up in students' small-group discussions. Students may want to talk about certain language used by Mars Bar, such as *fishbelly* and *honky donkey*. Ask them if they have any predictions about whom Maniac wants to bring to Piper's birthday party.

- If you want to take this opportunity to incorporate additional writing into the lesson, ask students to use their sequence charts to write summary paragraphs. Remind them that their paragraphs should not only list the story events but should have a strong concluding sentence. For example, they might draw a conclusion about what effect the events have had on Maniac.

Teaching Tip

The reference to the jump-rope song on page 142 lends itself to a creative-writing extension activity. You could ask students to take a heroic feat (one of their own, Maniac's, or someone else's) and turn it into a chant in the style of a jump-rope song. They can turn to the example in the "Before the Story" section of *Maniac Magee* (page 2) for inspiration.

Lesson 9

GOAL:
To have students create story graphs and discuss elements of plot

ASSIGNED READING:
Chapters 41–44
(pages 158–173)

Literary Elements:
Rising Action, Climax, Falling Action, Resolution

- This section of the reading contains the climax of the story, when Maniac brings Mars Bar to the McNabs' party. It is an opportune time to discuss rising action, climax, falling action, and resolution and to track these plot elements on a story graph.

- Introduce or review the concept of a story graph. Tell students that a story graph is a way to show how the events of a story (rising action) build to a climax (the most intense part of the story) and then slow down (falling action) as the book comes to an end. You might ask them what is creating tension in their minds at this point: What problem(s) are they anxious to see resolved?

continued on next page

continued from previous page

WRITING PROMPT:

- Draw a picture of a scene from today's reading. What words does the author use to help you visualize this scene?
- What was Maniac's purpose for bringing Mars to the West End? Why did he bring him to the Pickwells' and then to the McNabs'?
- What did Maniac learn from the birthday party experience?
- Has Maniac and Mars Bar's relationship changed? If so, how?
- Why did Maniac walk away at the end of Chapter 44?
- What scene do you think was the climax of the story? Why?

- Draw a story graph on the chalkboard, including a few of the events that have created tension so far. An example is provided below. Then ask students to watch for the climax of the story as they do today's reading.

- During community share, return to the story graph you started earlier. Ask students what they think was the climax of the story, and fill in the information on the graph. (If some students think that the scene on the trestle is the climax, explain that although this is an exciting scene, it is not directly related to the central conflict in the book, which is the tension between blacks and whites in Two Mills.) Tell students that the part of a story that follows the climax is sometimes called the resolution. During this part, any remaining conflicts are usually solved, and the book comes to a satisfying end.

Story Graph for
Maniac Magee

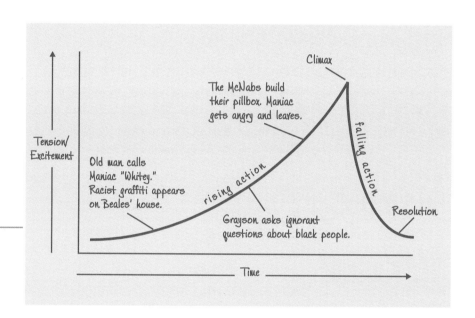

Lesson 10

GOAL:
To encourage students to think critically about what questions the author must answer in order to resolve the story's conflicts

ASSIGNED READING:
Chapters 45–46
(pages 174–184)

WRITING PROMPT:
- Why does Maniac tell Mars that he can't visit his house?
- What do you think of the way Amanda treats Maniac when she comes to get him? How does it make him feel?
- How do you feel about the way the author resolved the story's conflicts? Would you have ended the book any differently?
- Free write about your reaction to the book as a whole.

Response to Literature: Analyzing the Story's Resolution

- This lesson will give students a chance to think about the events of the book so far and then decide what conflicts still need to be resolved before the story ends.

- Before students begin today's reading, ask them to describe the different conflicts that have taken place in the book. Which of these conflicts do students feel have been resolved? How were they resolved?

- What do students feel the author still needs to address before the story ends? What do they predict might happen? (They can express their ideas in a class discussion or in their logs.)

- After students have had a chance to finish the book, write in their logs, and meet in their book club groups, you might invite them to discuss the book as a whole in community share. Are they happy with the way in which the author chose to resolve the conflicts? Why, or why not? What do students like most or least about the book? Why?

- If you have been tracking the story on a class story map, you can now add information about the resolution.

- An example of a student's free writing from this day in the lesson plan is provided on page 224.

Lesson 11

GOAL:
For students to assess their own performance during the *Maniac Magee* unit

ASSIGNED READING:
None

WRITING PROMPT:
Fill out a self-assessment form.

Student Self-Assessment

- See Lesson 12 of *Last Summer with Maizon,* page 80, for a fully developed self-assessment lesson.

- Distribute copies of the End-of-Book Self-Assessment sheet, or a similar sheet of your own design. (A blackline master is available in the Blackline Masters: Assessment section following page 281.) Tell students what your expectations are regarding their completion of the sheet, and give them time to write thoughtful answers.

Student Sample: Free Writing

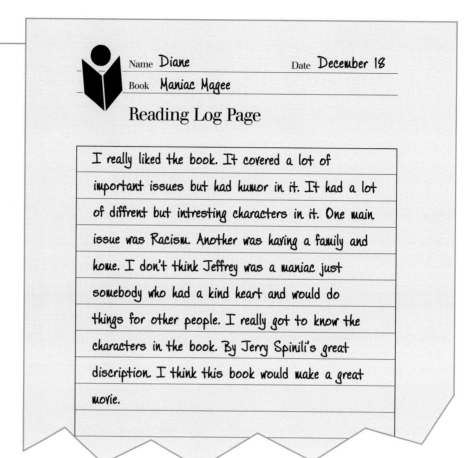

Name Diane   Date December 18
Book Maniac Magee

Reading Log Page

I really liked the book. It covered a lot of important issues but had humor in it. It had a lot of diffrent but intresting characters in it. One main issue was Racism. Another was having a family and home. I don't think Jeffrey was a maniac just somebody who had a kind heart and would do things for other people. I really got to know the characters in the book. By Jerry Spinili's great discription. I think this book would make a great movie.

Lesson 12

GOAL:
To inform students of the grades they've received for *Maniac Magee*, and to give them a chance to respond

ASSIGNED READING:
None

WRITING PROMPT:
Read over your grades and the comments I've written. Then fill out a Reactions and Goal-Setting Sheet.

Teacher Evaluation

- See Lesson 13 of *Last Summer with Maizon*, page 80, for a fully developed teacher evaluation lesson.

- Distribute copies of your grades and any other comments. (You can use the Book Club Evaluation forms from the Blackline Masters: Assessment section of this guide, or create similar forms based on your own curriculum.) Then allow students to read your evaluation and to fill out a Reactions and Goal-Setting Sheet, also available in the Blackline Masters: Assessment section. You can respond to students' comments as you're reading the Reactions form later on. An example of a student-teacher dialogue on a self-assessment sheet is provided on page 34.

Author Study: Mildred Taylor

Introducing the Books

Four powerful stories by Mildred Taylor provide an excellent opportunity to study several works by a single author. *Song of the Trees, Mississippi Bridge,* and *The Friendship* deal with the same family of characters, which will allow children to make intertextual links very easily. *The Gold Cadillac* features different characters but many of the same themes—prejudice, vulnerability, pride, family—allowing your students to make intertextual connections on a deeper level. The stories are all quite short and the vocabulary is not very challenging, although several are written in rural Southern dialect. The books can be used with grades four through six, depending on the maturity level of your class and how you think they will react to Taylor's honest and sometimes painful depictions of racism.

Summaries *Song of the Trees* is the first of Mildred Taylor's series of books about the Logans, a close-knit black family living in rural Mississippi. It takes place during the Depression, when Papa is forced to leave the farm to work on a railroad in Louisiana. The children—Stacey, Cassie, Christopher-John, and Little Man—stay home with their mother and their grandmother, Big Ma. Everyone loves the tall, old trees on their small farm. While Papa is gone, however, a white man named Mr. Andersen tries to cheat Big Ma into selling him the beautiful trees for lumber. The children are horrified by the thought, but Big Ma, moved by the family's need for money and Mr. Andersen's intimidation tactics, agrees to sells the trees. The children do not give up easily, however. As the men cut their trees down, they fight back in the best way they can. Papa returns and finally gets the men to leave the property by threatening to blow up the forest with dynamite. By the time the lumberers are scared off, though, they have already cleared many of the precious trees. The family stands by and sadly surveys the damage.

Paperback Editions. *Song of the Trees:* Bantam, © 1975 by Mildred Taylor, ISBN 0-553-27587-9. *Mississippi Bridge:* Bantam Skylark, © 1990 by Mildred D. Taylor, ISBN 0-553-15992-5. *The Friendship and The Gold Cadillac:* Bantam Doubleday Dell, © 1987 by Mildred D. Taylor, ISBN 0-440-41307-9.

Mississippi Bridge, another Depression-era story that includes the Logan family, is told from the point of view of Jeremy Simms, a shy ten-year-old white boy whose father is violently racist. Jeremy sits in the local store with his father, who is out of work, and sees small acts of racism unfold before his eyes on a daily basis. One day, the weekly bus stops in front of the store in the middle of a terrible rainstorm. Jeremy watches as the bus driver roughly forces black passengers off the bus to make room for more white passengers. Jeremy feels especially bad for his friend Josias Williams, a black man who was on his way to a rare job opportunity. The story takes a horrible turn when the bus veers off a rickety bridge and into the overflowing river. Despite Jeremy and Josias's courageous attempts to save them, many of the white passengers are drowned. When Josias recovers the limp body of a four-year-old girl Jeremy knew, Jeremy can only wonder why tragedies like this must happen.

In *The Friendship*, the Logan children are nervous when Aunt Callie sends them into town for medicine. They must go to the store owned by racist John Wallace, a place their parents have warned them never to enter. Just as they feared, the experience is humiliating and upsetting for them. Then they are forced to watch a confrontation between Mr. Wallace and Mr. Tom Bee, an elderly black man who dares to do the unthinkable: call a white man by his first name. Years ago, Bee saved young Wallace's life, after which Wallace promised his unending friendship. The older man takes this promise to heart, but Wallace cannot bear the humiliation of having a black man call him by his first name in front of his white customers. Bee continues to push the issue, and finally Wallace explodes into a rage, shooting the older man in the leg in front of the store. The children watch in horror as Mr. Tom Bee, crawling toward home with his shattered leg, continues to shout Wallace's first name in defiance.

The Gold Cadillac introduces readers to a new cast of Mildred Taylor characters. In 1950, 'lois and Wilma are thrilled when their father comes home one day with a brand-new gold Cadillac. Their mother, however, is angry about the purchase. They are saving for a new house, and he bought the car without consulting her. She refuses to ride in the car until one day when the girls' father decides to drive from their home in Ohio to visit his family in rural Mississippi. When the family crosses the state line—officially entering the South, where segregation laws are in effect—the girls learn what it is like to feel frightened because of the color of their skin. White people glare angrily at them in their fancy car. Then their father is stopped by white police officers for no reason, taken into custody, and held for three hours. The family, although hurt and humiliated, handles the situation sensibly and with a great deal of pride.

Themes Race relations in the United States, the strong ties of family, and issues of fairness are some of the most prominent themes in Mildred Taylor's works. Some Book Club teachers have used these books as a follow-up to a unit on the Civil War, showing students that racism and prejudice in the United States did not end with the surrender at Appomattox.

Special Classroom Library Any of Mildred Taylor's other books about the Logan family would be good choices for your classroom library. These include *Roll of Thunder, Hear My Cry* (Puffin Books, 1991), *Let the Circle Be Unbroken* (Puffin Books, 1991), *The Road to Memphis* (Puffin Books, 1992), and *The Well: David's Story* (Dial Books for Young Readers, 1995). Eve Bunting's book about race riots in Los Angeles, *Smoky Night* (Harcourt Brace, 1994), is another title you might consider. To allow your students to explore racial prejudice in other contexts, you could include books such as *Journey Home* by Yoshiko Uchida (Maxwell Maximillian International, 1992), *Maniac Magee* by Jerry Spinelli (HarperTrophy, 1990), *Year of Impossible Goodbyes* by Sook Nyul Choi (Houghton Mifflin, 1991), *Sing Down the Moon* by Scott O'Dell (Bantam Doubleday Dell, 1992), and *Tunes for Bears to Dance to* by Robert Cormier (Delacorte, 1992).

Lesson 1

GOAL:
To review Book Club format and the use of checklists; to review elements of author's craft such as imagery and the use of dialect

ASSIGNED READING:
Song of the Trees, pages 1–19

WRITING PROMPT:
Draw a picture of the forest.

Literary Elements:
Author's Craft—Imagery and Dialect

- A quick review of Book Club format and the use of checklists will help students to get the most out of this unit. Reading aloud and reviewing imagery and use of dialect will encourage students to hear and appreciate the language of the book.

- To begin the lesson, hold a brief review session of Book Club format and reading log checklists. You might ask students to discuss past Book Club experiences as part of the review. You might also choose to hold this review at the end of the lesson, just before students meet with their book clubs. (For fully developed lessons dealing with Book Club format and reading log checklists, see Lesson 1 for *Last Summer with Maizon*, page 57, and Lesson 1 for *Tuck Everlasting*, page 83, respectively.)

- NOTE: The first three stories that students will read are set during the Depression. Depending on whether your class has covered this era in social studies, you may want to build background about the United States economy in the 1930s and its impact on families.

- Ask students to look carefully at the book's front cover and predict what the story might be about. What could the title *Song of the Trees* mean?

- Read the day's reading assignment aloud to students, reminding them to listen carefully and to try to enjoy the book's language.

continued on next page

continued from previous page

- After the reading, review the terms *imagery* and *dialect.* Remind students that these are examples of author's craft—special ways in which a writer uses words to paint pictures in readers' minds or to make the story more interesting or realistic. Then ask them to scan the text that you read aloud to find examples of dialect and of imagery, especially words and phrases describing place. Record the words that students found on the chalkboard. Images that they are likely to notice include "shaggy-bark hickories"; "ambled into the coolness"; and "wrapped in jackets of emerald and gold." Ask students why an author might choose to write using dialect. Does it give the reader clues about where the story takes place? Does it make the characters of a story seem more realistic?

- One Book Club teacher asked each of her students to keep a "Wonderful Word and Phrase Book." Students enjoyed adding interesting words and phrases to the booklet as they read the four Mildred Taylor stories.

Lesson 2

GOAL:
To discuss with students how the author lets a reader get to know her characters, and to model character maps

ASSIGNED READING:
Song of the Trees,
pages 20–36

WRITING PROMPT:
- Make character maps of Mr. Andersen and Stacey, or write a paragraph describing a character in detail.
- What is Stacey doing in the story? Why? What would you do if you were in this situation?

Literary Elements:
Author's Craft—Characterization

- Mildred Taylor's characters are especially well drawn and memorable. This lesson will encourage students to think about the techniques she uses to create her characters.

- Discuss with students how readers can learn about characters by listening to what they say, by watching them interact with other characters, by reading direct descriptions of them, and by paying attention to their thoughts and feelings. Invite students to discuss what they know so far about the characters in *Song of the Trees,* and how the author has let them get to know the characters.

- If necessary, model how to create character maps (see page 63). If your class has been using character maps for a while, encourage them to move beyond this simple device. For example, you might ask them to write paragraphs about interesting characters, describing both *how* they act and *why* students think they act that way.

- At this point in the unit, you might begin to make regular rounds of the classroom during book clubs. Check to see that students are fully engaged in the discussions and that they're understanding the story.

Lesson 3

GOAL:
To discuss with students the sequence of events in the story so far and to model making a time line; to draw on students' prior knowledge of race issues

ASSIGNED READING:
Song of the Trees,
pages 36–52

WRITING PROMPT:
- Draw a time line of the events that happen from pages 36 to 52.
- What do you think the title of the book means?
- What would you have done if you were David?

Comprehension:
Sequencing; Building Background Knowledge

- Discussing with students the sequence of events in the story and modeling a time line as a visual tool for keeping track of the events will help them avoid getting confused as they read. Inviting students to discuss their ideas about race relations in the United States will help them become more involved in the themes of Mildred Taylor's work.

- Remind students that the story's sequence consists of the events of the story, listed in the order in which they happened. Ask students to discuss the sequence of events in the story so far.

- Model a time line of the events so far on the chalkboard or overhead projector. Tell students that they can keep a time line in their reading logs and update it as they read. This tool could come in handy during book clubs or community share when they need to remember important events of the story for the purpose of discussion. (Alternative formats for sequence charts appear on pages 140 and 179.)

- Give students a chance to read the day's assignment. Then meet as a class to discuss the ways in which this book demonstrates relationships between blacks and whites in the 1930s. Students should back up their statements with specific incidents from the book. In what ways do students believe black and white relations have changed since then? What events have happened to change relations? What do students feel people still need to work on in this area?

Teaching Tip

During this unit, one Book Club teacher invited a guest to her classroom to discuss Martin Luther King, Jr., with her students. This lesson marks an appropriate time to bring in such additional resources, if you wish to do so. Other options might include watching a movie or reading aloud a book about Martin Luther King, Jr., or about changes in African Americans' access to their civil rights since the 1930s.

Lesson 4

GOAL:
To present students with information and to hold a discussion about racism, prejudice, and segregation; to discuss point of view in the story

ASSIGNED READING:
Mississippi Bridge,
pages 7–22

WRITING PROMPT:
Write about the differing ways John treats his customers. How does he treat Rudine and her mama? How does he treat Miz Hattie McElroy and Grace Ann?

Comprehension:
Building Background Knowledge; Point of View

- Continuing the class discussion of racism, prejudice, and segregation will allow you to give students more historical background information. Reviewing the literary element *point of view* will prepare students to discuss how *Mississippi Bridge*—which is told from the point of view of a white boy—sounds different from *Song of the Trees,* which was told from Cassie's point of view.

- Building on your community share conversation in Lesson 3, begin a discussion about racism, prejudice, and segregation—both in history and in the world today—by asking students what they know about these topics. You might record their responses on the blackboard or overhead projector.

- Introduce students to the term *Jim Crow laws.* Explain that it refers to segregation laws that were passed in many Southern states after the end of the Civil War. Jim Crow laws separated black and white people in public places such as streetcars, trains, schools, and theaters. (Jim Crow was the name of a black character in a minstrel show.) Ask students how they would feel if they lived in a community controlled by Jim Crow laws. How might segregation have affected the way people felt about themselves and others?

- Ask students to define *point of view.* How does point of view affect the telling of a story? Are there times when a character's point of view helps make a story more realistic? Students might back up their responses with examples from other books they've read.

Lesson 5

GOAL:
To have students compare and contrast characters in the book using a Venn diagram

ASSIGNED READING:
Mississippi Bridge,
pages 23–37

Comprehension:
Comparing and Contrasting

- Explain to students that to compare is to examine the ways in which two or more things are alike, and to contrast is to examine the ways in which two or more things are different. Comparing and contrasting two people or things will give them a deeper understanding of each person or thing. You might give them practice by asking them to compare and contrast two people or items in the classroom.

WRITING PROMPT:

Where does Cassie want Big Ma to sit on the bus? Why? What do the people around her think?

- With the assistance of students, do a Venn diagram on the chalkboard or overhead projector in which you compare and contrast the Logans with Mr. Andersen from *Song of the Trees.* (A student's Venn diagram for the book *Hatchet* and examples of two other formats that students can use for comparing and contrasting appear on pages 184–185.)

- Encourage students to compare and contrast other characters in their reading logs as they read *Mississippi Bridge, The Friendship,* and *The Gold Cadillac.*

Lesson 6

GOAL:

For students to discuss the feelings and emotions of the characters and write about their own feelings about the story

ASSIGNED READING:

Mississippi Bridge,
pages 37–51

WRITING PROMPT:

Why does the bus driver make Josias get off the bus? What is Jeremy's reaction? How does Jeremy's father react toward Jeremy? How does this make you feel?

Response to Literature:
Feelings About the Story

- Discussing the feelings and emotions of the characters will help students gain a better understanding of the characters and the author's technique in sharing the feelings of the characters.

- Ask students to name the different feelings and emotions of the characters so far. To help them with this discussion, you might ask them to look over the scenes they have read, focusing on each character.

- Ask them to describe what the author does to let readers know how the characters are feeling. Does the author show characters' emotions in their words and interactions with one another? Does the author show characters' emotions by describing their gestures and facial expressions? Ask students to explain their responses and back them up with details from the story.

- The writing prompt for today encourages students to write about their own feelings about the story. Taylor's emotionally intense stories have produced strong feelings in the Book Club students who have read them. An example of a student's response to today's writing prompt is shown on page 232.

Student Sample: Feelings

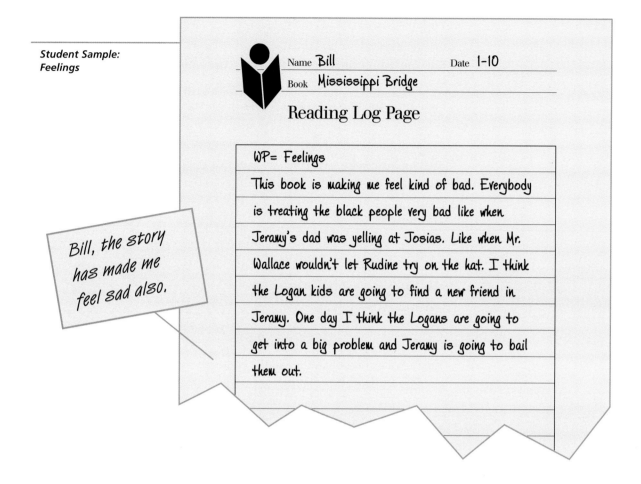

Name Bill   Date 1-10

Book Mississippi Bridge

Reading Log Page

WP= Feelings

This book is making me feel kind of bad. Everybody is treating the black people very bad like when Jeramy's dad was yelling at Josias. Like when Mr. Wallace wouldn't let Rudine try on the hat. I think the Logan kids are going to find a new friend in Jeramy. One day I think the Logans are going to get into a big problem and Jeramy is going to bail them out.

Bill, the story has made me feel sad also.

Lesson 7

GOAL:
To help students discuss the author's purpose and why people might want to write about true stories

ASSIGNED READING:
Mississippi Bridge, pages 51–62

WRITING PROMPT:
Why do you think Mildred Taylor wrote this story? What is her message?

Response to Literature:
Analyzing the Author's Purpose

- This lesson will help students examine the different reasons an author might have for writing a particular story.

- Ask students to describe any true stories or articles they have read. What did they learn from these stories? Why did the writers feel it was important to share these stories? Why do people write true stories?

- Explain to students the idea of author's purpose, or the particular message an author might be trying to share with a reader. Tell them that as they read the end of *Mississippi Bridge*, they should think about what the author is trying to say to them. What do they believe the author wants them to take away from the story? You might also mention that Taylor got the idea for this story from her father's oral storytelling. Why might she want to record such stories for others to read?

Lesson 8

GOAL:
To review the concept of intertextuality with students and to discuss the prejudice found in the opening pages of the book

ASSIGNED READING:
The Friendship,
pages 5–26

WRITING PROMPT:
What do you think is happening in this part of the story? Think about the other books you've read as you support your opinion.

Comprehension:
Making Intertextual Connections

- A review of the concept of intertextuality will help students make connections between the Mildred Taylor books they've read so far.

- Have students do today's reading **before** you conduct this lesson.

- Review with students the word *intertextuality.* Explain to them that often one book or movie might remind them of another book or movie because of similar characters, story lines, or themes. Invite them to make intertextual connections between books and movies they've seen. You might model ways to record intertextual connections, such as compare/contrast charts, Venn diagrams, lists, and so on.

- Explain that different stories by a single author often have common threads, simply because sharing certain messages, issues, experiences, and characters might be important to that author.

- After having read two stories by Mildred Taylor, what do students believe might be a theme in *The Friendship*? What examples of prejudice have they noticed in this first part of the story? Ask students to back up their responses with evidence from the text.

- Remind students that as they respond to today's writing prompt, they should remember their discussion of intertextuality and try to make connections between *The Friendship* and the other Mildred Taylor stories they've read.

Lesson 9

GOAL:
To encourage students to think about and discuss the story's title

ASSIGNED READING:
The Friendship,
pages 26–47

Response to Literature:
Personal Response

- A key word in this story is *friendship,* and this lesson will encourage students to focus on the concept of friendship and decide what it means to them.

- Ask students to describe what friendship means to them. What does it mean to be a good friend? When you promise to be someone's friend, what responsibilities do you have to that person?

continued on next page

continued from previous page

WRITING PROMPT:

Write about friendship and how friendship is defined in the story.

- What do students think of the "friendship" between Mr. Tom Bee and Mr. John Wallace?

- After students have done today's reading, written in their logs, and met with their book clubs, give them plenty of time during community share to discuss what they wrote about friendship and how they felt when John Wallace shot Tom Bee. Do they have any compassion for Wallace? What drove him to hurt his friend?

Teaching Tip

One Book Club teacher chose to read the last part of this book aloud so that the whole class could experience together the full impact of the story's powerful conclusion. In her classroom, students were stunned by the ending.

Lesson 10

GOAL:

To define *recurring theme* for students and then have them identify Mildred Taylor's recurring themes

ASSIGNED READING:

The Gold Cadillac, pages 53–87

WRITING PROMPT:

Consider the three stories you've read so far. What do you think Mildred Taylor's recurring theme, or repeated message, is?

Literary Elements:
Theme

- This lesson will encourage students to recognize themes that are repeated throughout the work of Mildred Taylor.

- Tell students that a recurring theme in an author's work is a repeated message or idea. An author might repeat in several different works the same message or idea about people, places, or issues. This is because an author is usually inspired to write about subjects and ideas that are important and familiar to him or her.

- After students have completed the reading assignment, the writing prompt, and book clubs, meet in community share to discuss Mildred Taylor's repeated themes. One Book Club teacher who taught this unit reported that community share was particularly exciting and powerful on this day. She found that students were able to make intertextual connections between Mildred Taylor's books and texts that they'd read previously (in other content areas) about such issues as the treatment of immigrant groups when they first arrived in the United States, European treatment of Native Americans, and other issues surrounding prejudices in today's world. This teacher decided to make a time line on the chalkboard that traced the historical events of African Americans in this country. Her time line was divided into the categories shown below.

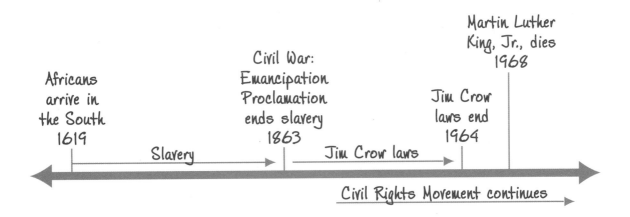

Teaching Tip

A good source of historical background for students is *Time for Kids*, a weekly news magazine published by *Time Magazine*. The students in one Book Club classroom are avid readers of this magazine and look forward to its appearance each week. As these students read and discussed the Mildred Taylor books, much of the historical background knowledge they had came from this magazine.

- Sample reading log entries about recurring themes appear on pages 236–237.

Name *Charlene*   Date *1/20*

Book *Mildred Taylor trilogy*

Reading Log Page

Consider the 3 books you have read. What do you think Mildred Taylor's reoccuring theme was?

I think the reoccuring theme was that black or colored people were not treated fairly. I think she wanted to show that life was not always easy. She wanted to show everyone how bad it was and she did this so that these bad actions wouldn't be repeated. I also think she wanted to show what it was like from a colored person's point of view, except for in Mississippi Bridge, where a white person who doesn't hate black people told. I think she wanted to show that not all white people hated colored people but those who did were real mean. If I had written a book like this I would have written the same kind of message, because I think we are really lucky, now.

Student Sample:
Recurring Themes #2

Name David   Date January 20

Book Mildred Taylor books

Reading Log Page

Consider the 3 books you have read. What do you think Mildred Taylor's reoccurring theme is?

I think that the reoccurring theme is the prejudice between whites and blacks. In Song of the Trees, Mr. Anderson and his crew "X"ed the trees before they had permission to create stumps and only paid them 60 frog-skins (dollars) for almost the entire forest when they said they would only chop down some of the trees (which were not to mention on the Logan's property). In Mississippi Bridge, Mr. John Wallace would let Miz Hattie try on a sky blue hat and wouldn't let Rudine try on the hat unless she bought it, no refunds. The bus driver forced the black people off the bus because of the Jim Crow Laws and let white people sit there, showing segregation. In The Friendship, Mr. John

©1997 Small Planet Communications, Inc.

Wallace pulled his shot gun of the shelf behind his desk and shot Mr. Tom Bee in the leg just because Mr. Tom Bee was calling John Wallace just John, not Mr. John or Mr. John Wallace. In The Gold Cadillac, just because the policeman saw a black family driving a really nice car, he pulled them over, gave him a speeding ticket, made him pay a fine, and put him in jail for three hours. The leson is never repeat prejudice.

Lesson 11

GOAL:
To begin to bring closure to the unit and to assess students' understanding of the books

ASSIGNED READING:
None

WRITING PROMPT:
See lesson at right for writing prompts.

Response to Literature:
Critical Response; Process Writing

- This lesson is designed to help you assess students' understanding of the books. Students' writing in response to today's prompts will create a valuable assessment artifact. One Book Club teacher chose to base her unit grades for the students on this final writing assignment.

- In community share, ask students to bring up any questions or comments they might still have about the three books. Then give them their choice of the following writing prompts and allow them to start their process writing.

  – Mildred Taylor's books teach us about life. What is the best lesson about life that you have learned from her books?

  – Which character from the four stories do you admire the most? Why? Give evidence from the story to support your choice. How does Mildred Taylor shape this character?

  – Mildred Taylor's books have themes of prejudice and racism. How have her books influenced your thinking about racism and prejudice?

  – Write about another issue in Taylor's stories that you think is important or interesting.

- You'll probably want to give students several days to complete the writing, and have them work on their process writing during a separate period of the day. When students have completed their first drafts, you can have them participate in peer conferences to get constructive criticism from their classmates.

Lesson 12

GOAL:
To give students a chance to assess their own work and set goals for the next Book Club unit

Self-Assessment and Goal-Setting

- NOTE: While students are completing their process writing, you can have them conduct a self-assessment as described in this lesson. Assessing their work in this unit and setting goals for the next gives students a valuable opportunity to reflect on the skills that they are gaining through Book Club and which areas still need improvement.

ASSIGNED READING:
None

WRITING PROMPT:
Complete a self-assessment sheet, or write a critique of your work in your reading log.

- Ask students to go through the work they've done in their reading logs in this unit and select the pieces that represent their best work.

- Ask students to identify their strengths and weaknesses. What might they like to improve during the next Book Club? What goals will they set?

- Students may write their assessments on a blank sheet of paper or they may use the End-of-Book Self-Assessment sheet in the Blackline Masters: Assessment section following page 281.

Lesson 13

GOAL:
To encourage students to focus on Mildred Taylor as an author and find the commonalities in her books

ASSIGNED READING:
None

WRITING PROMPT:
None

Literary Elements:
Theme and Other Common Elements in Taylor's Books

- NOTE: You may want to wait until students have completed the first drafts of their process writing assignments before conducting this final lesson. Your class discussion of the commonalities in Mildred Taylor's books will prepare them to comment on each other's writing and to revise their own.

- Discuss with students the common elements found in each of Mildred Taylor's books. Encourage students to use their reading logs for ideas as they contribute to the class discussion.

- Ask students what they enjoyed about the characters, settings, and themes in Taylor's books. What characters, settings, and themes made them uncomfortable?

- Give students a chance to hold peer conferences and to revise their process writing assignments. Encourage students to pay close attention to the work of their peers and give each other constructive criticism.

- A sample of a student's completed process writing is shown on page 240.

Teaching Tip

- At the conclusion of the unit, you may want to share some additional information about Mildred Taylor with the class. You can begin by directing students' attention to the information contained in the books

continued on next page

continued from previous page

themselves (e.g., Author's Note, About the Author). Some students may want to do research to find out more.

- One Book Club teacher ended her Mildred Taylor unit with a Reader's Theater activity. Her students enjoyed creating scripts based on the stories and presenting them to the class. For more about Reader's Theater, see pages 141–142 in the lesson plan for *The Fighting Ground.*

Student Sample:
Process Writing

CHRISTOPHER JOHN

The Mildred Taylor trilogy is three books. One is Song of the Trees. The second is Mississippi Bridge. The third one is The Friendship and the Gold Cadillac. Christopher John is my favorite character in the Mildred Taylor trilogy.

I like Christopher John because he has a sweet tooth and eats a lot. For example, in The Friendship when Christopher reached the store he ran to the candy jar and was eyeing the candy in the jar for awhile. Another example is in the Song of the Trees where he stayed up and ate bread all night. I also like Christopher because I can relate to him.

One way I relate to him is because we both have a sweet tooth and we both eat a lot. Also we are both slow runners and usually run out of breath quickly. Christopher John and I are both slothful. Both of us are kind of fat. Christopher John doesn't relate to me because he is easily alarmed.

He was petrified once when they were walking on the bridge. Christopher didn't want to go and stood there frozen. When he went he held Stacey's hand and closed his eyes as he walked. This happened in Mississippi Bridge. Christopher was scared when they thought Big Ma perished, but they were all scared. This also happened in Mississippi Bridge.

That is why Christopher John is my favorite character. He has a sweet tooth, is apprehensive, eats a lot, is a slow runner, and is slothful. The Mildred Taylor Trilogy had some great stories. For example, Mississippi Bridge. It had drama, action, and suspense. So I advise you to read the trilogy.

Multi-Book Units

Introduction

In schools today we hear a lot about giving children choices within which their learning can occur. In the Book Club program, we allow choice through the literature students choose to read, their written responses, and their membership in book club discussion groups. Multi-book units, in which each small group reads a different book that the children have selected, give students the greatest amount of choice and are thus a natural extension of Book Club. However, introducing too many choices overwhelms students just beginning the program. We've found it best to limit choices at first and then gradually allow more freedom as the year progresses.

Over the course of the year, we expand students' choice to include literature selection by moving to multi-book units in which four or five thematically or topically related books are offered as reading options. The children enjoy having a say in the choice of literature, and they feel motivated to read books that they've chosen themselves. They also gain several additional advantages in multi-book units. First, they are encouraged to develop and articulate their individual tastes in literature. Second, by hearing about the books their peers are reading, students are exposed to other texts that they may, in turn, decide to read themselves. Last, as several related titles are discussed in the classroom, students learn to make intertextual connections, relating ideas from their own reading to the books read by their peers. These intertextual connections help children construct meaning about the theme or topic and enhance content-area learning.

Theme and Curriculum There are many methods that teachers use to select themes for classroom study. Themes can take all year to develop, can connect to subject-matter learning, can exist within a grading period, or can simply be tied to a particular set of books. For example, for the year-long theme "Survival requires adaptation," you might focus units on American colonization, species adaptation, and the Civil War—all of which help children develop the theme. (For further reading about theme/topic selection, see Lipson, Valencia, Wixson and Peters, 1993, cited in the Bibliography.) The same methods that you use to select themes for other areas of instruction can be applied to Book Club, and especially to multi-book units.

Parallel to identifying a theme for study, you'll need to consider the curriculum needs of your students. There are several curricular foci for teaching through the Book Club program. During theme-based, multi-book units, students will learn about content, literature, and literacy. First, there may be general content knowledge that you want your students to gain. This content will be reflected in the theme or topic of the unit (e.g., civil rights, the Civil War, ecosystems, the life cycle). Second, your students will learn about literature as they read various titles and genres. Finally, there will be literacy curricular content in the areas of language conventions, literary elements, comprehension, and response to literature. (See the Book Club Curricular Target Areas chart on pages 26–27.)

Multi-book units provide as many advantages for teachers as they do for students. Instruction becomes more meaningful and more relevant when the students share a variety of books about a theme or topic. It can be easier to facilitate discussions in which children are eager to share their own book and use that book to develop an issue or idea with the whole class. Despite these advantages, though, multi-book units can be challenging to create and to teach. This chapter provides suggestions and ideas to help you implement multi-book units in your classroom.

Structuring a Multi-Book Unit

While there are many options for structuring a multi-book unit in Book Club, here we'll highlight three formats that we've found to be especially effective for literacy learning and content-area study. The chart on page 243 describes these three formats.

You'll want to think about several issues to determine the best format to use in your classroom at a particular time. And, since each class and situation is unique, you'll probably find yourself revisiting this decision as you plan each new multi-book unit. The relevant issues to consider include your thematic and curricular goals, the availability of books, the time of year and students' abilities in Book Club, and your own comfort level with the program.

Managing more than one title requires planning, organization, and specific strategies if the unit is to run smoothly and the students are to take advantage of the many opportunities for intertextual and content learning. As you read through the example unit provided here, think about the management system that's being used. Your reaction to that management system—whether or not you can imagine yourself doing it successfully—will be one indicator of your readiness to implement multi-book units.

Multi-Book Unit Formats

Option 1

You can use three or four short books (or picture books) to introduce a theme, with each group reading a different book. Then the whole class can read a single novel. This format is a good transition between single- and multi-book units.

Option 2

You can select three or four books on the same theme and have the class rotate through all the books: each group reads one book and then passes it along to another group, until all the groups have read all the books. Short books are best—students sometimes get bored reading several long books on the same theme. This format has worked well with genre studies such as folk tales or biographies.

Option 3

You can select several chapter books to be read simultaneously, with each book club reading a different title. This format uses three to five books on the same theme or topic—e.g., participating in the Civil War; friendships are something that we work to develop; the prelude to the Civil Rights movement; genre studies such as fantasy.

Now let's examine one successful multi-book unit. It will include: (1) objectives for the unit (including theme and curriculum areas), (2) literature selections, (3) descriptions of the inquiry and Book Club phases of the unit, (4) a structure for managing the unit, and (5) assessment measures used during the unit. This unit differs from the others in this guide in that we don't present a day-by-day lesson plan but instead suggest a format that you can use to plan your own multi-book units. We hope that you'll be able to use the single-book lesson plans and the format and decisions surrounding this unit as models to create your own effective multi-book units. Resources for several other multi-book units appear at the conclusion of this chapter.

The Civil War Unit

This unit was used as the final Book Club unit of the fifth-grade school year. The teacher was using Book Club to teach both reading and social studies. The structure of the unit followed Option 3, in which several groups read different novels simultaneously. An overview of the entire unit appears on pages 246–247.

Objectives The teacher had identified several goals for this unit, relating to content, literacy, and metacognition. She wanted her students to become more aware of and accountable for their own learning, as well as to acquire content knowledge about the Civil War through the use of various text resources. Her objectives appear below.

Objectives for the Civil War Unit

- As part of the social studies curriculum, the children will gain and demonstrate knowledge of the historical period surrounding the Civil War.

- Because point of view is an objective in the district's language arts curriculum, the students will be able to look at the war through the eyes of individuals involved, both real and fictional.

- As part of the Book Club curriculum, the children will be able to use a variety of reading log responses without a specific prompt and will be able to monitor the frequency of those responses.

- Crossing all three areas—social studies, language arts, and literature—students will examine and explore intertextual connections throughout the span of the entire unit, using many text resources.

- The children will take responsibility for their own learning and exhibit the metacognitive skills of planning, monitoring, and ownership.

The teacher also decided to share her goals with the class. She hoped this would help her students achieve the metacognitive goals (planning, monitoring, and ownership) set forth in her objectives. She divided the unit into three phases and used an overhead transparency of the chart shown on page 245 to discuss her goals with the class.

Civil War Unit Plan

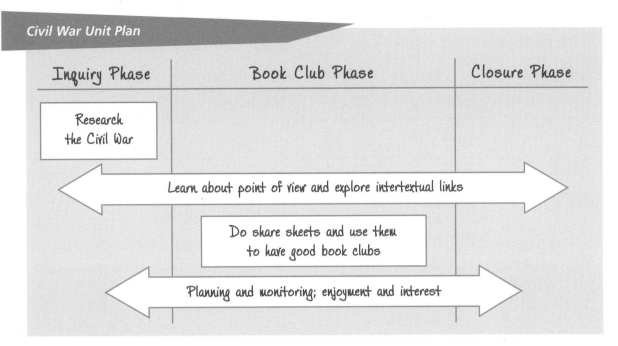

Inquiry Phase	Book Club Phase	Closure Phase

Research the Civil War

←— Learn about point of view and explore intertextual links —→

Do share sheets and use them to have good book clubs

←— Planning and monitoring; enjoyment and interest —→

Teacher Comment:

"I shared this unit plan with my class so they could see how I think about a unit before I begin teaching it. By doing this I was modeling the metacognitive skill of planning, which I wanted them to learn and practice themselves. The chart shows the three phases of the unit—inquiry, Book Club, and closure—and tells what my goals were for each phase. Some of the goals reached across all three phases."

Literature Selection Books were selected for this unit for many different purposes. There were the books for the social studies part of the unit (expository texts to teach content and context); a special classroom library that included novels, picture books, and nonfiction texts; the read-aloud novel; four novels that the students read for their book club discussions; and an additional read-aloud picture book used near the end of the unit. All books used in this unit are referenced in the chart on page 256.

The read-aloud book that began the unit was Irene Hunt's *Across Five Aprils* (Silver Burdett, 1993), which tells the story of one family's involvement with the Civil War. The four book club novels were chosen to provide a variety of ways to look at the war. *Behind Rebel Lines* by Seymour Reit (Harcourt Brace, 1991) tells the story of Emma Edmonds, a Michigan woman who entered the Civil War disguised as a man and worked as a spy for the Union forces. Carolyn Reeder's *Shades of Gray* (Avon Books, 1991) takes place after the war and centers around young Will, who comes to live with his uncle's family after his own family dies during the war. Will struggles in his relationship with his uncle, who chose not to fight in the war. *Turn Homeward, Hannalee* by Patricia Beatty (Troll Communications, 1990) portrays two Southern children captured by Union soldiers and forced to work as slaves in the North. *Who Comes with Cannons?*, also by Patricia Beatty (Morrow, 1992), explores the roles of the Underground Railroad and the Quaker people during the Civil War through the eyes of twelve-year-old Truth.

Overview of Civil War Unit

I. Purpose

To help students become more aware of and accountable for their own learning, and to help them acquire content knowledge about the Civil War

II. Outcomes

A. Content (knowledge of the Civil War historical period)
  1. Be able to identify reasons for/issues surrounding the war
  2. Be familiar with vocabulary relevant to this time period (e.g., *Confederate, Union, rebel, Underground Railroad*)
  3. Be able to characterize life during the war
  4. Become familiar with key historical figures
  5. Explore the impact the Civil War has on current issues

B. Literary: Point of view—Be able to look at the war through the eyes of those involved, both real and fictional characters (exploring issues of courage, bravery, family)

C. Literacy
  1. Reading logs and reading response
    a. Learn the share sheet format
    b. Take ownership of response choices (without being bound to checklist)
    c. Show evidence of using the log to influence talk (will need to tape record)
  2. Intertextual links
    a. Be able to examine links between the research/inquiry phase and the Book Club phase
    b. Be able to explore relationships between fictional characters in the several books being read for Book Club

D. Metacognitive: Planning
  1. Identify inquiry question
  2. Create plan for research
  3. Create plan for Book Club reading
  4. Be able to monitor this process

E. Attitude/Interest: Internal motivation and enthusiasm
  1. Demonstrate a good attitude toward learning
  2. Show a desire to learn about the Civil War
  3. Display excitement over taking ownership of learning

III. Portfolios

Portfolios will be used to show something from each of the outcomes to provide evidence of learning. Portfolio tools and artifacts are described below.

A. Tools
  1. Anecdotal notes taken during inquiry phase and book club groups
  2. Checklists
    a. Of content knowledge
    b. For interest and attitude
  3. Survey: At end of unit, ask how students liked the unit, how it compares to others they've done, if I should do it again, how to change it, etc.
  4. Informal interviews: Attitude/interest

III. Portfolios, continued

B. Artifacts

1. Writing samples
   a. "K" sheets done in pairs for KWLS
   b. "L" sheets done individually for KWLS
   c. Inquiry question/Note cards/Final report

2. Response log: To demonstrate understanding of . . .
   a. Point of view
   b. Use of share sheets
   c. Intertextual links

3. Audio tapes: Will be reviewed to determine if . . .
   a. Share sheets influence student discussion
   b. Intertextual links are being made
   c. Students make references to point of view
   d. Content knowledge is being used to make sense of novel

4. Plans
   a. For inquiry question
   b. For reading

5. Self-assessment
   a. To monitor plans
   b. To look at internal motivation and enthusiasm

The Inquiry Phase The first phase of the unit—the inquiry phase—lasted about three weeks and focused students on developing their knowledge of Civil War history. This was done primarily through individual research reports, for which students generated their own questions for study, methods and materials for studying, and formats for organizing and presenting the information to the rest of the class. (A sample lesson plan for the first day of the inquiry phase appears on page 249.)

Here's how the inquiry phase was conducted. First students worked in pairs to fill in the "K" section of KWL think sheets (found in the Blackline Masters: Think Sheets section following page 261). The KWL strategy helps children organize prior knowledge about a topic and think about how new information alters this knowledge. (See Ogle, 1986, for more information on this strategy.) *K* stands for What I **K**now, *W* is for What I **W**ant to Know, and *L* is for What I **L**earned. KWLS is an adaptation of this strategy in which *S* stands for What I **S**till Want to Know (Hoffman, 1994).

Students wrote down all the information they already knew about the Civil War. Then the whole class came together to fill in the "K" and "W" sections on a class chart. This was in conjunction with a lesson on good inquiry questions in which the teacher discussed what kinds of questions were worthy of lengthy study. She stressed that questions that elicited one-word answers or questions with obvious answers were not appropriate. Some examples appear in the chart on page 248.

Examples of Poor Inquiry Questions	Examples of Good Inquiry Questions
How many people died in the war?	What were the causes of the Civil War?
Which side won the war?	What was life like for an average soldier in the Civil War?
Did the North fight the South?	What were some important Civil War battles?
When was the Civil War?	What was President Lincoln's role in the war?

At this time the class identified four "W" questions to be studied as a whole group. The teacher then modeled each of the steps in an inquiry, providing her students with as much support as necessary while they worked on gaining content knowledge, making intertextual connections, and monitoring/planning their own learning. She modeled how to gather information from various sources, how to organize the information, and how to write a summary of the information. She researched the first question on her own and wrote a summary of her findings in the "L" section of the class chart. For the second question, she read some expository text aloud, took notes on chart paper, and then wrote a summary, thinking aloud for students the whole time. The last two questions she divided among the student groups for research, and the class worked together to fill in the "L" section of the chart based on what they learned.

Next, the class identified some questions that they still had and added these to the "S" section of the class chart. (Students can also work individually or in small groups to come up with these inquiry questions—see the Ideas for Inquiry Questions sheet in the Blackline Masters: Think Sheets section following page 261.) Some of the "S" questions were simply carried over from the "W" section, and others arose from the research students had done. Students then selected the questions from the chart that they would like to tackle for their independent inquiry reports. The teacher had students think about which questions they would like to do; then she called out their names in random order and allowed each child to pick his or her first choice from the remaining questions on the list. This provided a fair way to allow students to choose, and it avoided duplication.

The students then created plans for their independent research, writing down what resources they would use, how they would take notes, how they would present their findings, and so on. (A sample Inquiry Question Planning Sheet is provided in the Blackline Masters: Think Sheets section.) They took notes on note cards, wrote reports summarizing their information, and gave oral presentations to share their knowledge with the class. The teacher gave students the option of including their written reports in their portfolios. The oral presentations, which increased the amount of content encountered by the class, marked the end of the inquiry phase. Students now shared a common base of knowledge to draw upon during the Book Club phase of the unit.

Lesson Plan   Day 1: Start of Inquiry Phase

1. **Journal Focus:** Have students write in their journals about everything they know, have heard, or have seen about the Civil War. This will serve as a sort of rehearsal for filling out the "K" section of the KWL sheet, and will give children time to think in a risk-free context.

2. **Introduction:** Really build up the unit with students. Let them in on the unit plan (page 245). If you want them to learn to plan, it's important that they see evidence of your planning. Explain the five objectives. They need to become aware of what you expect and to take responsibility for working toward the objectives. They can also help identify what should be put in their portfolios when they have reached an objective.

3. **Bulletin Board:** Have bulletin board materials up for the first day to generate interest and provide some information. Also have KWLS on large chart paper posted on wall. (A description of these materials begins on page 252.)

4. **Group Brainstorm:** Students should use their think sheets to brainstorm with a partner or small group all the information they collectively know about the Civil War.

5. **KWLS:** Begin lesson by filling in the "K" section of the class chart.

6. **Begin Read Aloud:** *Across Five Aprils*

7. **Parent Letter:** Send a letter home to inform parents about the unit. Suggest films and books that they could watch or read at home. Offer topics of conversation that could be shared around these films and books. Ask if anyone has Civil War memorabilia or an ancestor who was in the war. Invite those with things to share into the classroom.

The Book Club Phase At the beginning of this phase, the teacher did a "book sale" in which she briefly described each of the four novels, including setting, main characters, point of view, plot, and readability/difficulty of the text. Students were asked to rank the books from the one they would most like to read to the one they would least like to read. Groups of four or five children were formed based on these selections, and most children received either their first or second choice of literature. As part of the fifth goal of the unit, planning and monitoring their own learning, groups planned their reading of the book. Given the length of the Book Club phase (twelve days), students planned when and in which ways (i.e., silently, in partners, as a group) they would read the book. (See the Book Club Reading Plan in the Blackline Masters: Think Sheets section following page 261.) Below is a sample lesson plan for the first day of the Book Club phase.

Lesson Plan

Day 14: Transition to Book Club Phase

1. *Across Five Aprils:* Continue discussion and chart as necessary.

2. **Presentations:** Allow remaining students to present the results of their research. Hand back reports with grades; talk about these grades and opportunities to improve them.

3. **Closure of charts:** Briefly review all the issues and ideas on the charts. Point out that the time line (see page 253) contains information from both the inquiry reports and *Across Five Aprils;* tell students that the class will add to it during the next phase of the unit.

4. **Book Club:** Pass back old reading logs; have students evaluate them, review the goals they set at the end of the last unit, and plan for their reading logs during this unit. Explain how Book Club will be different, both in log formats (share sheets) and reading assignments (students' own plans). Discuss the Reading Plan and how it will work. Pass out books. Have students work on their reading plans and make predictions about the books in their logs.

Book Club proceeded as usual during this multi-book unit. Each day began with a lesson focusing on a topic determined by the teacher's objectives. Students then read their own books in the manner and increments determined by their reading plans. Following the reading, students wrote in their response logs, focusing on using a variety of response types. Book club groups maintained regular book club conversations as they discussed their own books and responses each day.

Community share looks quite different in a multi-book unit. The focus remains on understanding and making meaning—however, it shifts from comprehension of a single title to a wider understanding of the theme or topic. During community share for the Civil War unit, the teacher focused specifically on some of her original objectives. She used it as a time for students to gain further content knowledge about the war, to model and make intertextual connections between books, and to explore multiple perspectives on the war. It also provided an excellent forum for students to construct new understandings based on sharing information from their respective books. Some of the issues that arose included the right of the South to secede, the issue of slavery, the "rightness" of war, and the idea of desertion. The students explored these issues from different points of view, such as the North versus the South, women versus men, young versus old, generals versus common soldiers, and through the specific eyes of the characters found in their books. (A sample lesson plan focusing on point of view appears below.) Therefore, community share became the most important place for making meaning during the Book Club phase of the unit.

Lesson Plan   ## Day 20: Point of View Lesson (Book Club Phase)

1. *Across Five Aprils:* Continue reading aloud from this novel.

2. **Focus Discussion:** Remind students of the unit goal of exploring various points of view, both in the novels they're reading and in the Civil War period generally. Ask students to give examples from the read-aloud book of different characters' points of view. Discuss how the story would be different if told from another character's point of view. Display this writing prompt: Write about a scene in your reading today from a particular character's point of view.

3. **Book Clubs:** Students read in their book club novels according to their reading plans. They respond to the writing prompt and then choose several other response types to add to their share sheets. They meet with their book club groups and discuss their responses.

4. **Community Share:** Update the community share chart (see page 254) by asking volunteers from each group to supply any important new information from today's reading. Ask each group to share what came up in their book club discussions about point of view. Ask students whether their reading and discussing is changing the way they think about the Civil War. Is one side or the other completely right or completely wrong? Can two people (or groups of people) hold opposite points of view in a conflict but still have some things in common?

Activities for Civil War Unit

Inquiry (2–3 weeks)	Book Club (3 weeks)	Closure (1 week)
• Introduction • KWLS • Read aloud: *Across Five Aprils* (extends through Book Club phase) • Inquiry Chart (I-Chart) • Selection of group inquiry questions • Group work for I-Chart • Discussion of I-Chart • Selection of individual inquiry questions • Independent research • Organizing and writing reports • Individual presentations • Important People Chart and Time Line (extend through Book Club phase)	• Selection of books • Development of group reading plan • Lessons – Point of view – Intertextuality – Quality reading logs – Quality book club discussions • Daily reading of historical fiction • Daily writing in response to literature • Daily book club discussion groups • Daily whole-class community share • Community Share Chart • Geography: U.S. map • *The Blue and the Gray* (video)	• Read aloud: *Smoky Night* • Whole-class discussion: Focus on intertextuality and big ideas/issues • Group discussions • Synthesis • Author's chair • Student self-assessment

Management   Throughout the Civil War unit, and especially during community share, the class explored and generated a wealth of ideas and information. The teacher needed to maintain a system for organizing all this information to help students get the most out of the unit. She decided to manage the unit through a series of classroom charts that she and the children constructed together. The charts stayed on display and were used as learning tools throughout the unit. Following is a list and explanation of the charts.

- *Across Five Aprils* **Story Chart**   This chart helped the class keep track of the read-aloud story and was organized into four sections: Setting, Characters, Point of View, and Issues. These categories helped the teacher focus on her objectives and helped the class focus on important aspects of the story.

- **KWLS Chart**   During the inquiry phase, this chart helped organize what the children knew about the war prior to beginning their study. Column "W" addressed issues and ideas students wanted to learn about. "L" reflected what the children had learned after teacher modeling and class information gathering. Questions that still remained were listed in column "S," and they formed the basis for the students' individual research.

- **Inquiry Chart** This chart reflected several of the children's original questions from the "W" section of the KWLS chart. It helped the teacher model and teach how to gather information about a question, how to organize that information, and to write up a summary using several sources of information.

- **Time Line of Events** This time line chart helped the class focus on the events in the Civil War, both from historical facts learned during the inquiry phase and from the events depicted in the various historical novels the class read during the Book Club phase.

- **Map** A map of the United States during the 1860s was kept on a classroom wall, and important battles and places were marked as the class learned about them (e.g., Gettysburg, Antietam, Andersonville Prison). The class also added the settings of their novels to the map.

- **Important People Chart** This chart listed biographical data about important historical figures. While fictional elements were included on some of the other charts, this chart was limited to real people—those discovered during the inquiry and Book Club phases of the unit.

- **Community Share Chart** This chart held information about the four novels that students were reading in their book clubs. It was organized into the same categories as the chart for *Across Five Aprils*. It helped the students and the teacher keep track of each other's story lines while allowing them to see parallel issues and ideas. Although the class could add information to any of the charts during community share, this chart was most often the focal point around which the conversation built. (A sample community share chart appears on page 254.)

While these charts added much to the development of the unit, the teacher's preparedness was equally essential. Since she had a clear set of objectives and a definite road map in mind, she was able to guide her students along the path of learning, even though she didn't know the specific content her students would address or which issues they would raise on a given day. The charts helped focus both the teacher and the students on the learning and were constantly referred to by students in their book club groups and during community share as they wove their own understanding of the Civil War.

Civil War Community Share Chart

Turn Homeward, Hannalee
by Patricia Beatty

- <u>Setting</u>: south, during war, Georgia (Savannah), mill town, on the road

- <u>Characters</u>: Hannalee Hannibal, Jem (Jemima), Rosellen, Davey, Ma, Quantrell, Sally, Miz Burton, peddler, Paulina, Marillae

- <u>Point of View</u>: southern, child

- <u>Issues</u>: south's right to secede

Behind Rebel Lines
by Seymour Reit

- <u>Setting</u>: beginning of war, north, Yorktown

- <u>Characters</u>: Emma, Mrs. Butler, Franklin Thompson, Cuff, Brigette (peddler), pet horse (Rebel), Charles Mayberry (fop), detective

- <u>Point of View</u>: northern, woman, spy

- <u>Issues</u>: existence of spies, role, right?

Shades of Gray
by Carolyn Reeder

- <u>Setting</u>: south, after the war, country setting (like Across Five Aprils), Virginia

- <u>Characters</u>: Will, Uncle Jed, Aunt Ella, Lizzy (friend), Meg (cousin), Matt, Doc Martin, Sam/Enos, Jim the Yankee

- <u>Point of View</u>: southern, boy

- <u>Issues</u>: choosing to fight or not, is war right?

Who Comes with Cannons?
by Patricia Beatty

- <u>Setting</u>: before the war, country farm (like Across Five Aprils), south

- <u>Characters</u>: Truth, Aunt Elizabeth & Uncle Matthew, Robert (cousin), Todd, Lucy, Squire, Elizabeth, Mary (Quakers)

- <u>Point of View</u>: Quaker, young girl

- <u>Issues</u>: treatment of human beings

Teacher Comment:

"This chart was used to help the whole class keep track of the novels that were being read simultaneously during the Book Club phase."

Assessment This kind of unit, unique in both its length (about seven weeks) and its depth, requires a variety of assessment methods to provide an accurate picture of the student and his or her growth. While the typical assessment (student self-assessment, teacher evaluation and grading, student reactions and goal-setting) was done at the conclusion of the Book Club phase, there were several additional assessments throughout the unit. Students' inquiry reports were used as an assessment measure from the content phase—including inquiry planning sheets, note cards, written report, and oral presentation. Several think sheets, such as the "K" of the KWL, were also collected and assessed in the way you might grade any kind of social studies assignment.

To further assess students' competence in Book Club, two performance-based assessments were used. Students were asked to read silently from a piece of expository text (Jim Murphy's *The Boys' War*) during the inquiry phase of the unit, and then from *Across Five Aprils* (the read-aloud book) during the Book Club phase. In each case, the children read, wrote in their response logs, and participated in a book club discussion—exactly the same format they followed every day. The only difference was that their reading log responses were collected and their book club groups were tape recorded and transcribed. These two artifacts gave the teacher a fairly accurate picture of each student's ability to "do" Book Club. Because one reading selection was fiction and one nonfiction, the picture was quite detailed. These pieces were maintained in a portfolio folder, along with other accumulated work of each student, during the span of the unit. (For more information about performance-based assessments in Book Club, see pages 24–34.)

The assessment procedures we've outlined here are just a few of the many options. The amount and kinds of assessments you use for a multi-book unit will depend on several factors, mainly your specific reasons for doing a multi-book unit and the time of year you do it. Because this Civil War unit was the final one in the fifth-grade year, the teacher wanted a complex and complete picture of her students' achievements. Therefore her assessment plans included more, both in quality and in quantity, than her previous Book Club assessments. She used performance-based assessments during the inquiry and Book Club phases, but the closure phase is also a good time to conduct a formal assessment. Other Book Club teachers have translated the assessments from multi-book units into separate history, writing, language, and reading grades. As with all components of the Book Club program, assessments are meant to serve your needs rather than dictate your classroom structure.

Classroom Resources for Civil War Unit

Classroom Library

Allen, Thomas B. *The Blue and the Gray.* Washington, D.C.: National Geographic Society, 1992.

Beatty, Patricia. *Charlie Skedaddle.* Mahwah, NJ: Troll Communications, 1988.

Donovan, Frank R. *Ironclads of the Civil War.* New York: American Heritage, 1964.

Fox, Paula. *Slave Dancer.* New York: Dell Publishing Co., 1991.

Hamilton, Virginia. *Many Thousand Gone: African Americans from Slavery to Freedom.* New York: Alfred A. Knopf, 1995.

Haskins, Jim. *The Day Fort Sumter Was Fired On: A Photo History of the Civil War.* New York: Scholastic, 1995.

Haskins, Jim. *Get on Board: The Story of the Underground Railroad.* New York: Scholastic, 1993.

Lunn, Janet. *The Root Cellar.* New York: Puffin Books, 1996.

O'Dell, Scott. *Sing Down the Moon.* New York: Bantam Doubleday Dell, 1992.

Smith, Carter. *1863: The Crucial Year: A Source-book on the Civil War.* Highland Park, NJ: Mill Brook Press, 1995.

Sterling, Dorothy. *Freedom Train: The Story of Harriet Tubman.* New York: Scholastic, 1987.

Winter, Jeanette. *Follow the Drinking Gourd.* New York: Dragonfly Books, 1988.

Independent Inquiry

Altman, Susan and Susan Lechner. *Followers of the North Star: Rhymes About African American Heroes, Heroines, and Historic Times.* Chicago: Childrens Press, 1993.

Bakeless, Katherine Little. *Confederate Spy Stories.* Philadelphia: Lippincott, 1973.

Davidson, Margaret. *Frederick Douglass Fights for Freedom.* New York: Scholastic, 1989.

Everett, Gwen. *John Brown: One Man Against Slavery.* New York: Rizzoli Publications International, Inc., 1993.

Freedman, Russell. *Lincoln: A Photobiography.* Boston: Houghton Mifflin Co., 1989.

Gauch, Patricia L. *Thunder at Gettysburg.* New York: The Putnam Publishing Group, 1990.

Levine, Ellen. *If You Traveled on the Underground Railroad.* New York: Scholastic, 1993.

Meltzer, Milton. *Lincoln, In His Own Words.* San Diego: Harcourt Brace and Co., 1993.

Murphy, Jim. *The Boys' War: Confederate and Union Soldiers Talk About the Civil War.* Boston: Houghton Mifflin Co., 1993.

Ray, Delia. *Behind the Blue and Gray: A Soldier's Life in the Civil War.* New York: Viking Penguin, 1996.

Wade, Linda R. *Andersonville: A Civil War Tragedy.* Vero Beach, FL: Rourke Enterprises, 1991.

Read Aloud

Bunting, Eve. *Smoky Night.* San Diego: Harcourt Brace, 1994.

Hopkinson, Deborah. *Sweet Clara and the Freedom Quilt.* New York: Random House, 1995.

Hunt, Irene. *Across Five Aprils.* Parsippany, NJ: Silver Burdett Press, 1993.

Polacco, Patricia. *Pink and Say.* New York: The Putnam Publishing Group, 1994.

Ringgold, Faith. *Aunt Harriet's Underground Railroad in the Sky.* New York: Crown Publishing Group, 1995.

Book Clubs

Beatty, Patricia. *Turn Homeward, Hannalee.* Mahwah, NJ: Troll Communications, 1990.

Beatty, Patricia. *Who Comes with Cannons?* New York: Morrow Junior Books, 1992.

Reeder, Carolyn. *Shades of Gray.* New York: Avon Books, 1991.

Reit, Seymour V. *Behind Rebel Lines: The Incredible Story of Emma Edmonds, Civil War Spy.* San Diego: Harcourt Brace and Co., 1991.

Other Sources

The Blue and the Gray. Directed by Andrew V. McLaglen. Parts 1 and 2. 295 min. RCA/ Columbia Home Video, 1986.

Newspaper accounts

Classroom computers: CD-ROM and WWW

Guest speakers: Civil War reenactors and local historians

Resources for Other Multi-Book Units

Now that you've seen how one Book Club teacher planned and implemented a multi-book unit on the Civil War, you're ready to adapt this format to your own curriculum and your own favorite books. The multi-book format is especially effective for creating interdisciplinary units—for example, combining reading with science or social studies. The charts on pages 258–260 contain lists of resources—books, magazines, internet, video, and so on—that can serve as building blocks for units on the environment, World War II, and coming of age.

The Environment Unit The resources we've recommended for this unit are geared mostly toward a fourth- or fifth-grade classroom. Many of the books available on this topic are nonfiction, so you may wonder if students will be able to maintain the same sorts of lively conversations that they've had while reading great novels. We've found that preserving the environment is a topic that our students feel very strongly about, and they do become deeply engaged in their book club and community share discussions. This unit is a natural for combining reading with content-area material from your science curriculum. It also provides opportunities for internet research because there are many sites on the World Wide Web devoted to environmental topics.

World War II Unit Depending on when your social studies curriculum covers the World War II era, you may choose to conduct a multi-book unit focusing on this topic. There is a wealth of excellent children's literature dealing with all aspects of this war, including its causes and its aftermath. It's also a rich context in which to discuss issues such as prejudice, racism, courage, compassion, death, and healing. Our resources chart suggests many fiction and nonfiction texts that can form the basis for your own unit on World War II. Because much of the literature contains mature subject matter and is aimed at older students, we recommend that this unit be taught in fifth or sixth grade.

Coming-of-Age Unit This unit is also appropriate for fifth or sixth graders. Coming of age is a fairly broad theme, and you certainly have your own favorite books that would work well in such a unit. We've provided a list of some of our own favorites, and those that our students have enjoyed exploring in Book Club. You probably won't start this unit with an inquiry phase, but you can create a shared context for the whole class by completing a short read-aloud book (such as *Missing May* by Cynthia Rylant) before students begin reading their book club novels. Issues that you might explore during the unit include change, loss, survival, self-acceptance, self-reliance, and of course growing up.

Classroom Resources for Environment Unit

Classroom Library

Baylor, Byrd. *I'm in Charge of Celebrations.* New York: Scribner's, 1986.

Baylor, Byrd, and Peter Parnall. *Desert Voices.* New York: Scribner's, 1981.

Caduto, Michael J. and Joseph Bruchac. *Keepers of Life: Discovering Plants through Native American Stories and Earth Activities for Children.* Golden, CO.: Fulcrum, 1994.

———. *Keepers of the Earth: Native American Stories and Environmental Activities for Children.* Golden, CO.: Fulcrum, 1988.

Cherry, Lynne. *The Great Kapok Tree.* San Diego: Harcourt Brace Jovanovich, 1990.

George, Jean Craighead. *The Fire Bug Connection: An Ecological Mystery.* New York: HarperCollins, 1993.

———. *There's an Owl in the Shower.* New York: HarperCollins, 1995.

———. *Who Really Killed Cock Robin? An Ecological Mystery.* New York: HarperCollins, 1991.

Heloise. *Heloise Hints for a Healthy Planet.* New York: Perigee Books, 1990.

Lasky, Kathryn. *She's Wearing a Dead Bird on Her Head!* New York: Hyperion, 1997.

Temple, Lannis (ed.). *Dear World: How Children Around the World Feel About Our Environment.* New York: Random House, 1993.

Van Allsburg, Chris. *Just a Dream.* Boston: Houghton Mifflin, 1990.

Independent Inquiry

Blashfield, Jean F., and Wallace B. Black. *Recycling.* Chicago: Childrens Press, 1991.

Crampton, Norman. *Complete Trash: The Best Way to Get Rid of Practically Everything Around the House.* New York: M. Evans, 1989.

Croall, Stephen. *Ecology for Beginners.* New York: Pantheon Books, 1981.

The Earth Works Group. *50 Simple Things Kids Can Do to Save the Earth.* Kansas City, MO: Andrews and McMeel, 1990.

Lauber, Patricia. *Seeing Earth from Space.* New York: Orchard Books, 1990.

Stille, Darlene R. *Soil Erosion and Pollution.* Chicago: Childrens Press, 1990.

———. *Water Pollution.* Danbury, CT: Childrens Press, 1990.

Walsh, Jill Paton. *The Green Book.* New York: Farrar, Straus and Giroux, 1982.

Wilcox, Charlotte. *Trash!* Minneapolis: Carolrhoda Books, 1988.

Read Aloud

Olaleye, Isaac. *The Distant Talking Drum: Poems from Nigeria.* New York: St. Martin's Press, 1995.

Stafford, William. *Learning to Live in the World: Earth Poems.* San Diego: Harcourt Brace, 1994.

Book Clubs

George, Jean Craighead. *The Missing 'Gator of Gumbo Limbo: An Ecological Mystery.* New York: HarperCollins, 1992.

———. *The Talking Earth.* New York: Harper & Row, 1983.

Krensky, Stephen. *Four Against the Odds: The Struggle to Save Our Environment.* New York: Scholastic, 1992.

Nirgiotis, Nicholas and Theodore Nirgiotis. *No More Dodos.* Minneapolis: Lerner Publications, Inc., 1996.

Other Sources

Caduto, Michael J. *Keepers of the Earth.* Sound recording. Golden, CO: Fulcrum, 1991.

E-Patrol: http://www.sprint.com/epatrol/

National Geographic *World* magazine

World online: http://www.nationalgeographic.com/ngs/mags/world/

Ranger Rick magazine

Ranger Rick online: http://www.nwf.org/nwf/lib/rr/

Classroom Resources for World War II Unit

Classroom Library

Coerr, Eleanor. *Mieko and the Fifth Treasure.* New York: G. P. Putnam's Sons, 1993.

Coerr, Eleanor. *Sadako and the Thousand Paper Cranes.* New York: Putnam, 1977.

Greenfeld, Howard. *The Hidden Children.* New York: Ticknor & Field Books for Young Readers, 1993.

Holliday, Laurel. *Children in the Holocaust and World War II: Their Secret Diaries.* New York: Pocket Books, 1995.

Innocenti, Roberto. *Rose Blanche.* San Diego: Harcourt Brace, 1996.

Maruki, Toshi. *Hiroshima No Pika.* New York: Lothrop, Lee & Shepard, 1980.

Morimoto, Junko. *My Hiroshima.* New York: Puffin Books, 1992.

Reiss, Johanna. *The Upstairs Room.* Boston: G. K. Hall, 1973.

Rol, Ruud van der. *Anne Frank: Beyond the Diary.* New York: Viking, 1993.

Tsuchiya, Yukio. *Faithful Elephants: A True Story of Animals, People, and War.* Boston: Houghton Mifflin, 1988.

Watkins, Yoko Kawashima. *So Far from the Bamboo Grove.* New York: Puffin Books, 1987.

Yep, Laurence. *Hiroshima.* New York: Scholastic, 1995.

Independent Inquiry

Hersey, John. *Hiroshima.* New York: Vintage Books, 1989.

Levine, Ellen. *A Fence Away from Freedom: Japanese Americans and World War II.* New York: G. P. Putnam's Sons, 1995.

Meltzer, Milton. *Rescue: The Story of How Gentiles Saved Jews in the Holocaust.* New York: Harper & Row, 1988.

Rogasky, Barbara. *Smoke and Ashes: The Story of the Holocaust.* New York: Holliday House, 1988.

Stanley, Jerry. *I Am an American: A True Story of Japanese Internment.* New York: Crown Publishers, 1994.

Zeinert, Karen. *Those Incredible Women of World War II.* Brookfield, CT: The Millbrook Press, 1994.

Read Aloud

Choi, Sook Nyul. *Year of Impossible Goodbyes.* Boston: Houghton Mifflin Co., 1991.

Hest, Amy. *Love You Soldier.* New York: Maxwell Maximillian International, 1991.

Kerr, Judith. *When Hitler Stole Pink Rabbit.* New York: Coward, McCann & Geoghegan, 1972.

Morpurgo, Michael. *Waiting for Anya.* New York: Viking, 1991.

Yolen, Jane. *The Devil's Arithmetic.* New York: Puffin Books, 1990.

Book Clubs

Adler, David A. *We Remember the Holocaust.* New York: Henry Holt, 1989.

Foreman, Michael. *War Boy.* New York: Arcade Publishing, 1989.

Frank, Anne. *Anne Frank: Diary of a Young Girl.* New York: Doubleday, 1995.

Lowry, Lois. *Number the Stars.* New York: Dell Publishing Co., 1996.

Uchida, Yoshiko. *Journey Home.* New York: Maxwell Maximillian International, 1992.

Other Resources

Guest speakers: family members who have stories to share; local historians

Grolier's World War II Page: http://www.grolier.com/wwii/wwii_mainpage.html

World War II Timeline (at The History Place): http://www.historyplace.com/worldwar2/timeline/ww2time.htm

Anne Frank Online: http://www.annefrank.com/

Library of Congress American Memory site— color photos from c. 1938–1944: http://rs6.loc.gov/fsowhome.html

Classroom Resources for Coming of Age Unit

Classroom Library

Avi. *A Place Called Ugly*. New York: Pantheon Books, 1981.

Babbitt, Natalie. *Tuck Everlasting*. New York: Farrar, Straus and Giroux, 1975.

Cormier, Robert. *Tunes for Bears to Dance to*. New York: Delacorte, 1992.

Crew, Gary. *Angel's Gate*. New York: Simon and Schuster Books for Young Readers, 1993.

Cushman, Karen. *The Midwife's Apprentice*. New York: HarperCollins Children's Books, 1996.

Farmer, Nancy. *The Ear, the Eye, and the Arm*. New York: Orchard Books, 1994.

Feiffer, Jules. *The Man in the Ceiling*. New York: HarperCollins Publishers, 1993.

George, Jean Craighead. *Julie of the Wolves*. New York: HarperCollins, 1996.

Hudson, Jan. *Sweetgrass*. New York: Scholastic, 1991.

Magorian, Michelle. *Good Night, Mr. Tom*. New York: HarperCollins Children's Books, 1982.

Marcus, Leonard S. *Lifelines: A Poetry Anthology Patterned on the Stages of Life*. New York: Dutton Children's Books, 1993.

Martin, Rafe. *The Rough Face Girl*. New York: G. P. Putnam's Sons, 1992.

Naylor, Phyllis Reynolds. *Shiloh*. New York: Atheneum, 1991.

Neuberger, Anne E. *The Girl-Son*. Minneapolis: Carolrhoda, 1995.

Neville, Emily Cheney. *It's Like This, Cat*. New York: Harper & Row, 1963.

Paulsen, Gary. *Brian's Winter*. New York: Bantam Doubleday Dell Books for Young Readers, 1996.

———. *Hatchet*. New York: Viking Penguin, 1988.

———. *The River*. New York: Dell Publishing Co., 1993.

———. *The Voyage of the Frog*. New York: Orchard Books, 1989.

Woodson, Jacqueline. *Between Madison and Palmetto*. New York: Dell Publishing Co., 1995.

———. *Last Summer with Maizon*. New York: Dell Publishing Co., 1990.

———. *Maizon at Blue Hill*. New York: Dell Publishing Co., 1994.

Read Aloud

Paterson, Katherine. *Jacob Have I Loved*. New York: HarperCollins Children's Books, 1990.

Rylant, Cynthia. *Missing May*. New York: Dell Publishing Co., 1993.

Book Clubs

Creech, Sharon. *Walk Two Moons*. New York: HarperCollins Publishers, 1994.

Cushman, Karen. *Catherine, Called Birdy*. New York: Clarion Books, 1994.

Fox, Paula. *Monkey Island*. New York: Orchard Books, 1991.

Lowry, Lois. *The Giver*. Boston: Houghton Mifflin Co., 1993.

Spinelli, Jerry. *Maniac Magee*. New York: HarperTrophy, 1990.

Taylor, Mildred D. *Roll of Thunder, Hear My Cry*. New York: Puffin Books, 1991.

Other Resources

Little Women. Directed by Gillian Armstrong. Videotape (VHS). 116 min. Columbia Tristar, 1994.

Stand by Me. Directed by Rob Reiner. Videotape (VHS). 87 min. RCA/Columbia Pictures Home Video, 1987.

Unstrung Heroes. Directed by Diane Keaton. Videotape (VHS). 93 min. Hollywood Pictures Home Video, 1995.

Blackline Masters: Think Sheets

This section contains blackline masters for nineteen "think sheets" that you can copy and distribute to your students. Think sheets give students a starting point for responding to their reading and for writing log entries that will inspire rich book club discussions. You'll probably find that think sheets are most helpful at the beginning of the year, when students are just getting used to Book Club and learning what kinds of written responses are appropriate.

The think sheets provided here are some of the most basic ones that we've used in our classrooms. You'll certainly be creating your own think sheets as you tailor the Book Club program to the needs of your own students, but we hope that the ones here will help you get started. Following is a complete list of the blackline masters in this section.

- Comparing/Contrasting
- Vocabulary
- Questions for My Group
- Reading Log Checklist*
- Reading Log Checklist (blank)
- Book Critique
- Venn Diagram
- Response Choice Sheets ("What can I do in my reading log?")—4 pages
- Response Choice Sheet (blank)
- KWL Chart
- Ideas for Inquiry Questions
- Inquiry Question Planning Sheet
- Project Evaluation, Parts 1 and 2
- Book Club Reading Plan
- Reading Log Page (blank)

*NOTE: All of the response choices mentioned on the Reading Log Checklist are described on the Response Choice Sheets.

Name _____   Date _____

Book(s) _____

Comparing/Contrasting

I am going to compare/contrast _____ and
_____

Things that are alike:	Things that are different:
_____	_____
_____	_____
_____	_____
_____	_____
_____	_____
_____	_____
_____	_____
_____	_____
_____	_____
_____	_____
_____	_____
_____	_____

Name _____ Date _____

Book _____

Vocabulary

Date	Word	Page	Meaning

Name _____ Date _____

Book _____

Questions for My Group

Date	Question

Name _____ Date _____ Book _____

Reading Log Checklist

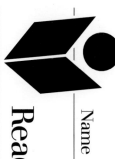

Choice	Dates																	
Prediction																		
Character Map																		
Picture																		
Special Story Part																		
Favorite/Least Favorite																		
Summary																		
Sequence																		
Questions for My Group																		
Compare/Contrast																		
Vocabulary																		
Feelings																		
Me & the Book																		
Title Explanation																		
Intertextuality																		
Critique																		
Author's Craft																		
Point of View																		
Wonderful Words																		
Interpretation																		

Reading Log Checklist

Name _____ Date _____ Book _____

Choice	Dates													

Name _____ Date _____

Book _____

Book Critique

I plan to critique (plot, character, setting?) _____

_____

What are some things the author did well? _____

_____

_____

_____

_____

_____

_____

What are some things the author could do to improve the story?

_____

_____

_____

_____

_____

_____

Name _____ Date _____

Book(s) _____

Venn Diagram

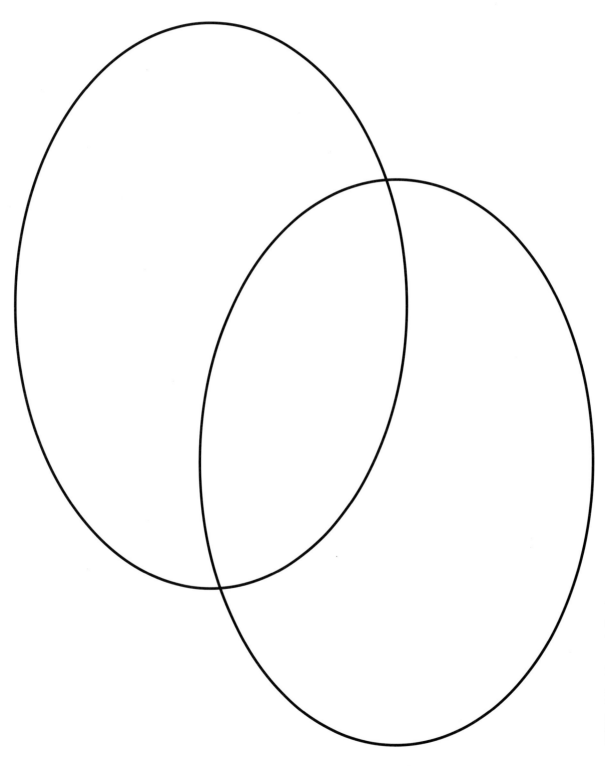

What can I do in my reading log?

COMPARE/CONTRAST

I can tell how two things are alike or different. Two characters, two books, myself and a character, a book and a movie—any two things that share similarities and differences. I can use a think sheet or create my own design in my log.

FAVORITE/LEAST FAVORITE PART OR CHARACTER

During a book, I usually have a favorite part or favorite character, and I usually have a least favorite part or character. I can write about any of these, making sure I tell why I like or dislike these parts or characters.

ME & THE BOOK

Sometimes what I read makes me think about my own life. I can write about an event or a character in a book that reminds me of my life. I need to tell what is in the book, and what it reminds me of in my life.

PICTURE

Every time I read, I get a picture in my head about the story. I can draw the picture from my head into my log. I need to write a sentence or two under my picture telling what it is and why I drew it.

INTERTEXTUALITY

Sometimes what I read makes me think about another text—a book I've read or a movie I've seen. I can tell what other text this story reminds me of and why it makes me think of it.

CHARACTER MAP

I can draw a map of a character in the story. I can include personality traits, descriptions, actions, and anything else I think is interesting about that character.

What can I do in my reading log?

SUMMARY/RETELLING
Sometimes it might be important to me to retell or summarize all or part of the story. I can write a summary and then tell why I decided to summarize this particular part.

SEQUENCE
Sometimes events in the book might be important to remember in the order they happened. I can make a sequence chart, map, or list of these events, and tell why I think they are important.

SPECIAL STORY PART
When I find a part in the book that I really like, I can write the page number in my log so I can remember where to find it. I can write a few sentences about why I think it is so special.

PREDICTION
I can think about the story so far and predict what I think will happen next. I can predict a whole book, the next chapter, or how the story might end.

QUESTIONS FOR MY GROUP
Sometimes there are things in the story that I wonder about. I can write questions to ask my group so they can help me understand the story better. Sometimes I might write questions to ask my group members to ask my group members how they feel about the story, or a certain part in the story.

FEELINGS
Sometimes a book makes me feel a certain way. I can write about that feeling, and why the book makes me feel that way. I can also talk about what the character(s) in the book might be feeling.

What can I do in my reading log?

AUTHOR'S CRAFT

Sometimes authors use special words, paint pictures in my mind with words, make me wish I could write like they do, use funny language, or write really good dialogue. I can give examples of things the author does to make me like the story.

CRITIQUE

Sometimes when I'm reading, I think to myself, "This is really great!" Other times I think, "If I were the author, I would do this differently." I can write about things the author did well, and things he/she could do better.

WONDERFUL WORDS

I can find some really wonderful words—words that are new, crazy, descriptive, or confusing. I can write them down with a sentence or two telling why I picked them, and the page number so I can find them again.

COMPARE/ CONTRAST

I can tell how two things are alike or different. Two characters, two books, myself and a character, a book and a movie—any two things that share similarities and differences.

POINT OF VIEW

Sometimes as I read about a character, I think that the author did not consider some ideas I think are important to understanding the character. I can write from the character's point of view to help explain those ideas.

INTERTEXTUALITY

Sometimes what I read about makes me think about another text—a book I've read or a movie I've seen. I can tell what other text this story reminds me of and why it makes me think of it.

VOCABULARY

Sometimes there are words in a story that I want to learn to pronounce, use correctly, and understand. I can list these words on a vocabulary sheet or in my log, with the page numbers. I can ask my group what they mean, or look them up later.

INTERPRETATION

When I read, I think about what the author is saying to me, what he or she hopes that I'll take away from the story. I can write down my interpretation in my reading log and share what I'm thinking with the rest of the group. I need to listen to others' interpretations to see if they have similar, the same, or different ideas.

TITLE EXPLANATION

Whenever I look at a new book or chapter title, I try to predict what the book or chapter will be about. After I read the book or chapter, I usually have a different idea of why the author used those titles. I can write about titles—what I think they mean before reading, and what they actually meant after reading. Some authors do not name their chapters. I can make up my own chapter titles and explain why I named them this.

What can I do in my reading log?

PICTURE
Every time I read, I get a picture in my head about the story. I can draw the picture in my log and write a sentence or two under my picture telling what it is and why I drew it.

FAVORITE/ LEAST FAVORITE PART OR CHARACTER
During a book, I usually have a favorite part or favorite character, and I usually have a least favorite part or character. I can write about any of these, making sure I tell why I like or dislike them.

SEQUENCE
Sometimes events in the book might be important to remember in the order they happened. I can make a sequence chart, map, or list of these events, and tell why I think they are important.

FEELINGS
Sometimes a book makes me feel a certain way. I can write about that feeling, and why the book makes me feel that way. I can also talk about what the character(s) in the book feel.

ME & THE BOOK
Sometimes what I read makes me think about my own life. I can write about an event or a character in a book that reminds me of my life. I need to tell what is in the book, and what it reminds me of in my life.

CHARACTER MAP
I can draw a map of a character in the story. I can include personality traits, descriptions, actions, and anything else I think is interesting about that character.

SUMMARY/RETELLING
Sometimes it might be important to me to retell or summarize all or part of the story. I can write a summary and then tell why I decided to summarize this particular part.

SPECIAL STORY PART
When I find a part in the book that I really like, I can write the page number in my log so I can remember where to find it. I can write a few sentences about why I think it is so special.

QUESTIONS FOR MY GROUP
Sometimes there are things in the story that I wonder about. I can write questions to ask my group so they can help me understand the story better. Sometimes I might write questions to ask my group members how they feel about the story, or a certain part in the story.

PREDICTION
I can think about the story so far and predict what I think will happen next. I can predict a whole book, the next chapter, or how the story might end.

What can I do
in my
reading log?

Name _____

Date _____

KWL Chart

What do I KNOW?	What do I WANT to know?	What did I LEARN?

Name _____

Date _____

Ideas for Inquiry Questions

Here is an idea for a good inquiry question.

_____

_____

_____

____ I would like to do this one myself.

____ I might like to do this one.

____ I'm not interested in this question for myself. Someone else can use it.

Here is an idea for a good inquiry question.

_____

_____

_____

____ I would like to do this one myself.

____ I might like to do this one.

____ I'm not interested in this question for myself. Someone else can use it.

Here is an idea for a good inquiry question.

_____

_____

_____

____ I would like to do this one myself.

____ I might like to do this one.

____ I'm not interested in this question for myself. Someone else can use it.

Name _____

Unit _____

Inquiry Question Planning Sheet

Inquiry Question:

Here is my plan for my inquiry question.

1. I will use these resources:

2. This is how I will show what I have learned (written form):

3. This is how I will present the information to the class:

4. Here are the enrichment activities I will do:

This plan will be accomplished by (date) _____ .

If I follow my plan, I will earn a grade of _____ .

Signature _____ Date _____

Name _____

Unit _____

Project Evaluation, Part 1

Self-Evaluation

My inquiry question was:

Here is a list of the sources I used for my research. (For books, please include the title and author. For people or movies, please tell what specific information they provided to you.)

Here is a brief description of what I will do for my presentation tomorrow. (Please check all that apply.)

____ I followed my plan.

____ I did my very best on this project.

____ I like my project.

____ I will be ready for my presentation on (date) _____.

____ I could have done better work.

____ I learned a lot from this project.

I believe I have earned a grade of _____on my project because:

Signature _____ Date _____

Name _____

Date _____

Project Evaluation, Part 2

Teacher Evaluation

I know that I will be graded in the following areas. I will turn all these items in with my folder so that I can be fairly evaluated. (Percent of the total grade for which each item counts is shown in parentheses.)

_____ Number and kind of sources used (10)

_____ Note taking (15)

_____ Organization (10)

_____ Rough draft of written report (10)

_____ Final copy of written report—length, content, mechanics (30)

_____ Plan and how well I followed it (10)

_____ Oral presentation—voice, information, eye contact (15)

_____ Bonus or extra work

_____ Total (100)

_____ Grade (to be filled in by teacher)

Comments from teacher:

My reaction to my grade and the teacher's comments:

Name _____   Date _____

Group Members _____

Book Club Reading Plan

Our book is entitled _____ . It is written by

_____ . This book has _____ chapters and _____

pages. We know that we have _____ days of assigned reading for

this book, and that we have _____ minutes of in-class time to do

the reading each day. Below is our plan for reading the book.

Pacing Schedule
Days

1	2	3	4	5	6	7	8	9	10	11	12	13	14	15

Reading Assignments (Chapters or Page Numbers)

Reading Options:

In class	At home	DEAR time	Silently	Partners	Taking turns

We have considered all of the reading options, and we have circled the ones that we will use most often.

This is how we will decide which reading option to use each day:

_____

_____

_____

_____

Signature _____

Name _____   Date _____

Book _____

Reading Log Page

Blackline Masters: Assessment

In this section you'll find blackline masters for nine forms that we've used for various assessment purposes. Some are for students to fill out, others are for your own record keeping, and others create a space for you to hold a conversation with a student about his or her performance and grades. As in all aspects of Book Club, we know that you'll be creating assessment materials to meet your own goals. Our forms are meant simply to give you some ideas. The following is a complete list of the blackline masters in this section.

For the Teacher

Book Club Observation Sheet

Fluency Checklist

Reading Competencies Checklist

Book Club Evaluation: Reading Log

Book Club Evaluation: Group Participation

For the Student

Daily Self-Assessment Checklist

Book Club Self-Assessment

End-of-Book Self-Assessment

Reaction and Goal-Setting Sheet

Date _____

Book _____

Book Club Observation Sheet

Student's Name	Shares Log	Shares Ideas	Listens & Responds	Questions	Off-Task Behaviors

Each ✔ means the student exhibited this behavior.

Overall rating (Mark next to name.)	Off-Task Behaviors Key
* exceptional + good/okay – not good 0 not participating at all	1. writing in log 2. playing with pencil or other object 3. digging in desk 4. talking with someone else in group, not about Book Club topic 5. getting out of group to wander

Comments:

_____

_____

_____

_____

_____

_____

_____

Date _____

Book _____

Fluency Checklist

Student's Name	Uses Expression	Observes Punctuation	Smooth	Appropriate Speed/Volume	Uses Decoding Skills	Miscues	Self-corrects

Name
_____

Teacher's Signature
_____

Reading Competencies Checklist

Strategies	1	2	3	4
Predicting				
Sequencing				
Organizing				
Representation				
Identifying important ideas				
Refining/Revising				
Drawing conclusions				
Comprehension	1	2	3	4
Recognizes story themes				
Recognizes purpose				
Synthesizes information across texts				
Expressive Abilities: Oral	1	2	3	4
Evaluates text using specific ideas				
Ideas are expressed clearly				
Expressive Abilities: Written	1	2	3	4
Evaluates text using specific ideas				
Ideas are expressed clearly				

Comments: First Grading Period

Comments: Second Grading Period

Comments: Third Grading Period

Comments: Fourth Grading Period

Key: + Excellent   √ Satisfactory – Needs Improvement

Name _____   Date _____

Book _____

Book Club Evaluation: Reading Log

You are graded in two areas—Quantity and Quality.

Quantity. During this book, you needed to demonstrate mastery of the following skills and strategies. You have demonstrated the ones I have highlighted. Others either were not attempted or were not mastered.

Prediction	Character Map	Picture	Questions
Summary	Favorite/Least Favorite	Feelings	Point of View
Sequence	Wonderful Words	Me & the Book	Title Explanation
Vocabulary	Compare/Contrast	Intertextuality	Critique
Author's Craft	Special Story Part	Author's Purpose	Interpretation

You have accomplished _____ skills and strategies out of a total of _____ . This is equivalent to a grade of _____ .

Quality. The quality of your reading log was determined by assigning a grade to the first 10 entries in your log. They were graded on completeness and accuracy of information, as well as length and amount of detail provided. They were not graded on spelling, mechanics, etc. I numbered them as I read them. Here is a record of your grades.

Excellent	Average	Unacceptable

Excellent	Average	Unacceptable

These ten grades average out to a grade of_____.

Overall Reading Log Grade. Your reading log grade is half quantity_____ and half quality_____. This gives you an overall reading log grade of_____.

Suggestions for improving your reading log:

Name _____ Date _____

Book _____

Book Club Evaluation: Group Participation

During this book, I observed your group twice, on these dates:

_____ and _____

I also audio taped your group twice, on these dates:

_____ and _____

Based on these observations, your participation in **book club group** was:

Excellent	Good	Okay	Not good
A	B	C	E

During this book, I observed your participation in **community share** on a daily basis. Your participation in community share was:

Excellent	Good	Okay	Not good
A	B	C	E

Based on these evaluations, your **grade for participation** for this book is _____.

Suggestions for improvement in participation:

Write your response to the grades and other comments above. Do you have any other thoughts about your group participation in this unit?

_____

_____

_____

Name _____

Book _____

Daily Self-Assessment Checklist

Date					
Did I read the assigned pages?					
When?					
Did I fill in a share sheet?					
How many spokes?					
The spokes were:					
Did I share during book club group?					
Did I listen to others?					
My book club today was _____ ?					

Important Comments

Date: _____

Date: _____

Date: _____

Name _____ Date _____

Book _____

Book Club Self-Assessment

1. How did your group do today?

_____

_____

_____

_____

_____

_____

2. What did you do to contribute to the group's success/failure?

_____

_____

_____

_____

_____

_____

3. What can you do to improve the group's level of success tomorrow?

_____

_____

_____

_____

_____

Name _____   Date _____

Book _____

End-of-Book Self-Assessment

1. Did you like this book?   Yes   No   Why or why not?

   _____

2. When you were reading the book silently, how did you find the reading?

   Easy   Just right   A little hard   Too hard

3. What is your favorite part of Book Club?

   Reading   Writing   Book clubs   Community share

4. What has been your favorite book this year?

   _____

5. I will soon be determining new groups. List, in order of preference, the three people you would most likely be able to work well with. I will try to give you one of your three choices.

   1. _____ 2. _____ 3. _____

6. Look through your log. Find the best entry you did. Write me a sticky note on that page, telling me why it is your best.

7. What is one thing you will do differently in your log next time? Why?

   _____

   _____

8. What grade do you think you deserve for group cooperation, sharing, and participation? Why?

   _____

9. What was the best thing about doing Book Club with this book?

   _____

Reaction and Goal-Setting Sheet

I received the following grades for my performance during this book:

_____ Reading log—quality and quantity of responses

_____ Group sharing and community share participation

How do you feel about these marks? Why?

_____

_____

_____

_____

What will you do differently next time to improve your grades? Please list specific goals you have set for yourself, in both writing and talking.

_____

_____

_____

_____

_____

_____

_____

Bibliography

Children's Literature and Media

Avi. *The Fighting Ground.* New York: Harper & Row, 1987.

Babbitt, Natalie. *Tuck Everlasting.* New York: Farrar, Straus and Giroux, 1975.

Beatty, Patricia. *Jayhawker.* New York: William Morrow Co., 1991.

Bellairs, John. *The Trolley to Yesterday.* New York: Dial Books for Young Readers, 1989.

Boston, Lucy M. *The Children of Green Knowe.* San Diego: Harcourt Brace and Co., 1989.

Bradbury, Ray. *The Halloween Tree.* New York: Knopf Books for Young Readers, 1988.

Bruchac, Joseph. *Gluskabe and the Four Wishes.* New York: Cobblehill Books/Dutton, 1995.

Bunting, Eve. *Smoky Night.* San Diego: Harcourt Brace, 1994.

Burnford, Sheila. *The Incredible Journey.* New York: Bantam Doubleday Dell Books for Young Readers, 1996.

Choi, Sook Nyul. *Year of Impossible Goodbyes.* Boston: Houghton Mifflin Co., 1991.

Collier, James L. and Christopher Collier. *My Brother Sam Is Dead.* New York: Scholastic, 1985.

Cooke, John P. *The Lake.* New York: Avon Books, 1989.

Cormier, Robert. *Tunes for Bears to Dance to.* New York: Delacorte, 1992.

Creech, Sharon. *Absolutely Normal Chaos.* New York: HarperCollins Children's Books, 1995.

———. *Chasing Redbird.* New York: HarperCollins Publishers, 1997.

———. *Pleasing the Ghost.* New York: HarperCollins, 1996.

———. *Walk Two Moons.* New York: HarperCollins, 1994.

A Cry in the Wild. Directed by Mark Griffiths. Videotape (VHS). 82 min. Culver City, CA: MGM/UA Home Video, 1991.

Curtis, Christopher P. *The Watsons Go to Birmingham—1963.* New York: Bantam Doubleday Dell Books for Young Readers, 1995.

Cushman, Karen. *The Midwife's Apprentice.* New York: HarperCollins Children's Books, 1996.

Fox, Paula. *Monkey Island.* New York: Orchard Books, 1991.

Fry, Virginia L. *Part of Me Died, Too: Stories of Creative Survival Among Bereaved Children and Teenagers.* New York: Dutton Children's Books, 1995.

George, Jean Craighead. *Julie of the Wolves.* New York: HarperCollins, 1996.

Griffin, Peni R. *Switching Well.* New York: Puffin Books, 1994.

Juster, Norton. *The Phantom Tollbooth.* New York: Knopf Books for Young Readers, 1988.

Lasenby, Jack. *The Mangrove Summer.* Auckland, N.Z.: Oxford University Press, 1988.

L'Engle, Madeleine. *Many Waters.* New York: Farrar, Straus and Giroux, 1986.

———. *A Swiftly Tilting Planet.* New York: Dell Publishing Co., 1981.

———. *A Wind in the Door.* New York: Farrar, Straus and Giroux, 1973.

———. *A Wrinkle in Time.* New York: Dell Publishing Co., 1996.

Lewis, C. S. *The Lion, the Witch, and the Wardrobe.* New York: HarperCollins Children's Books, 1994.

Lowry, Lois. *The Giver.* Boston: Houghton Mifflin Co., 1993.

———. *Number the Stars.* New York: Dell Publishing Co., 1996.

———. *A Summer to Die.* New York: Bantam Books, 1984.

Marcus, Leonard S. *Lifelines: A Poetry Anthology Patterned on the Stages of Life.* New York: Dutton Children's Books, 1993.

Marrin, Albert. *The War for Independence: The Story of the American Revolution.* New York: Atheneum, 1988.

McKean, Thomas. *The Secret of the Seven Willows.* New York: Simon and Schuster Trade, 1991.

Naidoo, Beverley. *Journey to Jo'burg: A South African Story.* New York: HarperCollins Children's Books, 1988.

O'Dell, Scott. *Island of the Blue Dolphins.* New York: Dell Publishing Co., 1994.

———. *Sarah Bishop.* New York: Scholastic, 1991.

———. *Sing Down the Moon.* New York: Bantam Doubleday Dell Books for Young Readers, 1992.

Paterson, Katherine. *Bridge to Terabithia.* New York: HarperCollins Children's Books, 1996.

———. *The Great Gilly Hopkins.* New York: HarperCollins Children's Books, 1987.

———. *Jacob Have I Loved.* New York: HarperCollins Children's Books, 1990.

———. *Park's Quest.* New York: Puffin Books, 1989.

Paulsen, Gary. *Brian's Winter.* New York: Bantam Doubleday Dell Books for Young Readers, 1996.

———. *Hatchet.* New York: Viking Penguin, 1988.

———. *The River.* New York: Dell Publishing Co., 1993.

———. *The Voyage of the Frog.* New York: Orchard Books, 1989.

Pitts, Paul. *Racing the Sun.* New York: Avon Books, 1988.

Rylant, Cynthia. *Missing May.* New York: Dell Publishing Co., 1993.

Smith, Doris B. *A Taste of Blackberries.* New York: HarperCollins Children's Books, 1988.

Speare, Elizabeth G. *Sign of the Beaver.* New York: Bantam Doubleday Dell Books for Young Readers, 1995.

Spinelli, Jerry. *Crash.* New York: Random House Books for Young Readers, 1996.

———. *Dump Days.* Boston: Little, Brown and Co., 1988.

———. *Maniac Magee.* New York: HarperTrophy, 1990.

———. *There's a Girl in My Hammerlock.* Old Tappan, NJ: Simon and Schuster Children's, 1993.

———. *Who Put That Hair in My Toothbrush?* New York: Little, Brown and Co., 1994.

Taylor, Mildred D. *The Friendship and The Gold Cadillac.* New York: Bantam Doubleday Dell Books for Young Readers, 1987.

———. *Let the Circle Be Unbroken.* New York: Puffin Books, 1991.

———. *Mississippi Bridge.* New York: Dial Books for Young Readers, 1990.

———. *The Road to Memphis.* New York: Puffin Books, 1992.

———. *Roll of Thunder, Hear My Cry.* New York: Puffin Books, 1991.

———. *Song of the Trees.* New York: Bantam, 1984.

———. *The Well: David's Story.* New York: Dial Books for Young Readers, 1995.

Thomas, Jane R. *The Princess in the Pigpen.* Boston: Houghton Mifflin Co., 1989.

Tsuchiya, Yukio. *Faithful Elephants.* Boston: Houghton Mifflin Co., 1988.

Uchida, Yoshiko. *Journey Home.* New York: Maxwell Maximillian International, 1992.

White, E. B. *Charlotte's Web.* New York: Harper, 1952.

Wiseman, David. *Jeremy Visick.* Boston: Houghton Mifflin Co., 1990.

Woodruff, Elvira. *George Washington's Socks.* New York: Scholastic, 1993.

Woodson, Jacqueline. *Between Madison and Palmetto.* New York: Dell Publishing Co., 1995.

———. *Last Summer with Maizon.* New York: Dell Publishing Co., 1990.

———. *Maizon at Blue Hill.* New York: Dell Publishing Co., 1994.

Yates, Elizabeth. *Amos Fortune, Free Man.* New York: Puffin Books, 1989.

Books Describing Book Club

McMahon, Susan I., and Taffy E. Raphael, with Virginia J. Goatley and Laura S. Pardo. *The Book Club Connection: Literacy Learning and Classroom Talk.* New York: Teachers College Press, 1997.

Raphael, Taffy E., and Elfrieda H. Hiebert. *Creating an Integrated Approach to Literacy Instruction.* Ft. Worth, TX: Harcourt Brace, 1996.

Chapters and Articles About Book Club and the Book Club Project

Goatley, V. J. (1996). "The Participation of a Student Identified as Learning Disabled in a Regular Education Book Club: The Case of Stark." *Reading and Writing Quarterly* 12, 195–214.

Goatley, V. J., and J. Levine (1997). "Participating in Student-Led Book Clubs: The Case of Jennifer." *Language and Literacy Spectrum* 7, 14–18.

Goatley, V. J., C. H. Brock, and T. E. Raphael (1995). "Diverse Learners Participating in Regular Education 'Book Clubs.' " *Reading Research Quarterly* 30(3), 353–380.

Goatley, V. J., K. A. Highfield, J. Bentley, J. Folkert, P. Scherer, T. E. Raphael, and K. Grattan (1994). "Empowering Teachers to Be Researchers: A Collaborative Approach." *Teacher Research: A Journal of Classroom Inquiry* 1(2), 128–144.

McMahon, S. I. (1994). "Student-Led Book Clubs: Transversing a River of Interpretation." *The New Advocate* 7(2), 109–126.

Raphael, T. E., and V. J. Goatley (1994). "The Teacher as 'More Knowledgeable Other': Changing Roles for Teaching in Alternative Reading Instruction Programs." In C. Kinzer and D. Leu (eds.), *Multidimensional Aspects of Literacy Research, Theory and Practice* (pp. 527–536). Chicago: National Reading Conference.

Raphael, T. E., V. J. Goatley, D. A. Woodman, and S. I. McMahon (1994). "Collaboration on the Book Club Project: The Multiple Roles of Researchers, Teachers, and Students." *Reading Horizons* 34(5), 381–405.

Raphael, T. E., and S. I. McMahon (1994). " 'Book Club': An Alternative Framework for Reading Instruction." *The Reading Teacher* 48(2), 102–116.

Internet and Multimedia Support for Book Club

Book Club: A Literature-Based Curriculum. Directed by Buzz Linnehan. Videotape (VHS). 32 min. Littleton, MA: Small Planet Communications, 1997.

Book Club on the World Wide Web: http://www.smplanet.com/bookclub/bookclub.html

Background Reading About Classroom Discussion

Almasi, J. F. (1995). "The Nature of Fourth Graders' Sociocognitive Conflicts in Peer-Led and Teacher-Led Discussions of Literature." *Reading Research Quarterly* 30(3), 314–351.

Alvermann, D. E., J. P. Young, D. Weaver, K. A. Hinchman, D. W. Moore, S. F. Phelps, E. C. Thrash, and P. Zalewski (1996). "Middle and High School Students' Perceptions of How They Experience Text-Based Discussions: A Multicase Study." *Reading Research Quarterly* 31(3), 244–267.

Cazden, C. *Classroom Discourse: The Language of Teaching and Learning.* Portsmouth, NH: Heinemann, 1988.

Gavelek, J. R., and T. E. Raphael (1996). "Changing Talk About Text: New Roles for Teachers and Students." *Language Arts* 73(3), 24–34.

McMahon, S. I., and V. J. Goatley (1995). "Fifth Graders Helping Peers Discuss Texts in Student-Led Groups." *Journal of Educational Research* 89(1), 23–35.

Paratore, Jeanne R. and R. McCormack (eds.). *Peer Talk in the Classroom: Learning from Research.* Newark, DE: International Reading Association, 1997.

Raphael, T. E., S. I. McMahon, V. J. Goatley, J. L. Bentley, F. B. Boyd, L. S. Pardo, and D. A. Woodman (1992). "Reading Instruction Reconsidered: Literature and Discussion in the Reading Program." *Language Arts* 69, 54–61.

Roser, N., and M. Martinez (eds.). *Supporting Children's Responses to Literature: Book Talk and Beyond.* Newark, DE: International Reading Association, 1995.

Short, K. G., and K. M. Pierce. *Talking About Books: Creating Literate Communities.* Portsmouth, NH: Heinemann, 1990.

Wells, G. (1990). "Talk About Text: Where Literacy Is Learned and Taught." *Curriculum Inquiry* 20(4), 369–405.

Background Reading About Assessment

Au, K. H., J. A. Scheu, A. J. Kawakami, and P. A. Herman (1990). "Assessment and Accountability in a Whole Literacy Curriculum." *The Reading Teacher* 43, 574–578.

Linn, R. L., E. L. Baker, and S. B. Dunbar (1991). "Complex, Performance-Based Assessment: Expectations and Validation Criteria." *Educational Researcher* 20, 15–21.

Paris, S., R. Calfee, N. Filby, E. Hiebert, P. D. Pearson, S. Valencia, and K. Wolf (1992). "A Framework for Authentic Literacy Assessment." *The Reading Teacher* 46(2), 88–98.

Tierney, R. J., M. A. Carter, and L. E. Desai. *Portfolio Assessment in the Reading-Writing Classroom.* Norwood, MA: Christopher-Gordon, 1991.

Valencia, S. (1990). "A Portfolio Approach to Classroom Reading Assessment: The Whys, Whats, and Hows." *The Reading Teacher* 43(4), 338–340.

Background Reading About Inquiry Learning

Hoffman, J. V. (1994). "Literature to Inquiry: Bridging Aesthetic and Efferent Responses in Thematic Teaching." Presentation at the Michigan Reading Association Conference, Grand Rapids, MI.

Ogle, D. M. (1986). "K-W-L: A Teaching Model That Develops Active Reading of Expository Text." *The Reading Teacher* 39(6), 564–570.

Additional Reading and Resources

Bauer, Caroline Feller. *Presenting Reader's Theater: Plays and Poems to Read Aloud.* Bronx, NY: H. W. Wilson, 1987.

Goatley, V. J., and T. E. Raphael (1992). "Non-traditional Learners' Written and Dialogic Response to Literature." In C. K. Kinzer and D. J. Lea (eds.), *Literacy Research, Theory, and Practice: Views from Many Perspectives.* Forty-first yearbook of the National Reading Conference (pp. 313–323). Chicago: National Reading Conference.

Lane, Barry. *After "The End": Teaching and Learning Creative Revision.* Portsmouth, NH: Heinemann, 1993.

Lipson, M. Y., S. W. Valencia, K. K. Wixson, and C. W. Peters (1993). "Integration and Thematic Teaching: Integration to Improve Teaching and Learning." *Language Arts* 70(4), 252–263.

Pardo, L., and T. E. Raphael (1991). "Classroom Organization for Content Area Instruction." *The Reading Teacher* 44, 556–565.

Rabbit Ears Radio: Program listings are available at the web site of WEOS, public radio from Hobart and William Smith Colleges: http://hws3.hws.edu:9000/weos/Rabbit.html. You can order tapes from the Public Radio Music Source, 1-800-75-MUSIC (1-800-756-8742).

Raphael, T. E., and C. H. Brock (1993). "Mei: Learning the Literacy Culture in an Urban Elementary School." In D. J. Leu and C. K. Kinzer (eds.), *Examining Central Issues in Literacy Research, Theory, and Practice* (pp. 179–188). Chicago: National Reading Conference.

Raphael, T. E., and C. S. Englert (1990). "Writing and Reading: Partners in Constructing Meaning." *The Reading Teacher* 43, 388–400.

Schloss, P. J. (1992). "Mainstreaming Revisited." *The Elementary School Journal* 92(3), 233–244.

Shepard, Aaron (ed.). *Stories on Stage: Scripts for Reader's Theater.* Bronx, NY: H. W. Wilson, 1993.

Short, K. G., and L. Kahn (1992). "The Literature Circles Project." A paper presented during K. Jongsma (Chair) symposium *Understanding and Enhancing Literature Discussion in Elementary Classrooms.* San Antonio, TX: National Reading Conference.

Sierra, Judy. *Multicultural Folktales for the Feltboard and Readers' Theater.* Phoenix, AZ: Oryx Press, 1996.

Index

This index focuses on topics discussed in the About Book Club section of this guide (pages 1–54). For a comprehensive listing of lesson topics in the Lesson Plans section (pages 55–260), turn to the Curriculum Overview of Lessons chart on pages 47–54.